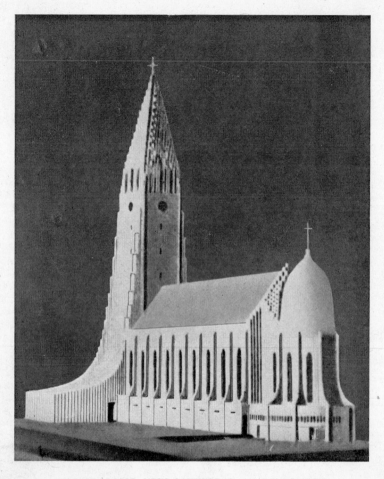

THE PROPOSED NEW CATHEDRAL AT REYKJAVICK

Frontispiece

ICELANDIC CHURCH SAGA

BY

JOHN C. F. HOOD, D.D.

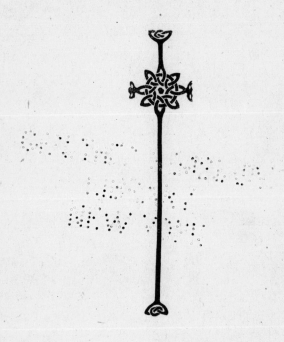

LONDON
SOCIETY FOR PROMOTING
CHRISTIAN KNOWLEDGE
NORTHUMBERLAND AVENUE, W.C.2

First published 1946

BOOK
PRODUCTION
WAR ECONOMY
STANDARD

THIS BOOK IS PRODUCED IN COMPLETE
CONFORMITY WITH THE AUTHORISED
ECONOMY STANDARD

MADE IN GREAT BRITAIN

TO

ELIZABETH

WHO LOOKED AFTER MY ROSES WHILE I WAS IN A COUNTRY
WHERE ROSES RARELY BLOOM

VIDIMYRI, THE OLDEST CHURCH IN ICELAND

Thy glory went through four gates, of fire, and of earthquake, and of wind and of cold.—2 *Esdras* iii, 19.

*   *   *

Thy spirit, independence, let me share,
Lord of the lionheart and eagle eye.
Thy step I follow with my bosom bare,
Nor heed the storm that howls along the sky.
Deep in the frozen regions of the north
A goddess violated brought thee forth,
Immortal liberty, whose look sublime
Hath bleached the tyrant's cheek in every varying clime.

TOBIAS SMOLLETT (1721–71).

*   *   *

It is impossible to enslave mentally or socially a Bible-reading people. The principles of the Bible are the groundwork of human freedom. HORACE GREELEY.

PREFACE

Two years in Iceland brought the British garrison into close touch with the Church in that isolated country on the edge of the Arctic Circle, whose bishop and presturs[1] freely afforded us the hospitality of their cathedral and other places of worship. We learnt that their ecclesiastical fittings and ceremonies bear a close resemblance to those prescribed by the Use of the Church of England. Further study showed deeper resemblances in their Church's early Celtic affinities, in its mediæval independence, its post-Reformation revival, rationalism, and mystic strain. The Lutheran Reformation made a break in episcopal succession, but, as in England, continuity in faith and worship was maintained.

No account of the Icelandic Church exists in English. Jón Helgason, Bishop of Iceland 1917-38, has published in Icelandic a valuable though undocumented history of the Christianity of his country (*Kristnisaga Islands*, 2 vols, Reykjavik, 1925-7). The only other history is the imposing Latin work of Bishop Finnur Jónsson in four quarto volumes complete to 1740 (*Historia Ecclesiastica Islandiæ*, Copenhagen, 1772-8), continued by Bishop Pétur Pétursson (1740-1840).

Original sources are markedly reliable. An early priest, Ari Thorgilsson (1067-1148), known as the Wise, set himself to collect accurate records of his country's origins, which are contained in *Islendingabók* and *Kristni Saga*, both composed about the year 1130. *Landnámabók*, the Book of the Settlement, compiled about the year 1150, gives a detailed account of the colonisation of Iceland (874-930). All these records pay special attention to Christian origins and development.

Ecclesiastical traditions are embodied in the early sagas, accounts of bishops and leading churchmen, written by authors evidently in touch with the events they describe; which as *Biscupa Sögur* were collected and published in two stout volumes by Mollers of Copenhagen in 1858 and 1872, a monumental work now out of print and almost impossible to obtain. They were presented to me on my

---

[1] The plural of this word is prestar, but just as sagas has become the anglicised plural of saga, by reason of our familiarity with those attractive writings, so with "prestur," our friendship with many of them has anglicised the plural. The word "pastors" has an un-Icelandic connotation.

leaving the country by the local printers of *The Midnight Sun* (a paper
I edited for the forces in Iceland), a typical gesture of goodwill.

These accounts carry us to about the middle of the fourteenth century, after which we have numerous and varied Annals, and a succession of Church and State documents, collected in the thirteen volumes
of the valuable *Diplomatarium Islandicum.* After the Reformation,
which led to a revival of interest in past history and literature, we find
a remarkably large number of personal records carefully drawn up by
a literary nation inspired by the noble ambition to make plain to
posterity that the same fresh springs of inspiration fed the apparent
backwater in which they lived as filled the larger stream which flowed
past them unconcerned.

Of the many travellers' reports and accounts drawn upon for
details referring to the eighteenth and nineteenth centuries special
mention must be made of the Reverend Ebenezer Henderson's delightful *Journal* (1813-4). Almost alone of scribacious visitors, he,
like the present writer, appears to have spent more than a month or
two in summer in the country and to have made contacts in all parts
of the hospitable island.

This account of the Church in Iceland has been given the title of
Saga not so much because of the appropriateness of the attractive
word (*adsit omen*) as for the non-abstract method it implies of letting
the story itself delineate the character of its heroes and the principles and problems involved.

This Icelandic Church Saga investigates the traces of early Christianity in the island among pre-settlement Culdees and early settlers,
and describes the militant missionary efforts which led to the official
adoption of Christianity in the year 1000.

It recounts the development and consolidation of the Church under
the first seven Bishops of Skálholt (1056-1211) and their contemporaries in the northern diocese of Hólar, including the story of
Iceland's two episcopal saints, St Jón and St Thorlak.

A survey is attempted of ecclesiastical influence on education
and letters, and of difficulties which arose over the introduction of
Canon Law, especially in the matter of church ownership. The independence of Icelandic churchmanship in the Middle Ages is illustrated in its different aspects. A description follows of the decadence
of the Church and nation in the fourteenth and fifteenth centuries
after the union with Norway in 1262 and a visitation of plague
and physical disasters; with an estimate of the forces in moral,

social, economic, and intellectual spheres making for a reformation.

After the Lutheran Reformation was imposed by force on an apathetic laity, bishops proved themselves in learning and letters the leading men of the age which followed. In a period of unusually severe volcanic devastations, followed by disease and famine, the mystical side of Lutheranism found expression in the poems of Hallgrimur Pétursson (†1674) and in the popular sermons of Bishop Jón Vidalin (†1720), though in the next century latitudinarianism prevailed. In the twentieth century Church and State carried into effect a growing dissociation from Denmark culminating in the Proclamation of Independence on June 17, 1941.

This war has intensified the country's isolation. The Icelandic Church is cut off from its sister churches on the Continent. It claims over 98 per cent. of the inhabitants, but even so it is a small community of 130,000 souls under a bishop and 109 presturs, administered through twenty-one rural deaneries, scattered over an unaccommodating country five-fourths the size of Ireland.

When the British suddenly appeared in June, 1940, to garrison the country, Icelandic clergy, regardless of misunderstanding and possible future consequences, offered to us as brethren in the Faith the hospitality of their cathedral and parish churches; and thus hundreds of our men, exiles on active service, preserved a link with their religion and their home. For this practical co-operation we are under an obligation to the Church in Iceland.

The British Forces have afforded material protection to the country; the British Council has helped its university by sending out a professor and offering bursaries. It would be well if the Church in England, in its sphere, could lend a hand. But before we can offer any real fellowship it is advisable to learn something of the spirit and achievements of the Icelandic Church. It is with this end in view that I offer this account, drafted beneath the midnight sun and in the long sub-arctic nights.

This book is written for ordinary readers by an ordinary unacademic writer, writing not so much as a Doctor in Divinity as the Editor of *The Midnight Sun*, the newspaper of the Icelandic garrison. Hence the use of homely transliterations such as Odin and Olaf instead of the doctrinaire forms Othin and Olafr. It must be admitted also that consistency has sometimes been sacrificed to (it is hoped) general readableness.

Military duties subsequently brought me within reach of Cambridge and Oxford, whose libraries are well equipped with Scandinavian books. Christ Church, Oxford, acquired the extensive Icelandic collection of Vigfusson and York Powell, to which also I am much indebted for providing off-duty opportunities for verifying references and giving body to my framework. The largest collection of modern Icelandic literature in England is to be found at Leeds University, which has established valuable liaison with the National University at Reykjavik. Even larger is the Fiske Library in Cornell University at Ithaca, U.S.A.

Following the scholarly tradition of their country, many Icelanders, not only in parsonages, farms and inns, but also in buses and ships, have proved able and ready to give information from their unrivalled ancient sagas, with which they are more at home than we are with the Bible. Such liberal assistance had the classic virtue of anonymity. In England it has been embodied in the ungrudging and thorough help in details received from Miss Ingibjörg Olafsson, K.I.F.

In the words of Adam (Canon) of Bremen, the first historian of Scandinavian Christianity (1072-5): "If I have not been able to write well, I have at least written truthfully, using as authorities those who are best informed about the subject."

JOHN C. F. HOOD.

St Jón of Hólar's Day, 1945.
Nuneham Courtenay.

CONTENTS

ABBREVIATIONS IN THE NOTES

Lndbk =*Landnámabók* (*c.* 1150)—Book of the first settlement.

Hv. =*Hungrvaka* (*c.* 1200)—story of the first five bishops of Skálholt.

S. =Saga—*e.g.*, Kristni S., Njál's S.

B.S. =*Biskupa Sögur*, a collection of Lives of Bps. 2 vols. Cpn, 1858-72.
B.S. II =2nd Series, post-Reformation.

Dipl. Isl. =*Diplomatarium Islandicum*, 13 vols., Cpn and Rvk, 1857-.

Annals =esp. *Islenzkur Annaler* (803-1430), Cpn 1847, Rvk 1922;
Gustav Storm: *Islandske Annaler* (−1578). Christiania, 1858.

O.I. =*Origines Islandicæ*, collection of early accounts, *Lndbk*, *Hv.*, etc.,
with trans., ed. G. Vigfusson and J. Y. Powell. 2 vols. Oxford, 1905.

Espolin = Jón Espolin: *Arbaekur Islands i Soguformi 1262-1832.* 12 vols.
Cpn, 1821-55.

F. J. =Bp Finnur Jónsson: *Hist. Eccl. Island* (History of the Icelandic
Church, in Latin, to 1740). 4 vols. Cpn, 1778.

P. P. =Bp Pétur Pétursson, Continuation of the above to 1840. Cpn, 1841.

E. H. =Ebenezer Henderson: Iceland (*Journal of Visit*, 1814-5). Edinburgh,
2nd ed., 1819.

J. H. =Bp Jón Helgason: *Kristnisaga Islands* (Hist. of Ch. in Iceland, in
Icelandic). 2 vols. Rvk, 1925-7.

Gj. =K. Gjerset: *History of Iceland.* N.Y., 1924.

Dic. C.V. =Rd. Cleasby and G. Vigfusson: *Icelandic-Eng. Dictionary.*
Oxford, 1874.

Bp =Bishop. Cpn =Copenhagen. Rvk =Reykjavik.

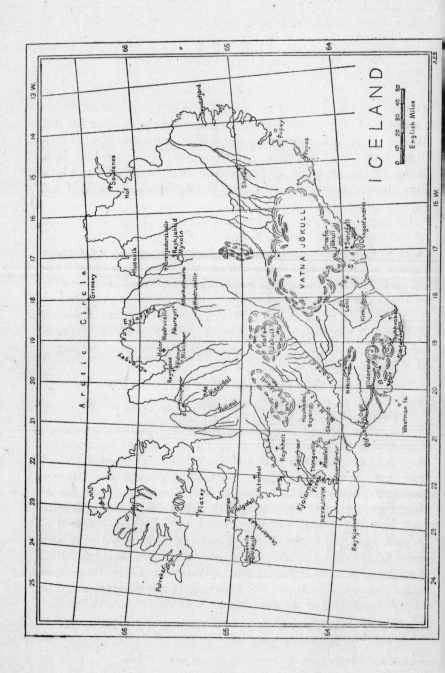

ICELAND

0 10 20 30 40 50
English Miles

xii

CHAPTER I

TRACES OF EARLY CHRISTIANITY

(i) Pre-Settlement Culdees (795)

During a pastoral tour in the second year of the recent war I was returning in the trawler *Tordensköld* down the east coast of Iceland. We passed the cliffs south of Seydisfjördur lost in admiration of their brilliant mineral blues, reds, and greens, and it was growing dusk. Before the Northern Lights began their winter night display a little light shone out from the shore, and the ship's captain said: "I was expecting that. It's Papey."

I thought it seemed an un-Icelandic name, and found that it is one of the oldest in the island, having been inherited by the original Norwegian settlers in the ninth century from earlier inhabitants. Near it is a fjörd called Papos and another called Papafjördur. The gleam from Papey lighthouse has historic symbolism. It marks the first touch of Christianity in Iceland.

(*a*) Unusual facilities exist for determining accurate details of Icelandic Christianity from the start, as an early group of Icelandic scholars took pains to set down authoritative accounts of the origins of Icelandic civilisation.

For this purpose the most valuable accounts are given in *Islendingabók*, written with unusual skill and accuracy by the priest Ari Thorgilsson, known as hinn Frodi—the Wise;[1] and in *Landnámabók*, an annotated List of Settlers, compiled by the Lawman, Sturla Thordarson, in the twelfth century.[2] The prologue to *Landnámabók* records a definite tradition about the earliest inhabitants of Iceland and connects them with Papey and kindred place-names: "Before the country was settled by Northmen (*i.e.*, Norwegians) those people were there whom the Northmen call Papar. They were Christian men, and people think that they must have come from the west of the sea" (*i.e.*, the British Isles), "because after they had gone they found Irish books and bells and croziers, and more things by which it might be perceived that they were Westmen. These things were found in the east, in Papey and Papyli. And it is also mentioned in English books that at that time there was traffic between the lands."

---

[1] C. 1067-1148. For details see under "References" *ad fin.*

[2] Lögsögumadr, Law-Speaker of the Icelandic Parliament or Althing, founded 930; first literally, as the Law was not written down, and afterwards resembling the Speaker of the British House of Commons, who bears his title (*Dic. C.V.*).

The mention in these records of Irish bells—*i.e.*, handbells—and staffs indicates that the Papar belonged to the Columban school, which laid great stress on these insignia. The Icelandic or old Norse word used for staff is "baglar," from the old Irish "bachall," Latin *baculus*, possibly suggesting itinerant missionaries.[1] But these Papar did not missionise anybody, and lived probably as hermits or Culdees. They appear to have lost also the true Columban courage. In earlier days guardians of the insignia would have defended them with their lives, rather than fleeing and leaving them behind. The reason for the monks' withdrawal is added in *Islendingabók*: "The Papar left because they would not dwell here with heathen men." They knew too well the "fury of the Northmen," bracketed in our old litanies with fire and famine, as it was due to devastations on Iona and other Irish monasteries that these Papar had sought security in this isolated sub-arctic island. The sequence appears to be: Danes ravage the Hebrides; Columban monks take refuge in Iceland; Norwegians invade the islands (865-80). Ketill Flatnose and other Northmen, driven from Iona and the isles by Harald Haarfagre, King of Norway, emigrate to Iceland, from which the Irish monks withdraw (870 *sq.*).

Ari suggests that they fled at the appearance of the first settlers, who arrived "at the time when Ivan Lodbroksson killed St Edmund, King of the Angles" (870).

All place-names associated with these Irish monks appear in the S.S.E. corner of the country. There, too, the traditional landing place of Ingolf and Hjorleif, the first settlers, is commemorated by headlands bearing their names. Between these historic sites lies the almost prehistoric Kirkjubaer, the traditional chief monastery of the Papar. A recorded saying of Ingolf shows him to have been a stalwart pagan, who would not readily have welcomed Irish priests, especially after Irish slaves had slain his comrade Hjörleif. Ingolf pursued these slaves to their refuge in the islands, called after them Vestmanneyjar, and slew them there.[2] It would not be surprising if the neighbouring Irish Papar at Kirkjubaer heard of this and fled, though their more distant fellow-countrymen at Papey and Papyli may not have gone at once, especially as Ingolf soon afterwards left to seek a settlement on the west coast.

The fact that some Irish place-names survived the settlement indicates that Irish Christian occupation was not completely obliterated.

[1] L. Gougaud: *Christianity in Celtic Lands*, pp. 131 *sq.*
[2] Westman Is. *Lndbk* I, 6, 7-8 (*O.I.*); *inf.*, p. 19.

These names, preserved even by heathen settlers, and handed down the ages, remain as memorials in Iceland of Celtic Christianity, to which much of the British Isles owes its civilisation.

(b) The reference in *Landnámabók* to records in English writings is borne out by passages in Bede, Adamnan, and an Irish traveller-monk called Dictuil.

Ultima Thule is used in ancient writers of different places, but Bede's mention of Thule "six days' sailing north of Britain" clearly applies to Iceland. In his commentary on 2 Kings xxix, 9, concerning the shadow on the dial, he gives an Icelandic illustration: "The people who dwell in the island of Thule . . . observe . . . every summer that the setting sun, below the earth to most observers, is yet visible to them all night. They see him go slowly back from west to east . . . as people of our own days, who come from these parts, tell us." The Venerable Bede died in 735, and his statements show that there was intercourse between Britain and Iceland at least 130 years before Norsemen settled in the country in 870.

Adamnan (†704) may take us farther back. In his Life of St Columba he tells of a prophecy of the saint concerning a hermit Kormak, who made three voyages in St Columba's days (521-97) in order to find a deserted spot in the ocean ("eremeum in oceano") —possibly the Faroes, though an apt description of Iceland even today.[1]

Dictuil, writing about 825, speaks of islands "now empty of anchorites on account of pirate Northmen."[2] He says that the Faroes had been tenanted by Irish for a century. From there they went on to "Thile, one day's journey from the frozen sea."

A homely touch authenticates Dictuil's report. "It is now thirty years [he writes] since I was told by Irish clerics who had dwelt in that island [Thile] from February 1st to August 1st [*i.e.* 75 years before the Norse settlers arrived] that the sun scarcely sets there in summer, and even at midnight always leaves enough light to do one's ordinary business. The light is so clear at midnight that one is able "pediculos de camisia abstrahere tanquam in præsentia solis." What St Francis later would have called "counting celestial pearls." Soldiers of our garrison in this war would have no doubt that this refers vividly to Iceland.

All this evidence makes it plain that more than a century before the settlers arrived Iceland had stray colonists, Christian hermits

---

[1] *Life of Columba* I, 6; II, 42. Gj., pp. 5-6.
[2] *Liber de Mensura Orbis Terræ* vii, 15.

from Ireland and the Western Isles of Scotland, who made no attempt at missionary work, but fled soon after the coming of the Northmen.

For a time the hammer of Thor drove out the cross, but a dim light remained shining in the darkness.[1]

(ii) CHRISTIAN SETTLERS (895)

Some half-dozen Norwegian settlers in Iceland, coming from the British Isles, definitely professed Christianity, and a few more had been impressed without being persuaded; but as no Christian priests took part in the migration, after the first generation Christianity almost lapsed.

(a) *Landnámabók* records about 400 names of settlers, including many "from Sodor, west of the sea" (*i.e.*, the Hebrides) and from Ireland. Diversity of opinion exists as to the relative percentages of British, or rather British-Norwegian, and purely Scandinavian settlers. But it has been estimated that 400 heads of families would mean about 1,000 immigrants, of whom the British Isles contributed 126, about 12·5 per cent.[2] Probably by the end of the Settlement in 930 the country would have a population of 45,000, of whom some 5,000 derived from the British Isles.[3] As a visitor travelling round the island is occasionally struck by the appearance of Celtic place-names, so he may notice that about one in ten Icelanders, not the least handsome, are conspicuously tall and have black hair.

These hundred-odd settlers, though originally they came from Norway, would have had opportunities of coming into contact with Christianity during their visits to North and East Ireland and the Hebrides, both at this time vigorous centres of Christianity, particularly of that refreshing form of it implanted by St Columba and his disciples. But no Christian teachers accompanied them to their new home, and they built there only one or two churches. *Landnámabók* gives the names of six settlers who "men say were baptised":—Ketill the Fool, Aud the Deep-minded, Ørlyg the Old, Helgi Bjolan, Helgi the Lean, and Jörund the Christian, "and most of them that came hither from the west of the sea," which probably means the families and retainers of those named. We can add three or four more names.

Of leading settlers, nine appear to have come directly from Ireland, and three times that number from the Hebrides. Some of them, and

---

[1] The swastika is the modern form of the sign representing Thor's hammer.

[2] Cp. Prof. Gudmundur Hannesson in *Rvk University Year-Book*, 1925.

[3] *Islandica*, Vol. XX, pp. 7-12.

almost all of their retainers, would have been born and brought up in those parts. Most of them would have lived there long enough to have imbibed something of the Christianity there established by St Columba (†597).

(b) The most conspicuous Christian family is that of Ketill Flatnose, driven out of Iona by King Harald (880), whose grandson was nicknamed Fiflski—the Fool, "because he was a Christian."[1] An account of his descendants is given in the first part of the famous Njal's Saga and in the delightful Laxdale Saga, both compiled, no doubt from traditional sources, about the middle of the thirteenth century.

His daughter Aud the Deep-minded, a great lady, came to Iceland in 895, after the death of her husband, Olaf the White, King of Dublin. With twenty retainers and many slaves she settled in the north-west on the shores of Breidafjördur (Broadfirth), which became one of the earliest centres of Christianity in Iceland. "She made an oratory in Krosshólar, where she had crosses set up, for she was baptised and of the true faith."[2] Her struggle with the sorceress Gulbra typifies the contest between Christianity and heathendom. Aud lived to a great age, and died sitting in her state chair, having dressed herself in her robes for the occasion. She is said to have been buried as a chieftainess, or rather as a chief, her body being laid to rest, as she had directed, in a ship below high-water mark, for she would not lie in unhallowed ground, since she was a baptised woman.[3] Afterwards her kinsmen turned Krosshólar into a High Place, and offered sacrifices there, for they reverted to paganism, presumably in the absence of Christian priests and teachers.

Another connection of the family, Ørlyg the Old, Ketill's nephew, had also been brought up in the Hebrides under a bishop named Patrick, who sent him to Iceland with timber for building a church, a gold coin (gullpening), an iron bell, a plenarium,[4] and consecrated earth to put under the corner posts to serve instead of consecration. The bishop told him to land where three promontories could be seen from the sea with a fjórd between each of them, and to build a church there, dedicating it to St Columba. While looking for the spot, Ørlyg wintered in a bay in the north-west, which he named Patreksfjördur,

---

[1] Olaf Trygg. S. 125-6.   [2] Lndbk II, 14, 8 (O.I.).
[3] Op. cit., III, 15, 15; Lax. S. vii.
[4] (Missale) plenarium, i.e., complete, as issued to missionary priests occasionally in the ninth century, generally in the tenth. Used of the complete book of Irish gospels given by King Athelstan to Canterbury Cathedral, now at Lambeth. Bæjarkirk possessed a plenarium (inventory c. 1463-70).

after his foster-father. With his wife, called Help (Hjalp), and his
sons, Ørlyg eventually settled at Kjalarnes under Mount Esja, at the
top of Faxafjörd. There he set up his church and dedicated it to
St Columba, but he proved so fervent and ill-instructed a disciple of
the apostle of Northern Britain that he appears to have worshipped
the saint instead of Christ.[1] He cannot have made much use of his
plenarium.

However, this church, though apparently it had no priest, is said
to have preserved an old gospel book, written in Celtic characters, no
doubt the plenarium, which was probably treated as a cathac or
mascot.

Hardby this solitary Christian outpost at Kjalarnes stood a heathen
temple or hof, dedicated to Thor, with its sacrificial stone, on which
bodies were broken after being condemned at the adjacent Circle of
Judgment (Domhringur), a miniature Stonehenge. Here one of the
largest local things or moots assembled before the general Parliament
(Althing) was established at Thingvellir in 930.[2]

Ørlyg's sons, though unbaptised, also put their trust in Columb-
kille. But they owe their mention in this early history to the fact
that they were ancestors of Thorlak, Bishop of Skálholt when the
work was compiled. It states also that Helgi the Lean was the ancestor of Ketill, Thorlak's northern colleague, who together were the
patrons of the book. It is not surprising to learn also that Helgi
Bjolan (in Irish, Beolan), Aud's brother, was the ancestor of Jón the
Saint, Ketill's predecessor at Hólar.[3]

Names are given of other notable Christians who came from
Ireland: Jörund, nicknamed in derision the Christian, who, though
surrounded by pagans, "steadfastly kept his faith until the day of his
death," and became the first of Icelandic hermits. His nephew Asolf
Alskik is said to have been such a strict Christian that he would not
fraternise with heathen men. He settled at Holt under Eyjafell with
eleven followers; which suggests that, except for his temperament, he
came as a missionary. When his companions died, Asolf was driven
away to Irá (Irish river), which owes its name to him. The suspicions
roused by solitary Christians in this period are shown in the alarm of
his neighbours at his unaccountable powers as a fisherman, which

[1] *Lndbk* I, 6, 1. Bp Patrick does not appear in the incomplete catalogue
of Bps of Sodor (South Is.—*i.e.* Hebrides) and Man.

[2] See Note on Human Sacrifices, p. 24. *Islendingabók* 3; Grettir's S. 10;
Eyrbyggja S. 4.

[3] For Helgi and his connections, see Viga Glum's Saga, trans. E. Head;
and Ljosvetninga S.

caused him once more to move on and settle finally near his uncle at Holm in Akranes, where he lived as an anchorite.[1] After his death a church was erected over his cell at Holm and dedicated to St Columba, though later on Asolf was venerated as a saint and the dedication changed to St Asolf.

These examples show that the distant, isolated country of Iceland should be added to the noble roll of lands in North-West Europe which first learnt Christianity through the disciples of St Columba. But the seed sown withered away untended, leaving but a mellowing memory.

(c) Tribute must be paid to those lonely Christians who maintained their faith with no outward religious support, surrounded by unsympathetic neighbours, in a harsh new land.

Definite believers were few, but there were a large number of half-Christians, perhaps more dangerous to believers than stalwart pagans, who in an age of transition treated Christianity as a form of paganism. For instance, Aud the Deep-minded set up her crosses as if they were heathen pillars. Prayers made before them were vague, as we can see from the recorded aspirations of Glum, who embraced Christianity in his old age: "Good ever be with the old; Good ever be with the young."[2] Some favoured a measure of the new religion without breaking with the past, as Aud's brother-in-law, Helgi the Lean, son of an Irish princess, Raferta, who called his new home Kristnes, "and yet on voyages, in bad stresses and in all things he most cared for, he called on Thor."[3] Others had abandoned Thor, but professed to trust in their own right arm. Witness the lament of the first settler, Ingolf, over his companion, Hjorleif, slain by his Irish slaves: "Such must ever be the fate of a man who refuses to sacrifice to the gods."[4] Ingolf's grandson, Thorkell the Lawman or Speaker, was carried out from his death-bed into the sunshine, and commended himself to the God who made the sun. Moreover, "he lived as cleanly as any Christian." We read of another Thor who, in spite of his name (always a favourite in Iceland), refused with his son Hall to offer sacrifice, and relied on his own might; and of Asgar, who gave up sacrifices of his own free will.[5]

Some settlers paid respect to the spirits of their strange new country, good and ill. Trolls who lived in rocky haunts and wrought

---

[1] Lndbk I, 7, 3-6; Olaf S. Trygg, 127-8.   [2] Lndbk I, 6, 5.
[3] Op. cit., III, 14, 3.
[4] Op. cit., I, 6, 7; E.H., p. 244; cp. Laxdale S. xl (of Kjartan).
[5] Lndbk III, 4, 4; IV, 3, 21.   As—one of the ancient gods.

mischief on their neighbours; berserks, who possessed men so that
they ran amok; and, in later ages, ghosts of the departed who "walked
after" (burial), and afflicted all that they deemed to have wronged
them—these relics of an older religion proved inveterate opponents
of the missionaries and priests of the new.

Some ideas of Scandinavian paganism acted as a bridge to Christianity. The Viking Cross at Gosforth in Northumberland (c. 1000)
displays Vidar with his booted foot rending the dragon's jaw, together
with Christ on the Cross exemplifying the same principle. Similarly,
Viking coins of Northumbria show the hammer of Thor alongside the
Cross of Christ (875-954), an example of historical transition. Such
was the conflate religion of Helgi the Lean, which could have been
quickened into a full Christianity by opportunities of instruction and
worship.

But for over a century no such facilities followed the settlers in
Iceland. It is therefore not surprising to read in the last sentence of
Landnámabók that such Christianity as the settlers brought with them
soon died away and "the land reverted to heathendom for a hundred
(=120) years" (i.e., 875-997).[1]

This is a general statement. The light of Christianity did not quite
go out. In the second missionary attempt a century later, when
Thangbrand came to Kirkjubaer in the south-east "Side," he found
living there Swart, son of Asbjörn, son of Thorstein, son of Ketill
the Fool, who had "all of them been Christians from father to son."
Ketill had taken over the settlement from Irish Christians after an
abortive attempt of a pagan settler to do so, "because the heathen
might not dwell there."

Later the place became a nunnery, and is now a church· and
prestur's farm-house[2]—the oldest Christian inhabited site in the
country, though the only vestige of mediæval days remaining, in
addition to the name, is a basalt memorial stone with an undecipher-
able inscription.[3] Nevertheless, Kirkjubaer provides a remarkable
instance of spiritual succession from the dawn of Icelandic history.

---

[1] The duodecimal system, used up to modern days by farmers and
fishermen in Iceland, is said to have come from Babylon. The long or great
hundred =120.   Cp. hundredweight =112 lb., U.S.A. =100 lb. So English
farmers in sales of cheese, etc., give 100 lb. =112, little hundred, 120 great
hundred. Mallet's *Northern Antiquities*, ed. Bp Percy, pp. 219-20; cp. *Dic.
C.V.*, s.v. hundrad.

[2] Prests-setur.   [3] E.H., p. 237.

(iii) First Missionary Efforts: Thorvald Kodransson and Bishop Fridrek (981-4)

The first attempt to preach the gospel in Iceland should be credited to Thorvald Kodransson, "the far-farer," friend of Sweyn Fork-beard, King of Norway, a noble Icelandic viking who accompanied Sweyn on his ravaging expeditions to the British Isles and ameliorated his excesses. Afterwards he travelled to Saxony, and was converted and baptised there by Bishop Fridrek.[1] The young viking then per-suaded the bishop to return to Iceland with him to evangelise his own folk, who had loved him little and treated him badly. The vicissitudes of this enterprise were picturesquely described 200 years later, in Thorvald's Saga, translated from the Latin Life written by the eru-dite Gunnlaug Leifsson (†1218), a monk of Thingeyrar.

For four years these pioneer missionaries (to use the words of the saga) "fared all round Iceland to preach the word of God" (Faro their vida um Island at boda Guds ord). They met with considerable opposition but made a number of converts in the north. Some men abandoned heathen sacrifices, already becoming unpopular, but would not give up their sacred pillars. At least two churches were built, at As and Holt, the first in Iceland. Moreover the Gospel was expounded at local and central Things. But after four years Thor-vald and his bishop were driven out.

(*a*) The missionaries arrived in Iceland in 981, and set up a farm at Laekjamot in the north-west, an early Christian centre. The story of the conversion of Thorvald's father Kodran illustrates the diffi-culty of Christian missionary work, the irrationality of the appeal made, and the apparent lack of instruction for converts. "On a certain high season, when Bishop Fridrek and his clerks were cele-brating the festival service, Kodran stood near, more from curiosity than sympathy. But when he heard the sound of the bells, and the clear singing of the clerks; when he savoured the sweet smell of the incense and saw the assistants clothed in white robes with bright coverings and the bishop in splendid vestments, and the fair white tapers shining with mickle brightness all around; then these things made a great appeal to him, and he came to his son Thorvald and said: 'Now I have seen and somewhat considered the service you offer to your God. It seems to me, your God rejoices in that light which our gods dread. This man whom you call your bishop, is your spáman, because you learn from him those things you offer us, on

---

[1] Kurtz, *Church Hist.*, 93, 5, questions the fact of his episcopate.

behalf of your God. I too have a prophet of my own who is of much
use to me. He guards my cattle and warns me what I must do, and
of what I must beware. Therefore I put great trust in him.' "

Then Thorvald, who did the speaking, as the bishop did not know
Icelandic, pitted the weakness of his prophet, the bishop, against his
father's strong spáman, premising that the bishop would use "the
strength of God the Creator, who lives in eternal light and fetches to
His glory all who believe in Him and serve Him faithfully."[1]

At this the bishop exorcised the heathen spirit from its rocky
haunt; and after that Kodran the bondi was baptised with Járngerda,
his wife.

(b) However, his son Orm would not let himself be baptised at
that time, nor would he accept the preliminary rite of prime-signing,
which would have enabled him to remain with his family. For in
those days Christians would not mix with heathen (cp. sup., p. 18); so
that pagans engaged in trade with Christians, and servants in Christian
households, at least up to the middle of the fourteenth century, let
themselves be prime-signed (with the Cross) without being fully
baptised or renouncing their old faith. Some of those thus prime-
signed became catechumens and proceeded to baptism. But in any
case they were admitted to part of Mass (primsignara messa), and
after death could be buried at the edge of consecrated ground.[2]

Orm nobly redeemed his obstinacy twenty years later as the
outcome of a striking incident, while the adoption of Christianity
was being publicly considered. A great band of pagans assembled
and agreed to offer some men as human sacrifices to the gods to avert
the loss of their religion. Christians then met and decided to outbid
the heathen. Whereas pagans were prepared to throw their weakest
men over the cliffs, the Christians called for the two best of their
adherents from each Quarter to offer themselves as living sacrifices,
a victory gift of their lives to Christ. Leading representatives immediately volunteered from all districts except the Western Quarter,
which produced only one. "Then up spake Orm: If my brother
Thorvald had been in the country, there would be no gap there. But
I am willing to fill it, if you will have me." They consented, and he
was at once baptised.

(c) Bishop Fridrek prime-signed one of the great chiefs of the
north, Thorvard, son of Baedwar the Sage, who ("some say") was

---

[1] Homiliu-bók, Introd. Fridrek Paasche, p. 8.
[2] Dipl. Isl. I, p. 382 (law); II, p. 545, 840 (Bps' Regs. to 1346); III,
p. 151; Grágas, 129, 320; Egil's S. 35, 50; Njál's S. 158.

afterwards baptised in England, from which he brought timber to build a church on his farmstead at As. That ineffective opposition was aroused is indicated by a story of Gunnlaug's that attempts to burn down the church at As were frustrated in a miraculous manner. The more reliable Kristni Saga adds a practical testimony: "This church was built sixteen years before Christianity was made Law in Iceland (*i.e.*, 984), and it was standing when Botolf was bishop of Hólar (1238-46), although it had only been repaired with a thatching of turves"—a homely practice which has lasted to this day.

Thorvald's father-in-law Olaf built a church on his homestead at Haukagil, for which Thorvald gave the wood.[1] Converts diverted their temple tax to the upkeep of this building, so that heathen priests were roused to opposition.

The Saga derives the name Haukagil from two berserks called Hauk, who challenged the bishop to an ordeal of walking through fire. Fridrek got the better of them by sprinkling the fire with holy water and passing over it in full robes and a mitre; whereas the berserks, biting the edges of their shields, yelling and brandishing their swords, fell dead. Gunnlaug is careful to add that he got this story from Glum, a veracious man, who heard it from Arnorr, son of Arndis, a cousin of Thorvald; so the legend may be founded on fact.

Another traditional derivation is connected with the church at Holt, near Managardur, and Manafoss, near Svinavatn. Bishop Fridrek baptised an anchorite named Mani, who became renowned for his devotion and benevolence and, like other notable early converts, was nicknamed "The Christian." His abnormal skill at obtaining salmon below the foss, which afterwards bore his name, averted a famine, so that the local fishing rights were vested in Holt church. In this remote spot traces of an anchorite's cell could be seen in Gunnlaug's day with the remains of a tún called Managardur, constructed by the hermit for his one cow.[2]

(*d*) Opposition from heathen spámen or soothsayers and priests did not stop the promotion of missionary work, for Thorvald and the bishop evangelised from place to place. But when Thorvald preached at the Althing, the centre of national government and religion, such opposition was evoked that two skalds or state poets made scurrilous verses against the missionaries. Matters were thus brought to a head, for Thorvald, who had won fame as a gentle viking, proved a vindictive Christian and slew two skalds; so that he was outlawed. Even the patient bishop was attacked, and he too had to leave the country.

[1] Melsted, Islendinga S. III, p. 7, questions Thorvald's S. in this.
[2] Thorvaldsvidförla S. 8. tún = fenced meadow-land, *inf.*, p. 37.

Fridrek returned to Saxony and died there, leaving a reputation for saintliness. Thorvald at first engaged in merchant expeditions, then he visited the Holy Land and Constantinople (called Micklegarth by old Icelandic writers), and finally settled in Russia, where he is reputed to have built a monastery on the Dnieper.

It cannot be maintained that this mission showed many signs of success. In a tolerant people it had rather provoked than allayed antagonism. But at least the challenge of Christianity had been thrown down. The cautious and conservative Icelanders at last were faced with the need for personal consideration in the matter, the ground was prepared for further efforts, and in the northern fashion, when the time came for the question to be settled one way or the other, having individually expressed their opposition, the whole community voted for the adoption of the New Faith.

NOTE ON HUMAN SACRIFICES IN ICELAND

Evidence is scanty except for topographical indications, a few stones and place-names, and some sub-contemporary historical references, especially those in the reliable *Landnámabók*—"Book of the Settlement" (*c.* 1150)—and Kristni Saga, based on the researches of the accurate Ari Thorgilsson (*c.* 1130).

More traces of pagan temples are found in Iceland than in the rest of Scandinavia, because the island's lack of wood led to the use of large rough stones, some of which remain *in situ*. Hof as a place-name, denoting a heathen temple, exists in all four Quarters, probably indicating the chief centres of heathendom, planted by the early settlers (870-930):

1. Hofstadir, in the N.W., built by Hall, a settler (*Lndbk* 19). The Annals for 1320 record a court or "thing" held here; presumably the settlers' court, near their temple, lasted until Christian times.

2. Hof at N.E. corner, on a mound, site of an exceptionally large hall of Broddi Thoresson. Tradition held that the strong wooden door of the church there had been taken over from the temple (Kristni Saga, App. 4, 2). E. H., pp. 165-6.

3. Hofstadir, near Myvatn in north, excavated 1908. Considerable remains of stone foundations indicate that pagan temples in Iceland were modelled on Irish churches, familiar to many settlers, who, though Norwegian, came via Ireland and the Hebrides (*Lndbk* IV, 7; Eyrbyggja S. 4; Gj., p. 31 *n.*).

4. Hof at S.E. corner, on top of the cone-shaped Godaborg, a foothill of the gigantic Øraefajökull; a large square stone of sacrifice, traditionally human sacrifice. (Henderson, *Journal* 1814-5, p. 207.) Gud=God, god=pagan deity, godi=chieftain-priest.

5. Helgafell, on Thórsnes in N.W., the "holy hill" dedicated to Thor by the settler Thorolf, godi from Moster in Norway, who brought the wood of his old temple with him. Helgafell was kept sacred from trespass of man or beast or any defilement. No one was allowed even to gaze at it with unwashed face. Here was a court, Thorsnesthing, and a hof with "Thor's Stone," on which men destined for sacrifice were broken. Here, too, was a doomring (dom-hringr), "in which men are condemned as victims"—a miniature Stonehenge. Helgafell became the site of a church and monastery (*inf.*, pp. 35-6). (*Lndbk* II, 10, 1-4; Eyrbyggja S. 4 *sq.*; E.H., pp. 336-9; Burton, *Ultima Thule*, ii, p. 104.)

6. Kjalarnes, at head of Faxafjörd; hof dedicated by Thorstein godi, with a sacrificial bog (Blót-kelda). Here was an important court in which several neighbouring godar united, until the general Althing was established in 930 at Thingvellir. (*Lndbk* I, 9; *Islendingabök* 3; Grettir's S. 10.)

It is evident that most godords or clans established a hof and a thing. Some had sacrificial stones. The Courts inflicted punishments, usually fines or outlawry. But some of the criminals in early days were sentenced to death at a thing, and executed or sacrificed to propitiate the offended deity. Three methods are indicated: they were broken on the stone (5), suffocated in the marsh (6), or thrown over a cliff (4). (Kristni S. 2; F. J. I, pp. 21-2.)

At the epoch-making Althing in the year 1000, when Christianity was adopted, some pagans wished to try to avert that event by making human sacrifices. Leading Christians retorted that whereas pagans offered only maimed and aged persons in sacrifice, they were ready to offer to live for Christ. We may conclude that such a practice was not then unthinkable. Such sacrifices would be akin to the exposure of infants which continued for some years after the adoption of Christianity. From the Christian taunt we infer that the practice was half-hearted; and the way was pointed from the external to the inward sacrifice. (Kristni S. 8, 7. Dasent, *Burnt Njal*, pp. xxxviii *sq.*)

Old religious rites are described in Eyrbyggja Saga, Viga-Glum's Saga, and Vatnsdaela Saga. These stories, though committed to writing more than a century after the period concerned, embodied traditions handed down by word of mouth. The fictional Kjalnes

Saga, with its story that Búi destroyed the temple with its human sacrifices, typifies the victory of Christianity.

That sacrifice of a human being as a great prayer or bribe to the deity was practised up to the twelfth century in Scandinavia is clear from notices in sub-contemporary records. Adam of Bremen gives vivid descriptions of such sacrifices at Upsala in Sweden and at Moster (Maeren) in Norway. Such blood offerings were forbidden by King Inge Stenkilsson, an unpopular course which led to his abdication. King Aun, or Una, of Sweden sacrificed his nine sons to Odin "in order to be granted a long life."[1] Icelandic Annals record a victory of Hákon, Earl of Norway, over the hitherto invincible Jómsvikings obtained "at the great price of the sacrifice of his eleven-year-old son to Odin." Hákon is called elsewhere in the Annals "Blót-Hákon" or "Blót-Jarl"—the sacrificer, and later the "Evil Jarl," so it appears that this action was not usual and brought him notoriety.[2]

Odin in Iceland never became a popular cult. Sacrifices of human beings there seem to have been penal and not propitiatory. As the country's learned antiquary Arngrim states in 1609: "Sometimes men were sacrificed at the Blót-kelda of Kjalarnes and at Thorsthing" (near Helgafell), "where the stone kept its dark stain for many ages." King Olaf Tryggvason did his best to stamp out such barbaric worship, which had had a long and painful history, as is shown by the story of Jephthah's daughter in Judges xi. We read of it in Heimskringla as late as 1021, when "a great blood-offering at Moster took place in midwinter";[3] but by then, even in the long dark nights of the North, men were learning to associate that season, not with the fierce powers of darkness, but with the birth of Christ, come to reveal the sacredness of all human personality.

---

[1] Ynglinga S. 25, in Snorri Sturluson's Heimskringla.

[2] Olaf S. Trygg. 42-50; cp. 134-5, 56, 239. The word Blót in Christian times came to denote cursing. Jomsberg was at the mouth of the Oder.

[3] Loc. cit. 108-9. In general cp. C. J. A. Oppermann, Eng. Missionaries in Sweden and Finland, pp. 16-24, Lond., 1937.

CHAPTER II

ICELAND ADOPTS CHRISTIANITY

(i) Olaf, King of Norway, takes Action (996-9)

The conversion of Iceland to Christianity was chiefly due to the initiative and compelling enterprise of Olaf Tryggvason, King of Norway c. 995-1000, and was completed in three stages: (a) Kjartan's abortive lay commission, followed by Stefnir's negative effort; (b) Thangbrand's aggressive campaign; and (c) the persuasion of the Althing by the chiefs Gizur the White and Hjalti Skeggjason.

(a) Olaf Tryggvason emerges from romance as a viking of commanding presence, crowning his adventures by plundering the coasts of England. Here he became a Christian and is said to have been confirmed by Alphege, Bishop of Winchester. Consequently he pledged himself never again to war against Britain. He determined however, to regain the throne of his fathers in Norway, and there became a viking on behalf of Christ. "No man durst gainsay him, and all the land was christened wheresoever he came."[1]

Iceland next became Olaf's special interest, for many leading Icelanders used to visit his country as a qualification for high status in their own land. The education of young chieftains was not considered complete until they had "fared overseas." On their return they brought back timber for building and fine raiment, gave an account of their travels, and, as it were, came of age. They acquired merit if they had been received at the Norwegian court, and still more so if they had been made hirdmen or liegemen of the king. To embrace his new religion might therefore be accounted a degree in continental civilisation.

This is well brought out in a tale that must have been recounted often in the long, dark Icelandic winters until it became woven for all time in many sagas. It illustrates the next stage in the story of Icelandic Christianity.

In the year 995, Kjartan, noble Icelandic grandson of an Irish king, fared overseas to Norway with ten highborn companions. They found that King Olaf " was ordering a change of faith in his country, and that the people took to it most unequally." Several Icelanders of high standing were waiting to sail home, but the king would not let

---

[1] Olaf S. Trygg. 32, 76 (V. 32, *Heimskringla*), Krist. S. 3, suggest that Olaf's Christian campaign in northern lands was advocated by Alphege; Olaf was baptised in the Scilly Isles (contrast Adam of Bremen ii. 34-5).

them go, because they refused to accept the new faith that he was preaching. Kjartan and his friends joined their fellow-countrymen at Nidaros, and bound themselves not to be baptised. However, Kjartan, a great athlete, was won over by the skill and charm of the king, who beat him at a swimming match in the Nid, and he finally succumbed to Olaf's preaching and the Christmas services. On the day that Kjartan laid aside his baptismal robes he became a hird or liegeman of the king, who then sent him back to his country "to bring men to Christianity by force or by expedients." Not until all Iceland became Christian would he let the hostages go. The king gave Kjartan a jewelled sword as a parting gift, and laid on him a charge to keep his faith well.

In spite of an apparent lack of instruction, we are told that Kjartan observed Lent, being the first man in Iceland to do so. But his new faith, though it inspired him to build a fine church, did not much affect his manner of life. He still took personal vengeance on his private enemies, for which the king's sword proved useful.[1]

(b) As foreseen by King Olaf, other leading Icelanders, as well as his retainers, followed the example of their popular young chieftain, Kjartan, and were baptised. Their preparation would be even less thorough than his own, and their practices less changed.

A notorious example of the unconverted baptised pagan appears in the sagas in the person of Hallfred Ottarson, one of Olaf's hostages. Like other reluctant converts, he made it a condition of his baptism that he should become the king's hirdman. Then he used his position as licence for committing acts of violence and even manslaughter. As we have seen, even Christian missionaries could not keep themselves from these viking outrages. But Hallfred stooped to un-Icelandic vice. To get even with a chieftain enemy Gris, he assaulted his wife. Later he became Olaf's principal court-skald or poet-laureate, saying: "What you taught me is not more poetic than my poetry."[2] At the death of the king in battle in the autumn of the year 1000, he composed a sincere lament of lofty tone, which suggests that Hallfred could have had great influence if he had been as loyal and devoted a hirdman of Christ as he was of Olaf. He died in 1007 and was buried in Iona, by the side of Macbeth. Kjartan did not do much, except indirectly, to forward Christianity in Iceland. But King Olaf's aggressive championship was beginning to tell. We read of a great traveller, Thorer, son of Skeggi, who had a merchantman he built

[1] Olaf S. Trygg. 88; Kristni S. 6, 3-4; Laxdale S. 40.
[2] Cp. W. A. Craigie, *Icelandic Sagas*, pp. 48-9.

blessed by Bishop Sigord the mighty, Olaf's court bishop, and afterwards was himself baptised. *Landnámabók* probably records this incident because doorposts made of ship's beams told the weather until the days of Bishop Brand (1163-1202)—*i.e.*, until shortly before the Settlers' Book was compiled.

King Olaf was not lacking in determination or resources. He followed up the commission to Kjartan by sending a priest, Stefnir Thorgillson, a great-grandson of Bjolan, one of the Ketill clan, pioneers of Christianity in the country, most of whom subsequently lapsed. Stefnir, an Icelander by birth, accompanied Olaf on his campaign on Britain and afterwards was baptised and ordained in Denmark. He went to Iceland in 996 with a bodyguard of nine retainers, and journeyed north and south, preaching with vigour. Since he evoked no response, he wrecked temples and burnt idols, which grossly offended the Icelandic principles of toleration. As Stefnir sheltered under the ægis of his chieftain connections at Kjalarnes, the Althing passed a law making Christianity *Fraenda skömm* (a family disgrace), putting the onus of prosecution on the offender's relatives. Consequently Stefnir was banished and returned to Norway. He then joined the missionary Thorvald the Far-farer, and travelled with him to Constantinople, returning to Denmark, where he lampooned Earl Sigvald and was put to death.

(*c*) Stefnir's negative effort was followed by the militant mission of Thangbrand,[1] Olaf's German court priest, "a passionate ungovernable man," "great in growth and mighty in strength."[2] Thangbrand had fled from Denmark because he had slain in a duel a man wanting an Irish slave-girl, whom he bought with silver given him by King Olaf in exchange for a shield emblazoned with a crucifix. The saga tells how the shield had been presented to Thangbrand by the Archbishop of Canterbury with the words: "Thou art to all intents and purposes a knight, so I give thee a shield. The crucifix marks thy priesthood." Olaf appointed Thangbrand as a priest of Moster in Norway, where he squandered the church funds and turned pirate to replenish them. Soon after Stefnir returned to Iceland in 996, the king summoned Thangbrand and told him he could have no robber in his service. Thangbrand begged to be sent on some hard errand; so the king sent him to Iceland to make the land Christian, which he attempted vigorously with the cross in one hand and a sword in the other.

[1] *Heimskringla* V, 65-74; Laxdale S. 41; Kristni S. 3 *sq.* etc.
[2] Olaf's S. Trygg. 80, 91.

The Icelanders' experience of missionaries had prejudiced them against Christianity, but a chieftain, Hall-of-the-Side, impressed on Michaelmas Day by a sermon on the glory of St Michael,[1] let Thangbrand's party winter in his tún, and was baptised with all his household in his own beck Throttá on Saturday before Easter. In summer Thangbrand, who was "clever of speech," rode with Hall to the thing and "dauntlessly pleaded God's errand before the assembly."[2] So that he baptised three chieftains later regarded, with Hall of the Side, as "the four patriarchs of the Icelandic Church"— Gizur the White, his son-in-law Hjalti, and Thorgils of Ølfusa. Njáll also was baptised, the noble hero of the most famous of all sagas, who had long been persuaded of the superiority of the Christian faith over paganism. Another Hall (of Haukadal) was baptised in 999 when he was three years old. He was destined to grow up to be the friend and counsellor of the first bishops of Skálholt, and his remarkable memory to a very old age was a great help to Ari the Wise in compilations of the early history of the country.

Once again pagan poets went into action against the spread of Christianity. Some of their hostile rhymes are preserved in Kristni Saga, but today do not seem to be worthy of attention.

One skáld said, "Drive away the foul blasphemer of the gods." Another, "I will not take the fly that Thangbrand casts." For this kind of insult the ruthless Thangbrand and his assistant priest Godleif killed two poets. Then another skáld sang, "Roodbearer slew a skáld with a sword." A more subtle attack was made by Steinvor, a temple priestess, who owned and served a pagan temple. She collected the temple toll and would have natural apprehension of the loss of her accustomed dues. She asked Thangbrand if he had heard that Christ dared not accept a duel to which Thor had challenged him. Thangbrand replied, "I have heard that Thor would be nothing but mould and ashes if God wished him not to live." As Sir Richard Burton says, "Thor died hard because he was essentially an Icelander; blunt, hot-headed, of few words and of many blows." Odin had little influence in Iceland, and has left few traces, but Thor remained popular in formations of Christian names, and the Icelandic week continued to begin on Thursday evening.[3]

Thangbrand travelled over most of the island, preaching, fighting

---

[1] *Homiliu-bók*, p. 8.   [2] Kristni S. 43.

[3] R. F. Burton: *Ultima Thule*, i, pp. 94, 150. Of men's Christian names in 1855, Jón = one-fifth, Thor and derivatives one-tenth. The commonest female name was Gudrun, after the heroine of Laxdale Saga. "M or N." = Jón or Gudrun.

and baptising. But he was disappointed with his reception, and in the summer of 999 went back to Norway in his ship *Ironbasket*. On his report that there was no hope of Iceland accepting Christianity, King Olaf took steps to punish the Icelanders he retained in his country.

That summer there were great debates on religion at the Althing, where the newly baptised chieftain Hjalti[1] retaliated on the pagan skálds by reciting a poem on the Law-hill calling Odin and Freyja dirty names. At this Runolf, the pagan high-priest, naturally sued him for blasphemy; but Hjalti was popular, and the powers of heathendom were waning, so that only with difficulty could he obtain a conviction; and then Hjalti was outlawed for three years. He set out for Norway, significantly accompanied by Gizur the White. They put the problem before the king in a more hopeful light than Thangbrand had done, and stayed his hand in the matter of reprisals against their fellow-countrymen, binding themselves to bring it about that Christianity would succeed in Iceland.

Thus the final stage was reached in Iceland's acceptance of the Faith.

(ii) St John Baptist's Day (1000)

Gizur and Hjalti sailed home early in the memorable year 1000 in order to arrive in time for the Althing. King Olaf had sent an impressive company of priests, headed by one Thormod. They came and rallied their party at Vellankatla, north-east of Thingvallavatn, where they were joined by fellow-Christians from all over the country. So they made a goodly array as they rode round the lake to the Assembly at Thingvellir. At sight of them the heathen chieftains rushed to arms with their followers, and a conflict in the sacred enclosure was avoided with difficulty. It was a promising sign that leading men who were not Christians strove to prevent civil war.

Next day, Sunday, June 23, Thormod and six priests celebrated Mass, and then the whole Christian congregation, headed by the priests in vestments and two large crosses, went in procession to the Lögberg. This was a Christian counterpart of the ancient legal mid-summer procession from the heathen temple to the Law-rock (Lögbergisganga). The crowds were much impressed by the incense and by the crosses, one of which had been made significantly the size of King Olaf, and the other the size of Hjalti, who was legally an outlaw.

By now Christianity had been adopted in all northern countries, and Icelanders who had travelled were familiar with its tenets. In

---

[1] His name suggests a connection with the Shetlands = Sholto.

their own country since 930, when the new Althing was established, some godar or leading chieftains had become sufficiently identified with the new Faith to remain outside the State organisation. Already the number of godar professing Christianity had increased to nine, nearly a quarter of the whole actual parliament. Moreover, they had King Olaf actively at their back ready to make reprisals on the hostages he held, which included Svarting, son of the heathen high-priest Runolf, and three other young chieftains.[1] Christian chiefs refused to join in heathen sacrifices, so the constitution itself was in danger. The nine chose Hall-of-the-Side as their own Lögsögumadr, Lawman or Speaker, and threatened to set up a separate thing.

Gizur and Hjalti addressed the Assembly and explained their mission in a harangue "surprisingly brave and telling," and made clear that King Olaf was supporting them. This courageous action was followed by awed silence and no heathen dared reply. Christianity had shown itself aggressive and paganism became passive. Then each side started to outlaw the other, when a strange interruption occurred. A man ran up and shouted: "Fire has broken out of the earth near Ølfus and is overrunning the homestead of Thorodd the (great heathen) godi." People said: "No wonder! the gods are wroth at the speeches we have just heard." But Snorri, the leading heathen godi, shrewdly asked: "Then what made the gods angry when the lava on which we are standing was pouring out?"

After that the Assembly broke up. It had become clear how things were shaping, so Hall-of-the-Side made a masterly decision. He approached the Lawman, a pagan priest called Thorgeir, and engaged him at a fee to put the Christian case in whatever judgment he should pronounce. Then Thorgeir returned to his booth for a night and a day and, covering his head with his robe, meditated in silence on the momentous issue. During this time the heathen held a meeting and agreed to offer human sacrifices to avert Christianity— a counsel of despair. The Christians countered by a call for volunteers to offer themselves as a living sacrifice to Christ.[2] Next evening, June 24, Thorgeir emerged to announce his critical finding. Today we can stand on the Rock from which he addressed the Assembly and the crowd, and imagine the proceedings. Drawn up beneath him on the slope down to the river stood the thirty chieftains of the old order and the nine adherents of the new, each backed by their armed retainers, spoiling for a fight. Behind him beneath the precipice thronged the women and children in much trepidation as to the

---

[1] *Heimskringla*, trans. Erling Monsen, p. 187.   [2] Kristni S. 8, 7.

outcome. The slanting rays of the sub-arctic sun, in the heavens there all that night, would be shining over the lake, touching the stern background of volcanic mountains with gracious colours.

Thorgeir mounted the Law-rock and urged on the people the folly of breaking the peace of their country by dividing into parties, which could only sweep away all they held dear. "Let us avoid extremes, and take a middle course; let us all have one law and one faith"(ein log ok einn sid).

The Assembly agreed and committed the decision to him. Then he made the memorable pronouncement that from henceforth the official religion of Iceland was to be Christian. All people were to be baptised at the earliest opportunity; but private worship of heathen deities was not forbidden, and some pagan customs were allowed to remain. Eating of horse-flesh and even the exposure of infants were permitted.[1]

Thus civil war was avoided, the constitution was preserved, and by mutual concessions, chiefly on the part of the heathen, the new religion was peacefully established.

All the heathen appear to have been baptised before they reached home. Thingvallavatn is a cold lake, being fed by deep icy waters emerging along sunless rifts from glacial mountains. However, over the eastern ridge lies Laugavatn, a lake of hot springs, and most of the people preferred to be baptised in its warm waters as they went home. The Westerners, under the influence of Snorri the godi, were baptised in their own warm springs in Reykjadal, afterwards called Krosslaug.[2]

Some might say that a certain tepidity has marked the Christianity of the nation ever since; others that the incident illustrates its practical common sense.

Hjalti was witness to the baptism of the heathen high-priest Runolf, his former enemy, and could not resist a dig at him. "Now," he said, "we'll teach the old priest how to mumble the salt."[3] The success of the Christian challenge to heathendom owed a great deal to Hjalti's wit, wisdom, and courage, more to the outstanding character of Gizur, and perhaps most to fear of King Olaf.

The Christian victory was externally complete, but the heart of the

[1] Islendinga S. 7; Kristni S. 11.
[2] Early Christianity permitted baptism in warm water: *Didache* 7.
[3] At baptism the candidate, after being signed with the sign of the cross, was given consecrated salt (cp. Matt. v, 13); cp. W. N. Cote, *The Archæology of Baptism*, p. 56.

people had barely been touched. It now remained to train the hastily acquired converts, organise their churchmanship, and instruct them in worship and character. And there were remarkably few people in Iceland at the time capable of doing this, so that the momentous decision of the Althing was not followed up for some years.

(iii) Strengthening the Stakes

(A) Church Building

It must be put to the credit of the national Assembly of Iceland that six years after its adoption of Christianity it officially prohibited duelling.[1] A duel as a settlement of grievances, whether judicial or private, often led to vendettas in which the families of bishops and leading churchmen became involved. For Christianity was nominal and churches were few. So the Althing's ideal was largely ignored, especially as its government, like the abortive League of Nations, which in a small way it resembled, had no executive power. Private feuds diminished, as the sagas show, but chieftains began to enlarge their domains, and these aggressions produced a conflict of clans as bitter and deadly as any which darken the pages of Scottish history, ultimately leading to the break-up of the country through civil war.

A few years after the Althing's prohibition one of the most far-reaching of early family feuds developed to such an extent that the protagonist on one side, the wise Christian chieftain Njál, was burnt in his house with his family; and the repercussions of this calamity broke up the Althing itself the following year in battle in the sacred enclosure.[2] Clearly the turbulent Icelandic nature, as hard and eruptive as the country of its adoption, had not been tamed. With their baptism the people had not put off the old Thor.

(a) Nothing much, in fact, was done to promote Christian order and worship in Iceland until the second Olaf, afterwards called the Saint, became King of Norway in 1016.[3] He found in his own country that almost all the Christianity that his namesake had forced on it twenty years before had not unnaturally disappeared. Those that remained Christian were merely so in name. Much the same must have

[1] Bogi Th. Melsted, Islendinga S., pp. 182, 186; Sir Geo. Mackenzie, *Travels in I.*, p. 39. The last legal duel (hólmganga—fought on an islet) was one between Gunlaug Ormstunga and Hrafn Ønundarson over Helga the Beautiful (Gunl. S. 11. *Inf.*, p. 143; see *Dic. C.V.*).

[2] Njál's S. xxvii, cxxxv; tr. G. W. Dasent.

[3] S. of Olaf Haraldsson, the Saint 111, 133.

occurred in Iceland, which had few priests and places of worship, and apparently not any teachers. Nevertheless, the seed had been sown at last, though the ground was stony and many briars grew strongly.

King Olaf persuaded Skapti Thoroddsson, the vigorous Lawman, who succeeded Thorgeir, to complete the adoption of Christianity by repealing all recognition of pagan practices. As a reward for this compliance, the king sent timber and a great bell for a church to be erected at Thingvellir (= Parliament Fields).

This building was burnt down a hundred years later, but it has been provided with successors down to the present day. A little church—the original cannot have been much smaller—occupies the same site by the river bank near a wishing well, overlooking the adulteresses' pool, and facing the Law-rock. Olaf's church at Thingvellir probably replaced the heathen temple.

(b) This royal benefaction gave an impetus to church-building in Iceland, which had been sparse and spasmodic even in the early days of Christian conversions, and later had almost lapsed. Settlers' foundations, such as St. Columba's Kjalarnes (pp. 17-8), had probably vanished before the arrival of the first missionaries, who left few churches (As, Holt and Hof). Snorri, the great godi, after his conversion, built churches at Helgafell and Tongue, where he was buried in 1031. Some say he also helped in the second church at Helgafell which Gudrun built.[1] Snorri's relative Styrr erected a church at Hraun (Lava), and Thorodd the Taxmonger had one built at his homestead at Froda "as soon as the Christian-making moot was over."[2] Sagas speak of other churches at Knapstadir, Vellir, Raudalæk, and at Hof in Vatnsdal. According to Runolf Dalksson, a twelfth-century priest, quoted in Bjarnar Saga, Bjorn the skald or poet, who died in 1024, composed a eulogy to St Thomas the Apostle, and dedicated a church to him, presumably in Hitardal, where he lived, destined like Helgafell to become a monastic centre.

A church was built at Borg in the west by Thorstein, son of the great viking-poet Egil Skallagrimsson. Here in 1003 Kjartan, Olaf's convert, was buried. His body was carried many miles, as there was no church near his home. At the time the church had just been consecrated, probably by a visiting bishop, Bernard of Saxony, and was still hung in white. Up to the last century travellers have

---

[1] *O.I.* II, p. 135. Vatnsdale Saga tells of Christianity in the N.W.

[2] Eyrbyggja Saga 48 and 65; Collingwood and Stèfansson, *Pilgrimage to Sagasteads of I.*, pp. 61-9. Thorodd was Snorri's brother-in-law.

been shown at Borg church a half-obliterated runic inscription commemorating "the brave Kjartan."[1]

Somewhat later the most famous church of early Christian days was built at Helgafell in the north-west by Gudrun, one of their most famous women, who had Kjartan slain. It was built soon after the adoption of Christianity, for her father was buried there in 1019. The early settler Thorwolf first established Helgafell as a sacred mountain dedicated to Thor—a place of judgment and prayer, and a sanctuary where no man or beast might be slain.[2] The fame of its subsequent monastic learning probably inspired the story in the Laxdale Saga (c. 1250) about the dying pagan chieftain who asked that his body might be laid to rest on the "holy hill, for that will be the greatest place about this countryside, for often have I seen a light burning there." It has been a sacred place for ten centuries.

Here Gudrun in her old age, having been four times married, lived as a nun or a recluse. "She was the first woman in Iceland to know the Psalter by heart, and, accompanied by her granddaughter Herdis, would spend long hours at night saying her prayers in the church she built."[3]

Gudrun's church was rebuilt in the next generation by her son Gellir "in a stately fashion," and, like so many of these wooden structures, was destroyed by fire. Its successor a hundred years later became a monastic centre, and a church stands there today.

The chief, Gizur the White, "who came with Christianity to Iceland," built on his homestead at Skálholt, on the Hvitá, twenty miles S.E. of Thingvellir, a church soon to become the mother church of Iceland.

About the year 1030, Oxi, son of Hjalti, the other Christian protagonist, built a church at Hólar reputed to be the largest church in the country. It had a wooden roof (trethak) covered with lead, and it was well furnished. "This church was burnt with all its fittings by the secret judgment of God."[4] Its successor became the cathedral of the north.

It is evident that, down to the twelfth century, places of worship in Iceland were built of wood, brought almost entirely from Norway. Such edifices were specially liable to destruction by fire, earthquake, or hurricanes, all frequent in this disquieted island.

[1] Laxdale S. li; Hooker in 1809 *Journal* i, p. lxxxii; Miss Oswald, *By Fell and Fjord*, p. 183; 1882. Borg continued in lay patronage until 1849 when by royal decree it "became a benefice."

[2] Eyrbyggja S. 4, 11 and 28; *Lndbk* II, 10. 2; see sup. p. 25.

[3] Laxdale S. lxxvi.   [4] Jónssaga 9. 1.

(c) In pre-Christian days chieftains had built temples on their estates and had acted as priests themselves. Some of them, like Snorri, attained eminence over a wide area by their second sight. They were prophets as well as priests, and, indeed, in their little goderds or clans, petty kings.

Some of these temples were converted into Christian places of worship. Other early churches were built by chieftains and enclosed within the turf walls protecting their farmsteads, which also contained labourers' bothies (buthir) and a "tún," the valuable cultivated meadow. We can see such homesteads still in outlying parts of the north. The arrangement and the name "tún" underlie our Scottish towns or touns. Adam of Bremen's strangely expressed observation, "Icelanders have their mountains for towns," probably means they make their "túns" on rising ground.[1] Chieftains are said to have been encouraged to build churches for more than their immediate circle—i.e., larger than private chapels—by the promise that each could admit into heaven as many as his church would hold.[2]

The godar were owners of the temples they erected or inherited, and when Christian churches were similarly built the founders claimed them as part of their estate, especially as they were expected to maintain them. This matter of ownership of ecclesiastical buildings became a most vexatious question argued between Church and chieftains for many generations.

(B) The Ministry and People

King Olaf Haraldsson took more definite steps for consolidating the infant Church by providing visiting bishops, whose names were given to the historian Ari by Teit, the son of the first native bishop. We note that almost all of them came from the British Isles.[3] In spite of this provision there was as yet no ecclesiastical organisation.

(a) Bishop Bernard Vildradsson, called the Book-learned, spent five years in Iceland (1016-21). He is said to have been English by birth and to have been brought to Norway by King Olaf as his court bishop. Nothing is stated of what he did while he was in Iceland,

---

[1] Adam of Bremen, *Hist. Eccl.* IV, 35; ed. G. Waitz. For tún, see Scott, *Waverley* IV. Tún meant the enclosed field (Njal's S. 112), and also the whole farmstead, including church (Nj. 23). Iceland had no proper towns before the twentieth century (*Dic. C.V.*).

[2] Eyrbyggja Saga 51, 53.

[3] *Hv.* 3; *Islendingabók* 8. At least they impressed their message on the language, for Iceland is the only Scandinavian country where the evangel is called by the English word Gospel (gudspjall).—*Dic. C.V.*

though his nickname suggests that he owned, and used, at least a small library, perhaps the first writing in a country of the spoken word. We may hope that he ordained priests and consecrated churches, and gave instruction to the people.

Four years later a Norwegian bishop, Kol, came over. He stayed with Hall of Haukadal, a pillar of the early Icelandic Church, who was baptised twenty years before by Thangbrand. Kol died four years after his arrival, and was buried at Skálholt, the nearest church to Haukadal. "He was the first bishop to be buried in Iceland and gave the church at Skálholt a prestige which it never lost."[1] This fact no doubt contributed to its subsequent elevation to be the first cathedral in the country.

Iceland appears to have been without a bishop for five years until Rudolf arrived, banished from Norway. He was a relative of Duke Richard of Normandy and had been brought over by King Olaf in 1015. He should be given the credit of establishing at Bae in Borgarfjörd Iceland's first monastery, where he lived for nineteen years with other monks,[2] and must have trained and ordained men for the priesthood. He retired to England in 1050, when he was made abbot of the monastery of Abingdon by his kinsman, Edward the Confessor, and died in 1052.[3]

During Rudolf's period in Iceland, Bishop Henry came from the Orkneys for two years, followed by Bishop Jón, who remained four years. The early account of the bishops, called *Hungrvaka*, cautiously adds: "Some men hold it for true that Jón afterwards fared to Vinland (*i.e.*, America, discovered by an Icelandic settler in 1000) and there turned many men to Christianity, and that in the end he fared through martyrdom to God." Adam of Bremen makes the more probable statement that this sincere and God-fearing missionary was martyred by the Vandals.[4]

Bernard, known as "the Saxon," was the most notable and longest resident of the six bishops, who for twenty years trained the infant Church of Iceland, until it produced its own bishop and established a certain measure of law and order. He stayed at Vatnsdal in the northwest and afterwards became Bishop of Selja, off Bergen in Norway. No account appears of episcopal activities, but of Bishop Bernard *Hungrvaka* quaintly records in the alliteration beloved of Icelandic

---

[1] *Hv B.S.*, I, 65.   [2] *Lndbk* I, 16.
[3] *Hist. Mon. Abingdon*, Rolls Series I, 463-4. Bruce Dickins on St Olave in Saga Bk of Viking Soc. XII, 2, p. 56 *n*.
[4] F. J. I, p. 87. For Vinland, see G. H. Gathorne-Hardy, *The Norse Discoverers of America*, London, 1922.

writers: "He hallowed many things, churches and cymbals, waters (*becki*) and wells, fords and fjörds, boulders and bells. These things are held to have afforded clear proof of his sanctity. . . . There is general opinion that of all these visiting bishops, Bernard was the most remarkable." We note the consecration of churches. Of the two kinds of "bells," one was not unlike the Columban handbell (see pp. 13-4). Rivers will have been prayed over, not only on account of the ever-prevalent danger in crossing them, but also to help salmon fishing. Boulders or rocks were blessed, because by that means trolls were thought to be exorcised.

(*b*) Bishops would have been required for the purpose of ordaining priests, for the supply of ministers was a problem of those early days. Eyrbyggja Saga, which pays careful attention to the development of Christianity in Iceland, sadly records that "there were no priests to say the hours at the churches even though they were built, for there were few in the country at the time."[1] Some chieftains hired untrained priests as an inferior kind of private chaplain. Such priests were regarded as so much a part of the household that, if they ran away, anyone who failed to return them to their master was outlawed.[2] They cannot have had any moral status or shown leadership.

Some church-building chiefs were ordained to look after their own churches, following the custom of heathen godar. This custom, like all great ideals, had its own dangers. But it led to a higher standard of education among the chiefs of Iceland in the twelfth century than was found at the time in any other countries in Europe. It produced some outstanding leaders of the nation, such as Ari, the first historian of his country (1067-1148), and Saemund the Wise (1056-1133); but for many priest-chiefs their priesthood had little influence on their lives, and so had little influence on the lives of their people.

Nevertheless, the absence of a narrow ecclesiasticism, a merely professional priesthood, made the Icelandic Church a really national institution, with a variety and width of interests that touched life at all its points.

During this time not only the Church but also the country was painfully acquiring civilisation. "The northern nations entered late into the inheritance of Roman civilisation which had survived in Western Europe."[3] When Iceland adopted Christianity in its own unique fashion, it possessed no literature and, indeed, no form of writing other than runic signs, painfully and infrequently cut on the sparse wood of the country or its intractable basalt rock.

[1] Eyrb. S. 48.   [2] Grágas 3.   [3] Phillpotts, *Edda and Saga*, p. 215.

(c) But a Church does not consist merely of its buildings and its ministers, and it has been a distinguishing mark of Icelandic Christianity in almost every age to produce lay men and women who have helped to strengthen its stakes, not only in the countryside, but also in the eternal values of truth, beauty, and goodness. Prominent among these early leaders we have noticed Jörund the Christian, pioneer of Christian perseverance, Thorvald the first missionary, Kjartan the chief convert of King Olaf, Hall of the Side and Hall of Haukadal, foster-fathers of the young Icelandic Church; and in particular Olaf's champions Hjalti and Gizur, valiant for truth. Among notable women the high-minded Queen Aud and Gudrun the penitent would find a place. Interesting stories are told of Thorodd's wife Thurid, sister of Snorri the godi, and of the immigrant Thorgunna from Tiree in the Hebrides, one of the first benefactors of the church at Skálholt.

Is it possible to trace the influence of Christianity on the rank and file of those days ?   Many sagas give vivid accounts of early Christian and pre-Christian times, but although they reflect traditions of the "saga-age," which finished a generation after Christianity was adopted, they were not written until a century after that, when the Faith had got a firm hold of the country. Indeed, so well established was their new religion that the Church was not afraid to let paganism fill a large and not unattractive part in the written saga. This is also a testimony to their truth. Most of the sagas centre round a blood-feud; but it is also significant that after Christianity had reached the country their descriptions of persons and events reflect something of the spirit of the new religion. We note a waning reliance on witch-craft, though the snakes of sorcery were never completely banished from Iceland.

It is only necessary to read some of the old sagas, with their philosophy of fatalism and their gruesome accounts of slaughters on almost every page, to see into what a dark world the light of Christianity was brought, and so to realise how deep and far-reaching was its influence.[1]

Conspicuously against the cruel and vengeful background of the old vikings is set the new virtue of kindness. We read of the generosity of Ingimund the Old to a pagan hag and her son, who repaid good with ill, for which Ingimund bore no malice; and of Thorvard "the Christian" at As, feeding many whom pagans were

---

[1] E.g., Njál's S. 62, 111, 144; Grettir's S. 40, 35; Laxdale S. 67, 55: "blackguardly and gruesomely done"; Olaf S. Trygg. 83, 87.

letting die of hunger.[1] The unheathen virtue of forgiveness is nobly illustrated in the saga about one of the finest of early Christians—the chieftain Njál. Njál bears no hatred in his heart and is "always ready to make up a quarrel." The last words of the dying Höskald to his treacherous assassinator were: "God help me and forgive you." In Flosi, Njál's principal enemy, the conflict of rival motives is exemplified, just as the viking Cross at Iona shows man between two lions. When Flosi determines on the unheroic deed of burning Njál in his home, he acknowledges his responsibility before God, "for we are Christian men ourselves." It is sometimes thought that this great battle-saga ends in anti-climax, for what the reader would expect to be the final battle-royal is dissolved in a handshake. But there is conflict other than that of arms; and when Flosi at last has at his mercy after a shipwreck Njál's son-in-law and avenger Kari, he asks him to stay in his house until winter ends. "Thus they were atoned with full atonement."[2]

The saga of Viga-Glum describes the long life of an old pagan worshipper and fighter whose religion and pugnacity brought him little profit, so that at last, old, blind, and in exile, he turned for comfort to Christianity.[3]

The kindly atmosphere cast over old stories when they came to be written down may have been due to a desire to turn them into Christian tracts. Nevertheless, even if they imperfectly represent the period depicted, yet they show the influence of Christian qualities in their compilers not long after the adoption of the new religion.

It marked a great advance when the Althing, consisting of chieftains, attempted to forbid personal conflicts so soon after Christianity "was taken up into the Law." This counsel of perfection, not even thought of in England for seven centuries afterwards, though it failed to prevent blood-feuds or duels, helped to mitigate the violence and vengeance of chieftains, and at least disseminated a spirit of forgiveness and consideration. Just as the recitation of old sagas proved easier than their transcription on vellum, so the proclamation of the new religion came more readily to Icelanders than the writing of Christian law in their hearts.

[1] Vatnsdale S. 22-6, trans. Baring-Gould; *Iceland, its Scenes and Sagas*, pp. 141 *sq.*; Olaf S. Trygg. 225.
[2] Njál's S. 158; Dasent, *The Story of Burnt Njál*, pp. clxxxvii-cxcv.
[3] Trans. E. Head. W. S. Craigie, *The Icelandic Sagas*, p. 43.

CHAPTER III

CONSOLIDATION OF THE ICELANDIC CHURCH

(i) The First Native Bishop—Islief (1056-80)

It had always been the fashion for the sons of chieftains to "fare abroad" in order to gain experience in foreign lands before settling down. On their return they described their experiences and displayed acquisitions to their family circle. These men came into touch with continental Christianity and thus indirectly prepared the way for the Church. Its consolidation and development waited until Icelanders themselves had been taught to supervise it. For Iceland makes little response to outside influence unless it is mediated by her own people.

(*a*) The adoption of Christianity in Iceland was largely due to the initiative of Gizur the White, who afterwards "set his whole mind to effect its strengthening."[1] He sent his son Isleif to be educated under the Abbess Godesti at the famous school of Herford in Westphalia, thus solving the main problem which confronted the undeveloped Christianity of the country—the training of a regular ministry. For after ordination Isleif settled on his father's estate at Skálholt and established there what the Bishops' Saga[2] naively calls "a good cure and a parish," apparently the first to be properly organised in the country.

When Isleif reached home "his kinsfolk thought it good that he should strengthen his position by taking a wife." For since the time of its foundation the Church in Iceland ignored papal decrees as to celibacy. Not for 120 years do we find a bishop, unmarried himself, attempting to force celibacy on his clergy; and the results of this attempt proved disastrous.

The story of Isleif's courtship is typical of the spirit of that day, with its robust independence and homely common-sense. With a friend he went to Asgeirsa in Vididal and told his errand to the girl's father Thorvald (a member of a great northern family, lately christianized), but met with the reply: "Good accounts are going of thee, but thou must dwell farther north, if thou wilt be wed." Isleif answered: "I do not agree to leave my parish; rather, we must part."

With that he and his companion mounted their ponies and rode

---

[1] Kristni S. 10, 1.

[2] This homely and personal story of the first five bishops of Skálholt is quaintly named *Hungrvaka* (The Appetiser); cp. *inf.* pp. 81-82.

off. Now Dalla, "the fairest of women," was up in a hayrick and called to her father asking who the men were, and when she heard, added: "I have the ambition to possess the best husband and the most famous son with him that were ever born in Iceland; therefore I think it is not inadvisable to send after them."[1]

Isleif and Dalla dwelt at Skálholt and had three famous sons: Gizur, bishop after his father; Teit, the learned instructor of the historian Ari; and Thorvald, "a mickle chief."

(b) In the year 1056 it was the counsel of the people to have a bishop over them; and Isleif, then fifty years old, was chosen as bishop "by the whole commonwealth of Iceland." He was bidden to go abroad for his consecration at the hands of Archbishop Adalbert of Bremen, who in 1053 had received authority over all Christians in northern lands.[2] On his way he went to see the Emperor Henry III, taking him a white bear that had come, no doubt on polar ice, from Greenland. That winter and the next were notoriously severe, lasting with snow until June and causing great mortality through famine.[3] The Emperor gave Isleif a pass, and then he went to obtain a brief from Pope Victor II. The Pope appointed Whit-Sunday for the consecration, "hoping that long honour might accrue to the bishopric if the first bishop of Iceland were consecrated on the day on which God adorned the whole world with the gift of the Holy Spirit." This was done, but it is significant that the date was noted in Icelandic story as "fourteen nights before Columba's mass" (May 26, 1056).[4] This reckoning not only avoids the ambiguity of a movable feast, but it also indicates the respect of the Icelandic Church for St Columba as one of their spiritual fathers, to whom some of their earliest churches were dedicated.

Bishop Isleif set his chair in Skálholt church, which then became the mother church of Iceland and the chief centre of culture in the island until the end of the eighteenth century.

(c) One of the first and greatest of Isleif's achievements was the establishment at his bishopstead of a school especially for ordinands, which was continued by most bishops down the centuries until the place was destroyed by an earthquake in 1784. Isleif admirably combined national traditions with European culture. To start with, the country had to be taught to write. Runes laboriously carved for

---

[1] *Flatey Book* ii, pp. 140-2; *Dipl. Isl.* I, No. 18.

[2] Adam of Bremen, *Hist. Eccl.* IV, 35. Bishop-elect=biskups-efni.

[3] "Everything was eaten that the tooth could bite on."

[4] A similar reckoning is used for Bishop Gizur's death (*inf.*, p. 48). The date, Columba-mass, appears as late as 1498.

memorial inscriptions on basalt pillars had not taken scribes far on the road to writing characters on parchment or vellum. Isleif had been trained at Herford on the Weser, and would introduce the continental script, in which his son Teit appears to have proved an apt pupil, passing on his knowledge to Ari, who was not slow to set down in writing lucid and enduring records. Chieftains seized this opportunity for sending their sons to Isleif, and many afterwards became good clerks. Two became bishops, Kol at Vik in Norway and Jón, son of Ogmund, first bishop of Hólar, the northern see in Iceland. It is remarkable that a small isolated country, hardly out of the nursery of civilisation, should train a priest so that he went to serve abroad and attained high office on the Continent, where education had flourished for centuries.

Jón used to pay a fine tribute to his foster-father. Whenever in later life he heard a man speak of any who were handsome, or wise, or worthy, he used to declare that Isleif came into his mind.

In the matter of temporalities for the see the new bishop had also to begin from nothing. He had little income, though Skálholt was to become the best farm in the country. But "there was much outgoing, and the bishop found it hard to live." He succeeded in getting sanction from the Althing for a toll (tollr), probably a head-tax, out of which other than personal expenses were met.

The bishop used his influence to mitigate external feuds between chieftains, which were beginning to satisfy their viking energies in place of the sea-roving, so vigorously denounced by King Olaf Haraldsson. Interest was growing in learning and literary pursuits fostered by the episcopal school, and in the development of the Commonwealth under Christian conditions. It is characteristic of the Icelandic Church that most men of standing were ordained, thus ensuring a general high level of scholarship.[1] But moral laxity had increased since the old days of faithfulness and devotion to duty, to such an extent that the bishop had to censure a Lawman who had married both a mother and her daughter.

(d) Isleif and his people were troubled by episcopi vagantes, one of the ecclesiastical diseases of the Middle Ages. Islendingabók gives the number of those "who said they were bishops" as five, and states their names. Three of them were Armenians, possibly of the Paulician sect.[2] They laid down easier rules than Bishop Isleif, so they found favour with evil men, "until Archbishop Adalbert issued a writ against them." In the bishop's latter days his greatness and

[1] Kristni S. 17.   [2] Cp. Gibbon, *Decline and Fall*, ch. 54.

goodness became manifest; so says the *Hungrvaka*, which illustrates his twofold gift of healing in one of its vivid and memorable pictures: "He blessed beer into which darnel had got and rendered it drinkable, and many mad folk were brought for him to lay his hands upon them, and they went away healed."

Isleif exercised great influence through the Althing. From the first the bishops were allotted seats in the Assembly, and more than filled the place of the heathen high-priests. For it was while Isleif, as chaplain, was celebrating Mass at the annual gathering that he fell ill. He had a room prepared for him in Skálholt cathedral church, from which he gave much final counsel. On July 5, "three nights[1] before the Festival of the Selja Saints," 1080, he died there after an episcopate of twenty-four years, that augured well for the Church in Iceland. The careful historian Ari adds: "I was there with Teit, my foster-brother, being twelve years old."

(ii) The Notable Rule of Bishop Gizur (1082-1118)

Isleif on his death-bed was invited by the Althing to nominate his successor. Thus a fortunate precedent was set in the method of electing the country's bishops. When the nominee refused, "the whole Althing turned to Gizur his son, and bade him fare abroad to be consecrated." In this way the nation paid a great tribute to the inaugural work of their first bishop. He had tackled the main problems before the young Church and State with resolution and tact, and laid down principles in which satisfactory solutions might ultimately be found. Before consenting, Gizur shrewdly obtained the Assembly's promise of support. Then he procured the Pope's brief, and was consecrated by Hardvig, Archbishop of Magdeburg, on September 4, 1082, being then forty years of age. Like his father, he had been educated at Herford and had travelled widely.

When Harald Hardradi, King of Norway, met him, he said: "Out of Gizur three men might be made. He is well suited to be a viking captain, and that he might be. He is well suited to be a king. But he is best suited to be a bishop, and this office he shall have, and be held a most notable man therein."[2] *Hungrvaka* says: "He excelled in all

---

[1] "Three nights"—the ecclesiastical reckoning of the day beginning with its eve at 6 p.m. (*inf.*, p. 48). The custom of counting time by nights rather than by days still continues and is of ancient origin; cp. Tacitus, *Germania* 2, nec dierum numerum, ut nos, sed noctium computant; and 11, "Night, the mother of the day"; cp. our fortnight (*Dic. G.V.*). For the Selja Saints see note, p. 54.)

[2] Harald Hardradi's Saga, *O.I.* I, p. 596. H. H. was killed at Stamford Bridge, 1066.

things that a man ought to know. . . ." On his return as bishop, the people received him joyfully, and he won such honour and esteem that "everyone was willing to sit or stand as he bade . . . and it would be true to say he was both king and bishop over the land while he lived."

He was practically the founder of the dioceses of Skálholt and Hólar; and he proved to be a great statesman as well as an ecclesiastic. A striking testimony to his strength of character is paid by the record that he kept such peace in the land that feuds between chieftains ceased and the carrying of weapons almost fell into disuse.

(a) His episcopate was marked by four great achievements.

1. He rebuilt the cathedral and endowed it with money and lands. After the death of his mother Dalla he gave the family house to the see, declaring that "there should always be a bishop's chair there while Iceland is inhabited and Christianity endures."

Alas for the frailty of human wishes! After a century of devastating volcanic eruptions and earthquakes, the last of which in 1784 destroyed the cathedral, this historic see was transferred to Reykjavik by Denmark in 1785 at the end of 700 years of service which survived the Reformation.

2. With a view to establishing a system of tithes, the bishop had a census taken of the bondi or yeoman farmers which gave the following interesting results: In the Quarter of the South, 1,000; of the East, 700; of the West, 900; and of the North, 1,200—a total (according to the duodecimal system) of 4,560. Allowing for dependants, Gjerset estimates that this would make the total population about 50,000.[1] These were scattered over, or rather round, an island five-fourths the size of Ireland, segregated into small communities by mountains, by unnavigable rivers, and by deserts of sand and lava, making administration an exacting enterprise.

3. By the help of two eminent counsellors, Saemund, priest of Oddi (1056-1133), "the most prudent and learned man of the day," and Markus Skeggisson (†1107), the Speaker, the bishop established in 1096, through the Althing, a system of tithes to be distributed in four parts: (1) for the bishop, (2) for the Church, (3) for the clergy, (4) for the poor. Such episcopal revenue had been authorised by Charlemagne and was the custom in Saxon England, but afterwards it had generally lapsed. By this establishment of tithe the clergy

---

[1] Kristni S. 13; *Islendingabók* 10, Gj., p. 67. (In 1790, after a century of volcanic disaster, there were only 40,000 in the island; in 1890 the total was about 70,000; in 1943, 125, 915, of whom one-third live in Reykjavik.)

obtained a fixed income and became less dependent for their living on the patronage of chieftains or on secular pursuits. The maximum stipend for priests was 12 marks (=5 cows), together with fees for funerals and masses for the dead.[1] Clerical tithe was abolished in 1914. The quarter-tithe earmarked for the poor reverted to the community to administer, a method unknown on the Continent, indicating the national character of the Icelandic Church.[2]

The author of *Hungrvaka*, writing after the Church had a century's experience of the importance of tithe and the intricacies of its collections, adds a suggestive comment: "There has been no such foundation in Skálholt for wealth as this tithe-tax, which was laid on by reason of the popularity and power of Bishop Gizur."

4. In 1105, at the request of the people of the north, "the thickest settled, most famous Quarter," Gizur granted them a bishop of their own; and "there was afterwards chosen by God and good men" Jón, son of Øgmund, pupil or foster-son of Bishop Isleif. After his consecration by the Primate at Lund, Bishop Jón set his chair at Hólar in Skagafjörd, and established there a centre of learning and civilisation in the north. Jón, who was afterwards venerated as a saint, had a distinguished episcopate which deserves a section to itself.

(b) In 1110 a bishopric was founded at Gardar in Greenland, which had been discovered by the Icelander Eirik the Red in 981, and Christianised by his son Leif at the instigation of King Olaf Tryggvason.[3] In his travels Leif "the Lucky" wintered in America.

In these early days the Church of Iceland took much interest in its daughter Church in Greenland. The Skálholt Annals record that Eirik, the first (according to one MS) Bishop of Greenland, went to search for Vinland, as Leif called the west coast of America, and was heard of no more (1112-21). The second bishop, Arnald, spent the winter of 1124-5 with Saemund at Oddi; and one of his successors was entertained at Skálholt in 1203 by Bishop Pál. The settlement was cut off from all outside communication during the Black Death of 1349 and probably perished, except a small remnant which was absorbed by Eskimos.[4]

An attempted resettlement perished like the first. The last bishop was Alf, who, according to the Annals, went out in 1368 and died in

[1] Grágás 6; *Dipl. Isl.* I (No. 22), pp. 70-162; *B.S.* I, 29 and 68.
[2] Gregersen, *L'Islande—Son Statut à travers les âges*, p. 40.
[3] Eiriks S. rauda, *Flateybk* III, p. 446; Gj., pp. 114-6.
[4] Cp. V. Stefansson, *Greenland*, pp. 118 *sq.* For list of eight bishops, see *Dipl. Isl.* III, pp. 21, 27.

Greenland in 1378. Ruins of ancient Norse churches there show traces of Irish architecture.

In former days missionaries to that bleak country had difficulties other than the climate with which to contend. The Eskimos had never seen sheep, so the metaphor of the Saviour as the Lamb of God had to be conveyed to them as "God's baby-seal."

(c) When Gizur had been bishop for thirty-six years, being then seventy-five years of age, he became dangerously ill, and sent to the Althing the name of Thorlak for election as his successor. His pain increased, and his wife Steinunn begged him to allow vows to be made to alleviate it. But the bishop said: "It is not permitted for a man to have himself prayed out of God's battle."

He died "12 nights before St Columba's day" (May 28, 1118). *Hungrvaka* adds: "Many men who were at Bishop Gizur's death-bed never forgot it as long as they lived; and it has been the opinion of all wise men that by the grace of God and his unusual talents he has been the noblest man in Iceland, both of clerks and laymen." So Ari similarly: "He was more beloved by his fellow-countrymen than any man we know to have lived in this land."

Of Gizur in particular Adam of Bremen must have been thinking when in 1100 he summed up Church rule among the Icelanders: "For a king they have their bishop, and to his nod all the people attend. Whatsoever he lays down from God or scripture or from customs of other nations, that they have for law."[1] Adam shows the same reserved enthusiasm for these early Icelandic bishops as Bede had for the Celtic missionaries. He praises their saintly sincerity of life (*sancta simplicitas*).

(iii) STORM, STRIFE, AND SCHOLARSHIP

Storm, strife, and scholarship marked the Icelandic Church almost throughout its history. For the people live on the edge of devastating volcanoes and have a natural propensity for personal quarrels and clannish feuds; and yet even in their most disastrous and bellicose periods they maintained an intense interest in literary pursuits.

During the constructive epoch of the first two bishops, Hekla and her fiercer sisters were quiescent, and men's passions followed suit, so that the era was known as the Peace Period. Furthermore, though

---

[1] Adam of Bremen, *Hist. Eccl.* IV, 35, cp. Giraldus Cambr., *Topographia Hibernica*, 13: "Their pontiff is their prince" (1187).

sagas were being preserved by recitation, and episcopal schools were teaching the art of script introduced by Christianity, Icelandic literature hardly began until shortly after Bishop Gizur's death, when the priest Ari Thorgilsson inaugurated a long series of historical writings of remarkable brilliancy.

(a) In order to mark the greatness of Bishop Gizur, *Hungrvaka* emphasises the atrociousness of the weather in the year in which he died. It is right that we should be reminded that the Icelanders' character and religion have been shaped largely by the trying climate and harsh conditions of their country on the edge of the Arctic Circle.

"There was such a storm in Holy Week that the clergy could not take services on Good Friday. Few could receive Corpus Domini on Easter Day." (This provides a timely illustration of pastoral work in Iceland, as we realised when our Forces were stationed there in the recent war.) "A merchant ship was cast up under Eyjafell and turned over keel upwards. Another storm came, as men rode to the Thing (in June), and killed cattle in the north. This destroyed the church of Thingvellir, for which the King of Norway had given timber. That summer thirty-five ships came to Iceland, but only eight went out to Norway, a week's journey."

"The fall of Bishop Gizur forboded a period of universal suffering in the country, shipwrecks and loss of life and scathe of cattle." The Annals call this "undraar," year of portents. Most of the calamities mentioned, including the first recorded eruption of Hekla in 1029,[1] actually preceded his death, so we feel that the real disaster to which they lead up is "the dissension and lawbreaking, and thereby such death of men in the land, that the like has never been seen since the country was inhabited." What Icelandic writers call Fridaröld—the Peace Period (1030-1118)—ceased on the death of Bishop Gizur.

(b) When his strong rule was removed feuds between chieftains recently suppressed broke into open conflict. How furious such feuds could be is shown in the sagas of Njál and Grettir. Those were days of personal vendettas, before Christianity got hold of men. Nevertheless, when religion closed the safety valve of viking sea-roving, chieftains sought outlets for their combativeness within the narrow confines of their country. Soon leading chieftains began to multiply their adherents and so upset the balance of power. The national régime formed a league of petty nations or clans without a police force, so that eventually the government broke down. The Church itself was not strong enough to maintain order, but leading ecclesias-

[1] *Hv.* 2, 23.

tics by their personal influence, especially in early days, sometimes
did so. For instance, in the year 1120, when rival chiefs appeared at
the Thing to assert their rights with their followers at their backs fully
armed, battle was avoided only by the intervention of Bishop Gizur's
successor, Thorlak Runolfsson (1118-35), with the help of the
venerated and now venerable Saemund the Wise.[1]

Icelanders are litigious by nature, and priests got into trouble for
taking too much time over lawsuits to the neglect of their parishes.
They found it a means of adding to their meagre incomes. Nor were
clergy themselves free from the lawless spirit of the age. We read
how a priest Ketill, who had heard that his wife Groa had been
solicited by a chieftain called Gudmund, attacked him on the high-
way, but got the worst of the encounter and lost an eye. However,
honour had been satisfied, and Ketill was afterwards made Bishop of
Hólar (1122-45). It is impossible not to admire the priest who took
the law into his hand in a lawless age, and it is gratifying to note that
later, when Gudmund fell into poverty, the bishop offered to look
after him.[2] Ketill later used this personal episode, with its conclusion
in peace of mind won by forgiveness, to assuage the anger of a
vindictive chieftain.[3]

The old law of Iceland, hitherto proclaimed by the Lawman from
the Law-mount at the Althing, was for the first time written down in
1117-8 at the Lawman's dictation. Following this lead, Bishop
Thorlak took in hand the transcription and codification of all existing
Church Law, being assisted by Bishop Ketill, the learned priest
Saemund, and Ozur, the Primate of Lund. This Kristinrettr was
passed by the Althing in the years 1122-33, and incorporated in the
law of the land.[4] This was Thorlak's great achievement, and made a
notable advance in ecclesiastical administration, actually anticipating
the collection of Canon Law in the Decretum of Gratian completed
about 1140. Copies of the law were kept at the bishopsteads, the final
authority being the copy at Skálholt. To this copy the odd title of
Grágás was afterwards given, probably on account of its binding of
grey goose skin.[5]

It is characteristic of Iceland that this ecclesiastical law was administered by the Althing and not by the Church. Breaches of
ecclesiastical discipline were dealt with by an ecclesiastical tribunal of

---

[1] Sturlunga S. I, 5-27.   [2] Ljósvetinga S. 31.
[3] Sturlunga S. I, 7-39.   [4] Dipl. Isl. I, No. 98.
[5] First in Bp Gissur Einarsson's valuation, March 26, 1548; Cod. Reg.
Grágás, Introd. Olason. See inf. pp. 149, 151.

the Althing called *prestadomr*, but civil and criminal cases were brought before the ordinary courts.[1]

(c) Iceland was beginning to take pride in its own history. National consciousness had sprung to birth, fostered chiefly by the school at Haukadal, where Bishop Thorlak had been trained. Thorlak encouraged Ari and Saemund in their work on history. He continued the training school for clergy at Skálholt, in which he was ably seconded by Torfi, the former bishop's grandson and chaplain, who appears to have been a model priest. "A splendid man," says *Hungrvaka*. He was always of the same temper and never unoccupied. Every day he sang a third of the Psalter slowly and meditatively, and between his devotions he studied, taught and transcribed the Scriptures. He gave healing advice to those who needed it and came to visit him. Though he had the reputation of being close-fisted in many things, he was ready with alms. Torfi was burnt to death (see *inf.* p. 58). We learn from a letter of Bishop Brynjolf, written in 1658, that in memory of this outstanding chaplain a prebend was founded at Skálholt, endowed with a farm named Torfastadir.

For about a year before his death Bishop Thorlak was confined to his bed in the dormitory which he shared with his priests. As his illness grew, the bishop had read to him Pope Gregory's greatest book, *De Cura Pastorali*. "When that was done he seemed to all to await death more cheerfully than he did before." Although learned Icelanders had access to Catholic culture, yet insular tradition prevented many from taking kindly to it.

They were acquainted also with Catholic hagiology. After having been bishop for fifteen years Thorlak died in 1133 "on St Bridget's Eve." "At the same moment," *Hungrvaka* adds with reserve, "a priest named Arni was faring on his way in the north, when he heard over his head fair singing from *St Lambert's Martyrdom*, 'Sic animam claris cælorum reddidit astris.'[2] Many thought there was much in this circumstance, and never let it fall out of memory."

Bishop Thorlak's foster-father, Hall, son of Thorarin, who had been responsible for his love of learning, was a remarkable man. He lived over fifty years at Haukadal, fifteen miles north-west of Skálholt, in a district now wild and barren, just north of the great Geysir. He had been a friend of King Olaf the Saint, and remembered his own

---

[1] Grágás 28; Gregersen, *L'Islande—Son Statut à travers les Ages*, p. 40. The Icelandic custom resembled the procedure at the Witanagemot.

[2] 'So he gave back his spirit to the bright stars of heaven;' from anon. poem ap. Bollandists, Sep. 17. Lambert was Bp of Maestricht (*c.* 633-700).

baptism at the age of three at the hand of Thangbrand in the year 999. He had remembered, too, most of the great events since then. Like all true scholars, he was most generous with his knowledge, which he passed on to another foster-son, Teit, son of Bishop Isleif, and through him to Ari, the author of *Islendingabók*, who also was a pupil at Haukadal from the age of seven; so that if Ari be styled the father of Icelandic history, Hall of Haukadal is its foster-father. He died in 1089 at the age of ninety-three.

Thorlak in his turn became the foster-father of Gizur, Teit's grandson, and predicted rightly that he would become a man of mark. This Gizur became a notable Law-man or Speaker, "one of the treasures of Iceland," who lived to the age of eighty, and was a friend of five bishops of Skálholt (†1206); so says the author of *Hungrvaka*, acknowledging his indebtedness to "that learned man."

Thus for 200 years the lamp of knowledge was passed on from generation to generation in this obscure northern outpost of civilisation, and the clear beams then kindled illuminate us yet.

The priest Ari Thorgilsson the Wise (1067-1148) was a great-grandson of Gudrun, the heroine of the Laxdale Saga and descendant of Hall-of-the-Side, one of the first Christians to be baptised. He was foster-son and pupil of Teit, son of the first bishop, and learned much also from Thurid, Snorri the godi's daughter, "who was both wise and truthful."[1] Ari devoted his life to establishing the details of the foundation and Christianising of his country, summing them up admirably in the *Islendingabók*, his Libellus, which he made for Bishops Thorlak and Ketill, the earliest historical work in the native tongue (probably 1122-33). He based his conclusions on careful enquiry, stating his authorities and weighing the evidence. "This I learned from Teit, who learned it from one who was there." His reading extended to the works of Bede, whom he quotes. Ari's researches also underlie *Landnámabók*, the unique and invaluable Book of the Settlement. Snorri Sturluson (†1241) pays him a worthy tribute in the prologue to his famous *Heimskringla*: "It is not surprising that Ari was excellently informed about early events . . . since he had learned from old men and wise, and was himself eager to learn, and had a good memory."[2]

Saemund hinn Frodi, the Wise (1056-1133), grandson of Hall-of-the-Side, counsellor of three bishops, is described in the saga of St

[1] *Islendingabók* 1. For Ari see Arnór Einarsson, *Ari Frodi*, Rvk, 1942.
[2] Cp. Vigfusson, Sturlunga S. I, pp. xxvii *sq.*, and especially the article in *Islandica*, Vol. XX, by Halldor Hermansson.

Jón of Hólar as "the man who of all others has been the greatest help to the Church of God in Iceland." He was educated in Paris, and, returning about 1078 to be ordained, settled in his father's farm estate at Oddi in the south, where he built a large church dedicated to St Nicolas.[1] Here, too, he founded a school, passing on his culture through his sons Eyjolf and Lopt. Saemund as a mediaeval scientist practised astrology, and so acquired a reputation as a magician, a wizard almost of uncanny arts.[2] Eyjolf Saemundsson became the greatest teacher of the day, and trained Bishop Thorlak, one of the two national saints. From the school of Oddi emerged in the next century the *Heimskringla* of Snorri, foster-son of Jón Loptsson, grandson of Saemund.

Academic chroniclers tend to forget that history is lived before it can be written. Hence the weakness of monkish annals. The soundest history is based upon experience, a living concrete happening taken into the life of the recorder. The schools of Skálholt, Haukadal and Oddi, though cradled and fostered in the Church, went farther. Their writers were themselves vigorous shapers of the events they vividly recorded. This literary productivity would not have been possible had not the runic alphabet been translated into roman letters, an achievement said to have been brought about by a carpenter at the beginning of the twelfth century, though no doubt foundations of a national script were laid by Bishops Bernard and Rudolf and followed up at the four great schools. The oldest extant Icelandic manuscript dates from 1150.[3]

A little later a masterly piece of mathematics was carried out in adapting the old computation of years to the Julian kalendar, introduced into the country by Christianity.

Icelanders still like to reckon only two seasons in the year, and observe as holidays the first day of summer and winter, April 24 and October 25, in a semi-pagan or, rather, delightfully historic fashion that the matter-of-factness of modernity has not succeeded in obliterating.

A significant feature about this great Icelandic prose literature indicates the patriotic and independent spirit of the country and its Church. Almost all the writing, ecclesiastical as well as secular, was in the vernacular. Except, perhaps, in actual devotions, the language of the Church, like the language of literature, was the language of the people.

---

[1] *Islendingabók* 9; *B.S.* I, p. 320.   [2] *B.S.* I, pp. 227-9.
[3] *Icelandic Illuminated MSS of the Middle Ages*, Introd., p. 9.

NOTE ON THE SELJA SAINTS

Seljamen's Mass, the festival of the Selja Saints, appears on July 8 in the Norwegian and Icelandic kalendars and breviaries. It is also included in the Scots Menology, a memorial of the period 1152-1472, during which the Orkneys were under the jurisdiction of the Archbishop of Nidaros, afterwards Trondhjem.

The festival was popular in Iceland, especially in the southern diocese. Bishop Magnus (1134-48) changed the Church day, the annual festival of Skálholt Cathedral, from Holy Cross day in spring (May 3) to Seljamen's Mass, which followed after the annual meeting of the Althing, held twenty-five miles off at Thingvellir, and made a good climax to that legal and social Assembly.

This festival was used in the ordinary way to mark a date—e.g., Bishop Isleif died in 1080 "three nights before Seljamen's Mass." Selja saints' vigil is the date of a fray reported in the Annals under 1362, in which a tax-gatherer called Smith was killed (Gj., p. 248).

Selja is an island off Bergen in Norway, where in the days of King Olaf Tryggvason (according to his saga) a workman found a luminous skull. He took this to the king, knowing his fanatical zeal in the cause of the Church. Then sailors in passing ships reported the appearance of a strange light coming from a heap of rocks, underneath which the king found a female body intact, and other bones. The body was believed to be the remains of an Irish princess, Sunniva, who set out from Ireland in a vessel without sails or rudder, to escape the unworthy attentions of a heathen chieftain—a Scandinavian version of the story of St Ursula and her companions.[1]

King Olaf built on the island a church and a monastery dedicated to St Alban, the proto-martyr of Britain, evidence of the close connection between the two churches in the days of early Norwegian Christianity. England repaid the tribute by extensive devotion to the cult of St Olaf (Haraldsson), the patron saint of Norway. This devotion links England, Norway, and Iceland.[2]

In 1170 the Selja relics were removed to St Michael's Monastery in Bergen, which received additional endowment in 1280 from Arni Thorlaksson, Bishop of Skálholt, by the gift of the Westman Islands. In 1545 the monastic possessions were vested in a leper hospital in Bergen.

[1] T. B. Willson, *Church and State in Norway*, pp. 47-8, 119-20. Sigrid Unset, *Kristin Lavransdottir*, note, pp. 931-2. ? St Alban = Sunniva's brother.

[2] Bruce Dickins, "Cult of St Olave in the British Isles," art. in *Saga Book of the Viking Society* XII, ii, 1940.

CHAPTER IV

CLIMAX OF THE ICELANDIC CHURCH

(i) Two Chieftain-Bishops

(A) *Magnus* (1134-48)

In this imperfect world it is easy to criticise prince-bishops and parson-squires. The Barchester novels show how they tend to become more secular than spiritual, like the "half-priest" mentioned in one of the sagas.

In specialist days such criticism is sharpened. In cities the artisan who shapes the chair-leg will have nothing to do with the seat or the fixing. In the country still a single craftsman will take pride in turning out the job complete. So the early bishops in Iceland, who held that Christianity should influence all sides of life, proved master-craftsmen of the Church.[1]

If Isleif may be termed the St Paul of the growing Icelandic Church and Gizur the St Peter, then Thorlak may be termed its St John and Magnus its St Barnabas.

(a) Thorlák's successor at Skálholt, Magnus, a grand-nephew of Hall-of-the-Side, had been well grounded in letters and religion by his father and stepmother, Einur and Oddnya, daughter of Magnus, priest of Reykholt. *Hungrvaka* gives a characteristically long genealogy and a long alliterative list of his good qualities, out of which emerges the fact that he earned popularity as a priest for charm, generosity, and peace-making.

Thorlak Runolfsson died in February, 1133. Magnus Einarsson in the customary way was elected at the summer Althing, but owing to storms, although a good seaman, he could not go abroad until the following summer, when he was consecrated by Ozur, Archbishop of Lund. King Harald of Norway gave him many valuable gifts, including a loving cup, which the bishop made into a chalice.

He returned home the year after, reaching Eyjafjörd in the north while the Althing was in session. He went straight over the mountain passes to Thingvellir, where the chronic litigation between chieftains had reached a dangerous stage. But when a messenger announced to the Law-man, "Now rides Bishop Magnus to the Thing" (Thá ridi Magnus biskup á Thingit), dissension dropped.

---

[1] It is significant that the usual word for organised religion was Kristni—Christianity, and not Kirkja, which almost was confined to the building (*Dic. C.V.*). Cp. p. 39 *sup.*

On arrival the bishop climbed the mound in front of the church and gave the Assembly and the crowds an account of his experiences in Norway, thus lifting their provincial thoughts into a wider world; "and all men thought a great deal of his eloquence and dignity."

Travellers' tales formed a welcome element in Icelanders' education. Young men of standing travelled to Norway and sometimes beyond it, to Sweden, Germany, even to Paris and Rome, and on their return retailed their experiences and news of world happenings to appreciative but critical home circles. These travellers' tales had to pass the renowned Icelandic standard of truth. Among conspicuous ecclesiastical travellers we have already mentioned Thorvald the Far-farer, Kjartan, Hall of Haukadal, Isleif, his sons Teit and Gizur, and Saemund the Wise. It will be noted that the Church provided a valuable link in this educational process. Small sailing vessels that braved sub-arctic seas in those early years were more numerous every summer than were the larger ships which steamed across them in the nineteenth century.

Sailing boats in a fair wind took about five days to cross from the north of Ireland to the south-west corner of Iceland,[1] and the steamers from Leith took not much less time (although in the recent war fifty-two hours was a good journey from Reykjavik to the Clyde, and I flew from Skerjafjörd to Milford Haven, 1,000 miles, between breakfast and tea).

(b) "Bishop Magnus rides to the Thing" would make an attractive subject for a picture of a great churchman's influence on the turbulent passions of his half-tamed people.

In the rock-walled valley in the clear northern sunshine we would see at the head of the tranquil lake thirty-nine chieftains in their resplendent uniforms, drawn up in rival clans, backed by their retainers, armed with battle-axes and swords. Their anxious women-folk, richly robed, with their long fair hair plaited and diademed, would be grouped by the booths which line the rocky banks of the Oxará.

As angry clamant shouts assail the Law-man and re-echo in the valley, a messenger runs up and points northwards, where through a gap in the great mountain wall a small company of ponies is seen approaching, and the joyful cry runs round the assembly: "Thá ridi Magnus biskup á Thingit."

In spite of his popularity and accession of power, the youthful

---

[1] *Lndbk* I, 1; Olaf S. Trygg. 112, where day = 24 hours, though generally in Iceland = 12 hours (*Dic. C.V.*).

Magnus retained towards all the same humility as he had shown before he became bishop. "Therefore he was more beloved than most other men, and was able to do many great deeds."

He spared neither time nor money in order to settle disputes, and so there were no quarrels and no litigation while he was bishop.

Magnus enlarged his cathedral at Skálholt, and changed its festival (kyrkjudagr) from Holy Cross day in spring (May 3) to the festival of the Saints of Selja—Seljamen's Mass (July 8). This favourite commemoration would associate the cathedral festival with the memorial of the first bishop's death, and, falling later in the season, following the session of the Althing, would better suit the convenience of visitors.

The bishop presented the cathedral with a costly altar frontal which he had brought from abroad. He also brought over purple from which was made that cope called, says the *Hungrvaka*, "Skarbending."[1]

He endowed the see with numerous lands, in particular purchasing the Westman Islands, in which he proposed to establish a monastery on the lines of that founded at Thingeyrar in the north in 1133, under the auspices of Ketill, Bishop of Hólar.

(c) Both Magnus and Ketill came to an untimely end. When Ketill reached seventy years of age he desired to retire from his bishopric, and commended himself to the prayers of the synod of priests at the Althing. Then Magnus invited him to his dedication festival at Skálholt, in connection with which he gave a banquet, serving a goodly supply of mead, the whole "so elaborate that it had scarcely a parallel in Iceland." At this feast no doubt, in accordance with the Christianised version of an ancient northern custom, a bumper (Icelandic "bumba") would be drunk to departed relatives, then one to Christ (Kristsminni), and a third to the patron saints.[2]

After supper on the Friday following both bishops went to bathe in the adjacent hot springs. Consequently the aged Bishop Ketill died. Great sorrow fell on the festive company until the close of his funeral, when "the comforting speech of Bishop Magnus, and the excellent drink provided, made men forget their sorrows sooner than they would otherwise have done."

Three years later Bishop Magnus went to Hitardal to keep Michaelmas, when it happened the night afterwards that the house in which

---

[1] *V.l.* skarmendingr; a full chasuble, an Icelandic fashion. Or ? curiously fastened; cp. Skaru-bunden in Beowulf, cunningly bound, with a curious artistic clasp. Cp. Bp Audun's gift to Hólar, *inf.*, p. 119.

[2] Hakon's Saga 16. 1.

he was staying was burned down. Seventy-two men were burnt to death, including seven priests, among whom was Torfi, faithful chaplain of three bishops. Tidings were sent to Hall, son of Teit, and Eyjolf, son of Saemund, the most eminent clergy in the country, who took in hand the funeral of Bishop Magnus and Torfi at Skál-holt (October 10, 1148). "So great was this calamity that everyone seemed to have lost his best friend."

These disasters emphasise the fact that it comes natural to Icelandic churchmanship to fulfil the apostolic injunction to be given to hospitality, and illustrate the difficulty and dangers of such social intercourse.

The life of Bishop Magnus is a fine illustration of Adam of Bremen's testimonial to the character of Icelanders: "They are remarkable for their charity."[1]

(B) Klaeng, Bishop of Skálholt (1152-76)

The Althing elected Hall, son of Teit, as successor to Magnus, which would have put learning once more on the episcopal chair, and carried on the line of Isleif, the first bishop.[2] But Hall died on his way to be consecrated, a reminder that to fare overseas could be a trying experience. Then Klaeng, son of Thorstein, was elected.

(a) In 1152, the year of Klaeng's consecration, the English cardinal Nicolas Breakspear, afterwards Pope Adrian IV, visited Norway and established an archdiocese at Nidaros, under which the two sees in Iceland could be more strictly supervised. An archbishop at Nidaros provided the King of Norway as well as the Pope with a closer opportunity for direct intervention in political and ecclesiastical affairs in Iceland. When Eystein Erlendsson was appointed Primate in 1159, he attempted by correspondence to strengthen the hands of the two bishops in their efforts to stop the violence and immorality of chieftains and contumacious priests. The weapons used were those of ecclesiastical ban and excommunication. But Icelanders are not the sort of people to kiss the rod; and later bishops tended to use their rights for the aggrandisement of the Church. Nor did Icelanders welcome interference with their independence by an external power. A survey of the first two centuries of Christianity in Iceland under the notable first five bishops of Skálholt and their northern colleagues shows that the greatest influence in the land came from patriotic

[1] Adam of Bremen, *Hist. Eccl.* IV, 35.
[2] "The language of every land he visited he spoke as a native." (Hv.)

prelates and priests of character and repute. It proved to be no use elaborating ecclesiastical machinery without improving the status and calibre of ecclesiastics, who, after all, have to run it.

Klaeng was a bishop of the old school. He was a northerner trained by Bishop Ketill and was an eloquent preacher and a skilful poet. "He became a great lawyer and chief. In every great suit, the bishop's advice was sought." Like Magnus, Klaeng settled the feuds of the chieftains.

Nevertheless, what was afterwards known as the Stone-Throwing Summer, 1163, occurred in Klaeng's time. In a fight which broke out on the sacred soil of the Thing, a priest, Halldor Storrason, was killed, which shows how difficult it is to be in the world and yet not of the world. The fact that at this time similar feuds raged incessantly in Europe does not justify this secularity though it provides some extenuation. Halldor was a member of the Snorri clan, whose conflicts in the next century were to lead to the loss of Icelandic independence.

After his consecration Klaeng fell in with Gizur, the son of the Hall who had been elected bishop. Gizur was on his travels, but was persuaded by Klaeng to return home for the good of Iceland. The *Hungrvaka* adds: "This gave the country the opportunity of welcoming the two men most valuable to it." Gizur became a Law-man and settled at Haukadal, where he kept up the reputation of that house for sound—that is, sacred—learning. He had eight children, including Hall, also elected Speaker, who afterwards became Abbot of Helgafell (†1225), and Magnus II, Bishop of Skálholt (†1237).

(*b*) Klaeng also brought back from Norway timber for rebuilding the cathedral. Iceland has never been able to grow trees of any size. Its graceful birches and rowans, refreshing in a land of rock and lava, are not much more than shrubs. All the churches constructed in these early centuries depended on timber procured by private benefactions, brought overseas and then pulled by ponies upcountry over rough tracks and passes in the mountains. For repairs driftwood from the shore was used.

The cathedral at Skálholt had been built on his farm by Gizur the White, father of the first bishop, about 998, rebuilt by his grandson Gizur, the second bishop (1082-1118), enlarged by Bishop Magnus (1145), and now rebuilt by his successor, probably about 1153. As a Saxon church-nave of upright half-timbers has lasted at Greenstead in Essex for a thousand years or more, there may be more to be said for the English climate than we think. But as the enlargement by

Bishop Magnus indicates, reconstructions of Skálholt cathedral were carried out chiefly in response to a call for more accommodation.

It is clear that the engaging author of *Hungrvaka* was present at the rebuilding of the cathedral, for he paints an enthusiastic first-hand account of the new building, "which surpassed all the country in wood and workmanship." He gives the name of the principal artificers: Arni chief architect, and Björn Thorvaldsson the Skilful. Illugi Leigsson shaped and cut the wood.

Icelandic sagas contain woven into their narratives short poems which hardly reach the high standard of the prose. *Hungrvaka* observes both these principles here, for it adds that when the church was all finished, Runolf, son of Bishop Ketill, sang this song:

> "Strong the temple that is fashioned
> Unto Christ the merciful,
> Firmly founded by the counsel,
> Of the ruler bountiful.
> Happy fate that Igultanni
> Here the house of God should build;
> Holy Peter owns with favour
> Björn and Arni, workmen skilled."[1]

Here it is in twelfth-century Icelandic, which is remarkably close to the current language of the country today;

> Hraust var Höll, fú er Kristi
> Hugblidum let smida,
> Gód er rót er rádum,
> Rikr stiórnar slikum
> Gipta vard that er giördi
> Guds rann Igultanni;
> Petr hefr eignaz itra,
> Arna smid oc Biarnar.

(c) The bishop presented his cathedral with a chalice of gold, set with gems, and directed that the service books be rewritten "in the best script." Two schools of script had been introduced into the country.[2] The continental script would be that learnt by Bishop

---

[1] Trans. by Mrs. Disney Leith. Igultanni is an Icelandic "kenning" or poetical circumlocution:=seabiter=bear=Björn. For kenninger, see Snorri's Edda. *E.g.*, Kross-madr=a soldier of the cross, a Christian; lifs-kenning=life's doctrine=the Gospel; to depart to the other light=to die.

[2] *Icelandic Illuminated MSS of the Middle Ages*, Introd., p. 9.

Isleif in Westphalia, and taught on his return. But Klaeng was a pupil of Ketill, associated in the Canon Law transcription with the first Bishop Thorlak, who was trained by Hall of Haukadal, the friend of St Olaf, patron of English visiting bishops, and they would teach the Saxon script. We conclude that Bishop Klaeng's order as to his service books meant the supersession at Skálholt of the continental script by the Saxon.

The cathedral was consecrated on St Vitus' Day, June 15: the outside by Bishop Klaeng, the interior by his colleague, Björn of Hólar. The sermon was preached by Nicolas Bergsson, the eloquent and much travelled abbot of the newly founded monastery at Thvera. Afterwards, in bountiful Icelandic fashion, the bishop invited to a sumptuous breakfast all the congregation, who sat down "not without difficulty to the number of 700"—*i.e.*, according to the reckoning of the Scandinavian long hundred, 840. The whole affair is a good illustration of Icelandic ecclesiastical fellowship in the early days.

Klaeng was a great builder and founder, and in his day (though *Hungrvaka* strangely omits to record it) Augustinian monasteries were established at Hitardal, Thykkvabaer, Flatey, and a Benedictine nunnery at Kirkjubaer.[1]

Klaeng maintained the episcopal school and theological college, and himself took pains to instruct the students in copying the Scriptures and singing the psalms in the approved manner.

In spite of his ecclesiastical magnificence, Klaeng proved more ascetic than his predecessors "in watchings, in fastings and in raiment." Often by night in frost and snow he would go barefoot. Such austerity led to his final illness at the age of seventy. On signifying to the Althing his desire to retire, they let him choose his successor, and he nominated Thorlak Thorhallsson, the saintly abbot of Thykkvabaer, destined to be canonised after his death. Klaeng then took to his bed and died in the following winter, February 28, 1176. The *Hungrvaka* adds: "It seems to us for many reasons that Iceland has never had a man of such magnificence[2] as Bishop Klaeng; and we believe that his munificence will be remembered while the country is inhabited."

Such a characteristic aspiration encourages a recorder of today to pass on the stories of these pioneers, which bring home the spirit, method, and effectiveness of the early Icelandic Church in the face of an intractable country and people.

---

[1] *Inf.* pp. 74-80. [2] *Skörúngr*, cp. *inf.* p. 207.

(ii) Two Episcopal Saints

(A) St Jón of Hólar (1106-1121)

Jón Ogmundson, the first bishop of the northern diocese of Hólar, developed a side of episcopal administration that was new to Iceland. He exercised his ministry not so much as pastor or administrator, but as priest. His pioneer work in founding the see with its cathedral and school, and in particular his inspiring life, led to his local canonisation within a century of his death.

(a) Like Bishop Magnus, Jón was descended through his mother from Hall-of-the-Side, one of the earliest chieftain champions of Christianity in the country. It would be difficult to exaggerate the influence of a few great families on the early centuries of Icelandic church life. We have noted the leading parts played by Gizur the White and his episcopal son and grandson, and by Hall of Haukadal and his learned disciples, Ari and Saemund, both descendants of Hall-of-the-Side. Most of these leaders were married priests, and their children carried on their work; so that the general ignoring of papal injunctions to celibacy by ecclesiastics in Iceland proved of far-reaching value to the Church.[1]

Jón was trained by Isleif, first Bishop of Iceland, and his life and work paid a great testimonial to that training. Sagas like to begin their lives with a genealogy, followed by a glowing description of personal characteristics. Jón's saga says of him that in his youth he gave great promise of future greatness by his ordered life and mastery of sacred learning. He is depicted as tall, strong, and handsome, "with uncommonly fine eyes; and withal gentle and lowly."

After his ordination as deacon, like other chieftains' sons he desired to travel, "to observe the ways of good men and to continue his education." He visited Norway, Rome, and Denmark, where he became a favourite of King Sweyn, who was attracted to him on account of his "noble and clear" reading of the story of the Passion.

He accompanied Magnus, King of Norway, on a marauding expedition to the Hebrides. *Heimskringla* tells how they visited Iona, where King Magnus opened the door of the small chapel-shrine of St Columba, hastily shutting it with the words, "No one should be so bold as to enter here." On this "holy isle" Magnus intermitted his devastations.

[1] Decretum Gratiani, Dist. 81, c. 15 (Gregor. VII, *c.* 1037); Dist. 27, c. 8 (Sixtus II, 1123). A MS of *c.* 1220 lists 40 high-born priests living in 1143.

On returning to Iceland, Jón conferred a great boon on his country by bringing back with him his cousin, Saemund the Wise, "the man who of all others has been the greatest help to the Church of God in Iceland." Popular legends make play with the notion that Jón rescued Saemund from a School of Black Magic, which had no windows and all its doors facing north, where, in mastering Black Arts, Saemund had forgotten his own name. Saemund's real contribution to his country was his foundation of the school at his homestead of Oddi.

(b) In the year 1105, as has been recorded, the second Bishop of Iceland was asked by the people of the north to grant them a bishop of their own, on account of their distance from Skálholt and the vast size and comparatively large population of their Quarter. With the consent of all the priests and laymen in the north, the bishop nominated Jón Øgmundson, then aged fifty-four, serving as a priest at his home at Breidabolstad. After much hesitation, owing to his humility, Jón agreed and went overseas to Ozur of Lund, the primate.

The saga records a story that illustrates one of the unusual gifts of the bishop-elect, and also the friendliness of high ecclesiastics of those days and their devotion to the daily offices. Jón arrived in Lund late one evening when vespers were almost finished, and he began to sing them with his clerks outside the choir, so that the archbishop looked down the church to see who was chanting. Afterwards the archbishop's clerk said to him: "Now, my lord, have you not yourself broken your rule against gazing about the church during divine service?" To which the archbishop replied: "True, indeed! but I have never heard so angelic a voice."

Jón went to stay with the archbishop, and when he disclosed his errand and presented his papers Ozur said: "I see thou hast about all the qualities that fit thee for a bishop. But as thou hast been twice married I cannot proceed with the consecration without the sanction of the Pope." A dispensation was granted, and Jón was consecrated on Sunday, April 29, 1106.

(c) The north of Iceland has the largest population of the four Quarters. The people live widely scattered along the fjords that stretch out to the Arctic Ocean. Winters there are longer, snows deeper, storms more frequent. For weeks from October to April in the deeper valleys the sun is not seen, with the tiring compensation that in summer the sun never dips below the horizon. Consequently, in the northern diocese the problems of isolation and distance increase the normal difficulties of supervision.

Early settlers, not least those who had Christian affinities, favoured the north and north-west. Most of the converts made by Thorvald and Fridrek lived in those regions, which contained some of the earliest notable churches—As, Holt, Holm, and Helgafell.

Hólar was chosen as the seat of the northern bishopric because none of the northern chieftains would give up his heritage and his home, except Illugi, a priest and owner of Hólar, who withdrew to Breidabolstad, Jón's homestead and former parish.

Hólar is finely situated in the rich green valley of Hjaltadal, "the garden of the north," leading down to Skagafjörd and the Arctic Ocean.

Here the new bishop established his see round his cathedral and a school. He had brought a shipload of timber back from Norway, and he built well. The cathedral, though constructed of wood and exposed to fierce buffeting of arctic storms, lasted for two centuries, after which it was rebuilt in stone by the munificent Bishop Audun. Bishop Gizur of Skálholt transferred a quarter of his income towards the endowment of the new see, which, of course, received the tithes of the northern Quarter, and became unusually wealthy. At the Reformation it tempted the Danish Crown to confiscate its 300 farms with their pasturage for 15,000 cows, and its historic rock-island of Drangey, though the grasping officials ignored its valuable rights of driftwood along a long stretch of coast.

(d) Jón also built an extensive bishopstead and an elaborate school, which spread culture and civilisation, and so provided one of his chief direct methods of meeting the difficulties and dangers of the day, due to the undisciplined nature of leading chieftains and priests, aggravated by isolation and ignorance.

The idea of the school Jón took over from his foster-father Isleif, and developed it more thoroughly, especially by the provision of foreign teachers. As head he imported from Gothland a learned young priest called Gisli, who combined teaching with a lectureship at the cathedral. The bishop appointed his "chaplain and great friend" Rakinne (Racine), a Frenchman, to teach singing and verse-making, a favourite Icelandic accomplishment. Thus from the first at this northern Christian outpost two main functions of a cathedral were established: it became a centre of sacred music and a home of sound learning. A twelfth-century French Psalter, used as a palimpsest after the Reformation, was brought from Iceland by Arni Magnusson in the seventeenth century and is preserved at Copenhagen University.[1] It may well have formed part of the equipment of the French precentor Rakinne.

Not the least striking thing in the story of the celestial singing heard in the north when Bishop Thorlak died, is the fact that so sequestered a part of the world at that time should be familiar with the hagiography of Christendom.

One of the masters was Isleif, son of Hall, whom the bishop wished to succeed him. And most remarkable of all was a successful teacher of Latin, a maiden called Ingun, who had Latin books read to her while she did needlework. A story in Jónssaga illustrates the effectiveness of the Latin teaching and the aptness of the ordinary Icelander as pupil: when the Latin class was meeting in summer, sitting in the sunshine, the builder, on the roof of the cathedral he was constructing hard by, picked up the language so readily that he became a competent Latin scholar.[2]

All candidates for the priesthood in the north had to pass through this college, and most chieftains' sons went there, so that many afterwards in high positions owed their training to Bishop Jón. Among them the names are recorded of Klaeng, afterwards Bishop of Skálholt; Björn, third Bishop of Hólar; Vilmund, first abbot, and Hreinn, third abbot of Thingeyrar; and Bjarni, priest and arithmetician.[3]

(e) By improving the quality of the clergy rather than by setting up or developing ecclesiastical machinery, the bishop adopted the only sound method of dealing with their loneliness and independence, and through them of improving the faith and morals of their people.

For the principal problem which faced the Church at this time arose largely from isolation, which caused much turbulent independence in franklins and chiefs. Loose living and aggressive self-seeking led to strife; local things or courts fostered rather than settled quarrels. Jón's first business, after attending the Althing and arranging there with his colleague of Skálholt rules of church administration, was, in accordance with ecclesiastical law, to go round on a visitation of his diocese. He inculcated daily prayers in church, or at a wayside cross, and ordered worship on holy days and frequent doctrinal sermons. He abolished heathen charms, lewd plays and

[1] *Icelandic Illuminated MSS of the Middle Ages*, Introd. by Halldór Hermansson, p. 9 (a magnificent volume); Cpn, 1935.
[2] *B.S.* I, pp. 235 *sq.*
[3] Klaeng was rebuked by Bishop Jón for studying surreptitiously Ovid's *de Arte amoris*. For Vilmund see *inf.*, p. 75.

poetry, and made a severance with paganism unique in Europe by abolishing the heathen dedication of weekdays to Tyr, Odin, and Thor, in favour of Third-day, Mid-weekday, Fast day and the like.[1] The ancient five-day week (fimt) by then was beginning in Iceland to give place to the seven-day week of Christendom, and Jón's changes stabilised the modern kalendar and gave its days an ecclesiastical colour. The saga thus sums up all these reforms: "In short, Christianity in the north never showed such blossom as it did in the days of the holy bishop Jón."

Jón's indirect influence in promoting righteousness lay in his own personal sanctity. He had not long been bishop before "he began to raise men's ways on to another level that they had not been on before. He rebuked those of evil life, and showed in his own life that what he taught he followed himself. He loved his people as his brothers and sons, and rejoiced when it went well with them and condoled over all that went otherwise." He was not satisfied unless everyone in his diocese came to see him at least once a year. Crowds made the journey to Hólar, especially at festivals, to join in the cathedral services, so well were they performed there, and to hear the moving sermons of the bishop or the teacher Gisli. Jón was praised for his fine addresses. Gisli is recorded to have preached from a book on a desk in the choir, an unusual custom due to his youth and humility; but he is given credit because "his sermons did not contain empty or ostentatious words."[2] At Eastertide, according to Jónssaga, more than 400 (*i.e.*, 480) would attend. Some of them brought their own food, but most of them had to be fed by a committee or chapter, which the bishop appointed to assist his wife Valdis in the management of the bishopstead.

Some families came to live at Hólar near the church and school, a good example of how towns grew up. In these more secularly civilised days we string together a monstrous conglomeration of houses without planning for church and religious school, and so often the people have no focus of worship and Christian fellowship and the youth get out of hand.

After Jón had been bishop for fifteen years, at the age of sixty-nine, he died (April 23, 1121). As he died he was reciting the psalm "My soul shall make her boast in the Lord: the humble shall hear

[1] R. F. Burton, *Ultima Thule*, p. 73. Jón's names were introduced into the southern diocese and still obtain in Iceland, Saturday being known as Laugardagur or "bath-day."

[2] *Homiliu-bók*, Introd. Fridrek Paaske, pp. 9, 18, 21-2.

thereof and be glad"—a verse which effectively sums up his ministry of love, joy, and peace.

His body was buried in the cathedral garth, but eighty years later, after "God had made manifest His grace by sure tokens," "his halidom" was placed before the altar by Bishop Brand, and the Althing paid him the honour of canonisation.

(B) St Thorlak (1178-93)

Thorlak Thorhallsson, afterwards called hinn helgi, the Saint, developed the type of episcopacy introduced by Jón of Hólar, and his life and work produced the hagiographical style of chronicle usual in the Middle Ages, but not before adopted in Iceland. He took the first steps to assert the bishops' right to churches and glebes, and was the first to use the power of ban and excommunication. These claims led to opposition, but his life of devotion and self-denial won universal veneration, which was increased by stories of posthumous miracles and so led to speedy canonisation by the Althing.

(a) Thorlak was born in 1133, the year the elder Bishop Thorlak died, at the farm of Hlidarendi in the south country, famous as the home of the heroic Gunnar in Njál's Saga. He was the product of noble lineage and a good home. His parents taught him the Psalter and good manners, and sent him to be educated at the neighbouring school at Oddi, which had become under Eyjolf Saemundsson the foremost school in Iceland. He was ordained deacon by Bishop Magnus († 1148), so that he cannot have been more than fifteen years old. Afterwards he devoted himself to book-learning and especially writing, not neglecting "prayers in the midst of these." His mother also taught him family history and genealogy, always an Icelandic speciality. At the age of seventeen or eighteen he was ordained priest and travelled abroad, spending six years in the crowded lecture-rooms of Paris and at Lincoln. The fact that Geoffrey of Monmouth († 1154) brings Iceland into his romantic history as one of the countries in subjection to King Arthur has not the historical significance that Geoffrey would desire, but his reference indicates that at this time English people were interested in Iceland.[1] And Thorlak's lengthy visit and many references in Icelandic Annals show that the interest was reciprocated. On Thorlak's return it was remarked that he had retained his humility (an un-Icelandic virtue commended

---

[1] Hist. Reg. ix, 10, 12; cp. Dipl. Isl. X, No. 1, 1169: King Henry II of England accepts a Norwegian hawk and an Icelandic falcon. Cp. Giraldus Cambrensis, 1187, ut sup., p. 48.

in these Lives of early bishops) and "gave kindly countenance to his sisters."

Thorlak's unusual departure from the almost universal custom of priestly marriage is embodied in the story of a dream he had when he was staying at a farm where he had gone to seek a wife. By night a saintly figure appeared to stand by his side telling him: "There is a much higher bride destined to thee, and none other shalt thou take."

Next morning he bade farewell to his intended wife, and went to live with a learned priest at Kirkjubaer, until in 1168, after six years of great contentment, he was chosen to take charge of a monastery just founded in the neighbourhood at Thykkvabaer. Here he instituted a strict mode of life which impressed many visitors with its order and devotion. Many men with various ills came to him, and "he chanted over them, so that they went away whole." Valuable cattle, too, were cured by incantations. However, we read that some men found a difficulty in recognising this holiness.

After he had been six years abbot he was elected by the Althing as Bishop Klaeng's successor at Skálholt, but owing to dissension at home and difficulties with Norway it was two years before he was consecrated. When he returned to Skálholt as bishop in 1178, though he might have dispensed with the monastic rule, he kept it "alike in dress, in watchings and fastings, and in prayers." He was a monk in heart to the end and never an administrator.

(b) Thorlak's episcopacy was marked by a call to priests to more faithful performance of their sacred office and to a more converted life. Laity, too, he urged to greater continence. But his moral reforms did not cause such an outcry as his vigorous attempt to restrict lay ownership of churches and advowsons.

He had been consecrated by Eystein, Archbishop of Nidaros, an ecclesiastical reformer, from whom he received letters patent to enforce the rights of the Church.[1] Eystein had little success in Norway, and in the greater isolation and independence of Iceland Thorlak met with much opposition.

The situation is illustrated in a story recorded in the Oddaverja Saga in which Bishop Thorlak's own sister and Jón Loptsson, the most learned and powerful chieftain of the day, are concerned. The incident vividly shows the bishop's courage and the difficulties with which he had to contend, and brings out the strange mixture of character in a leading Icelander of the period.

---

[1] Gj., pp. 158-60 (who translates the archbishop's letters in full from F. J.). Eystein visited England in 1182 (Annals; *Dipl. Isl.* I, Nos. 53-4).

Jón, son of Lopt, governed Oddi as one of the godar or leading chieftains. He was also in deacon's orders, "with a fine voice in holy church," and had shown himself an energetic churchman. Nevertheless, for many years he had lived in adulterous union with Ragnheid, the bishop's sister. Their son Pál had been one of Bishop Klaeng's nominees (with Thorlak) as his successor, and actually was a great friend of Thorlak.

In the place of two churches on Jón Loptsson's estate blown down in a storm he "built an elaborate new church, and the bishop came to consecrate it." Thorlak asked him if he knew the primate's mandate as to the bishop's rights in the matter. To which Jón answered: "I am minded to hold him at nought. I think he knows no better than my forebears, Saemund the Wise, and his sons. Laymen should rule those churches which their forefathers gave to God, handing on their authority to their successors." The bishop then refused to consecrate and rebuked Jón for reducing the number of clergy for whom he was responsible, and finally for living in sin. He put him under ecclesiastical ban and threatened him with excommunication. At this Jón made plans to capture the bishop, and his son lay in wait for him with an axe, but the plans miscarried, seemingly miraculously. Then Jón gave way. The church was consecrated and the bishop joined in a family banquet. Jón, however, refused to put away Ragnheid at the bishop's request, though later he did so of his own free will "at God's bidding," and Ragnheid and he received absolution and penance from the bishop. Their son Pál became the bishop's chaplain and succeeded him at Skálholt.

The bishop had similar controversies with other chieftains, notably Sigmund, son of Orm, who, like Jón Loptsson, refused to recognise the right of Eystein and other foreigners to interfere with Icelanders' privileges. The bishop would not consecrate their churches and put them under ecclesiastical ban. Then they threatened violence, but finally yielded.

Thorlak appears to have taken notice of moral misdemeanours only when they accompanied breaches of ecclesiastical order. Snaelaug, daughter of a rich priest called Högni, had an illegitimate child, and after the death of its father, Hreinn, married a priest called Thord. Her father built a church and, as was customary, desired to retain the advowson. The bishop refused to consecrate the building, and denounced the daughter's marriage, as the husband was Hreinn's fourth cousin—a not uncommon relationship in Iceland, as almost everyone was descended from the first few settlers. The couple protested strongly, but finally agreed to live apart in order that the church might be consecrated. Subsequently, however, they had three children.[1]

(c) It cannot be concluded that Bishop Thorlak's church policy met with any real measure of success, as regards either chieftains or clergy. But his courage, restraint, and personal piety won him high esteem. He was at heart a priest rather than a preacher or administrator. "He often taught precepts of virtue, and therefore it was a great misfortune that his words were hard and slow."[2]

Again (according to his saga), "he feared nothing much except the Assembly and the Ember days " (some modern bishops might agree with him in that respect)—the Althing because of the excessive weight put upon his words, and ordinations on account of the unworthiness of the candidates.

The bishop introduced the feasts of St Ambrose, St Cecilia, and St Agnes, and ordered fasting on the eves of festivals of apostles and of St Nicolas. He effected the change in names of weekdays, as Jón had done in the north. He laid stress on abstinence on Fridays, the name of which Jón and he changed to Föstu-dagr, "fast-day," allowing only one meal and restricting himself to vegetables (a luxury in Iceland today). He drank water, but "was not fastidious at feasts, and blessed ale in its brewing so that it never burst." He was a popular host, as he liked music and good stories.

After fifteen years as bishop, Thorlak resolved to resign and retire to his monastery, but before he could do this he died, on the night before Christmas Eve, 1193. During his illness he was attended by the wise chieftain Gizur, Hall's son, who "sorrowfully made up the church accounts so that all should be handed over in good order." Pál, his sister's son, was also present. When he was dying he lifted up his eyes and called out, "Whither fared Thorkell just now?" referring to the founder of his monastery, come, as Gizur averred, "to lead him to the heavenly life."

Gizur made an oration at his funeral. A more telling eulogy was the presence in church of a leper whom Thorlak had saved and cared for.

(d) The veneration in which Thorlak was held is shown by the record that 230 wax candles were burnt at the memorial service on

---

[1] Oddaverja S. 3, 1 ; Bogi Th. Melsted, Islendinga S., Vol. III, pp. 288-91.

[2] Cp. Giraldus *l.c.*: "Icelanders use very few words, and speak the truth. They seldom converse and then briefly, and take no oaths, for they know not what it is to lie." He might have known Thorlak.

the first anniversary of his death. His successor, Bishop Pál, asked Brand, Bishop of Hólar, and a popular northern priest, Gudmund Arason, to deal with Thorlak's posthumous reputation, and at their recommendation he was canonised by the Althing in 1199. The previous year Pál had "a shrine made for his relics which (says his saga) now stands to this day over the high altar." Dr Uno von Troil saw St Thorlak's coffin, denuded of its gold and gems, at Skálholt in 1772. The shrine was sold in 1802 when the bishopric was transferred to Reykjavik, and now no man knoweth of his sepulchre.

The pre-eminence of St Thorlak in the select hierarchy of Icelandic saints is indicated by the appearance of his figure in the centre of a mediæval altar-cloth used at Hólar Cathedral until recent years. Hólar's own saint Jón and the Blessed Gudmund are depicted as supporters of the country's patron saint.[1]

Among mediæval robes preserved in Reykjavik is one with an embroidered picture of a ship on which a bishop in his vestments stands admonishing or blessing the crew. This is held to represent an incident in which Thorlak in God's name forbade a crew to overload a ship in which he was a traveller.

The name of Thorlak hinn helgi often appears in the Annals as denoting a date, or receiving vows of shipwrecked sailors (1360), or being accredited with posthumous miracles (1388).

St Thorlak is commemorated by two days in the Icelandic kalendar: December 23, the anniversary of his death, and July 20, the day of the translation of his relics.

Except by the Althing, Thorlak was never formally canonised, yet not only was he long venerated in the northern lands, but according to a later saga his cult extended to England.[2] At Kynn (? Kyme in Lincolnshire), one Audun put up in a church a statue of the Blessed Bishop Thorlak.[3] A local priest, being told who it was, ran and fetched a sausage, and offered it to the image, saying, "Wilt thou, man of suet? Thou art a suet bishop," referring, as an English beef-eater, to the Icelandic custom (still common) of living on mutton. The priest's hand was then smitten with cramp, and was only restored in response to earnest prayers of bystanders, which God and the Blessed Thorlak heard. About the middle of the fourteenth century, Bishop Laurence uses this story to rebuke similar arrogance on the

---

[1] Baring-Gould, *Iceland : Its Scenes and Sagas*, p. 236.
[2] F. J. I, p. 298 (except Sweden, according to the learned Swede von Troil, Letters, p. 78).
[3] E. Magnusson, Rolls Series 65, pp. 10-11.

part of a visiting Norwegian priest.[1] In the next century Bishop Wilkin enshrined St Thorlak's head in silver.

The fame of St Thorlak reached the Middle East, for at Constantinople, which Icelanders called Micklegarth, the church of the Varings, Scandinavian bodyguard of the emperor, was dedicated to him.[2]

No adventitious reasons led to such widespread renown. The Althing must have been impressed not merely by the posthumous miracles advanced in favour of his canonisation, but also by the courage with which he stood up to the chieftains, his celibacy and personal piety, and his powers of healing.

The Althing acted without any thought of referring the matter to Rome, and history has justified their decision. With the possible exception of the great statesman-prelate Gizur, the Icelandic Church has produced no finer leaders than Jón and Thorlak.

[1] *B.S.* I, p. 357; Lárentius S. 19.
[2] Varings or Varangians was the name given by Greeks and Slavs to Northmen who fought in the East in the ninth and tenth centuries. They were Christianised by Vladimir in 988, and a bodyguard of them was retained for the Emperor at Constantinople until it fell in 1453. (See Saga of St Olaf 219; Grettir's S. 85; Laxdale S. 73; Scott, *Count Robert of Paris*; Anna Comnena, Life of (her father) Alexias, Emperor of Constantinople; *ap.* Migne, *Pat. Gk.*, No. 131.)

CHAPTER V

SPIRIT, MIND, AND BODY

(i) The "Religious" Life

It is noteworthy that the pioneers in Iceland of the life technically called " religious" came of the same race and adopted the same profession as the Columban Culdees of the pre-settlement period, who fled when the new settlers arrived. After a succession of hermits, two Benedictine monasteries were founded—Thingeyrar 1133, and Thvera 1155; followed by five Augustinian foundations—Thykkvabaer 1168, Flatey 1172 (moved to Helgafell 1184), Videy 1226, Modruvellir 1296, and Skrida 1493.[1] Two Benedictine nunneries were established—Kirkjubaer 1185, and Reynistad 1296. Most of these religious houses made a great contribution to the country as homes of learning and teaching, and produced some notable books, until in 1551 the Crown, under the guise of the Reformation, swept them away and confiscated their valuable property.

(*a*) The first authenticated hermit was an Irishman, Jörund, contemptuously nicknamed the Christian, who in the midst of his derisive neighbours stuck to his religion to the day of his death, and, to enable himself to do so, in his old age built himself a cell at Gardar in Akranes, "intent on prayer and meditation day and night."

His nephew Asolf Alskik had arrived in the country with eleven followers and settled at Holt, probably with a view to establishing some kind of Columban evangelistic community. When his companions died he refused to mix with his heathen neighbours and went to live as a hermit near his uncle.[2]

Gudrun, the interesting heroine of the Laxdale Saga, "the goodliest of women who grew up in Iceland," after the vicissitudes of four marriages, two of which were brought to an end by murder, one by divorce, and the last by shipwreck, turned for peace of mind to the religious life, and spent her days, like aged Anna, never off the doorstep of the church she built at Helgafell. Such was the tradition, doubtless founded on truth, though embroidered picturesquely a century afterwards in one of the most romantic of sagas.[3]

Gudlaug, the eldest son of Gudrun's counsellor, Snorri the godi, prominent in the later heathen and early Christian life of his country, found no niche in Iceland where he could lead an ascetic life, so in

---

[1] Dates and details in Annals: cp. F. J. IV, pp. 1-121.
[2] *Lndbk* I, 7, 3-6; *ut sup.*, pp. 18-19.
[3] Laxdale S. 32 and 76 (*ut sup.*, p. 36).

1016 he took vows and went to live as a recluse in England, perhaps at the suggestion of the visiting bishop, Bernard, reputed to be of English birth.[1]

It has already been noted that another of the visiting bishops, Rudolf, made the first attempt at a monastic establishment in Iceland at Bae in Borgarfjördur, where he lived for nineteen years (1030-49). On his departure for England he left behind him three monks, of whom we hear nothing further.

A century had to pass before Christianity in Iceland had sufficiently developed to establish its own monastic life. No more male hermits are mentioned, but we hear of a woman semi-recluse, Groa, daughter of Bishop Gizur and wife of Bishop Ketill, "best of matches," in defence of whose honour her husband lost an eye. After his death Groa lived for many years as a nun at Skálholt, dying in the days of Bishop Klaeng (1152-75), who himself lived an ascetic life and founded three monasteries.

Groa's example was followed by Ketilbjörg, who lived at Skálholt in the days of Bishop Pál. At the same time, Ulfrun, another anchoritess, lived at Thingvellir, so obsessed by a love of solitude that she refused to see her only son when he paid her a visit. These recluses took the place of the heathen spá-women or prophetesses, as is shown by a visit paid to Ulfrun by Gudmund, when in doubt as to whether he should accept consecration as Bishop of Hólar.[2] That they were not infallible is clear from the ill effects of the advice she then gave. Gudmund, a successful and popular priest, had none of the qualities which make a good bishop.

(b) Bishop Klaeng's predecessor, Magnus, bought most of the Westman Islands in order to found a monastery there, but he lost his life in a fire before he could begin the work (†1148).

By then a Benedictine foundation had been established at Thingeyrar, the place of the spring moot. Its large church owed its origin to Jón, the first Bishop of Hólar (1106-21). Soon after his consecration, and at the end of an exceptionally bad winter, the earth showed no signs of growth when the Thing met on the last days of May; consequently, in Old Testament fashion, the bishop made a vow to build a church if the drought broke. He marked out the building, and, as often happens in arctic lands, spring burst on the country in a week. Shelley's dream came true, and "bare winter suddenly was changed to spring." But the monastery was not established until 1133, when it was put in the charge of the learned Vilmund Thórólfsson,

---

[1] Islendinga S. 11, 30 (ut sup., pp. 37-38).   [2] Sturlunga S. 3, 14.

trained at the episcopal school at Hólar, a godly man and an able administrator.[1]

This community became famous for historical work. Here, in the middle of the thirteenth century, Gunnlaug Leifsson (†1218) and Odd Snorrason (†1200) composed sagas about King Olaf Tryggvason, while their abbot, Karl Jónsson, wrote a spirited Life of King Sverrir of Norway, in which the king co-operated, though he was a pronounced anti-clericalist.[2] Gunnlaug also compiled Latin Lives of the country's episcopal saints, Jón and Thorlak, and paraphrases of Merlin. It is clear that at least in the thirteenth century Iceland maintained some contacts with the wider world. Another monk, Arngrim, wrote one of the sagas on the buccaneering Bishop Gudmund. Another Gudmund, about 1310-39, is praised in the Annals for his "usefulness" in training erudite priests.

A second Benedictine monastery in the north was founded in 1155 at Thvera, later called Munkathvera, by Björn, Bishop of Hólar. Its first abbot, Nicolas Bergsson (†1159), acquired a reputation as a great traveller, another far-farer, and wrote a guide-book to the Holy Land called Leidavisir, and a poem on St John the Evangelist. A versatile fourteenth-century abbot, Berg Sokkason, translated Latin Lives of saints to meet the taste of the day, and was known as an orator and musician. He resigned in 1334 by reason of his humility.[3]

In 1203 and 1212 the Annals record the deaths of two abbots of a monastery at Saurbaer, also near Eyjafjörd, a short-lived foundation about which little else is known.

(c) The first steps for establishing conventual life in the south were taken by Thorlak, afterwards bishop and saint, who lived under rule for six years with Bjarnard, priest-owner of Kirkjubaer, until a neighbouring chieftain gave his farm at Thykkvabaer "to Christ and His saints," and by the counsel of Bishop Klaeng founded an Augustinian Priory there, with Thorlak as its head (1168-74). Many visitors came from parts of Iceland and abroad "to learn for the first time the value of the holy life he led and enjoined."

Thykkvabaer, later called Ver and Alftaver ("haunt of swans"), possessed a fine library and had some learned abbots, one of whom, Brand Jónsson, became Bishop of Hólar 1263-4. He was the author of

---

[1] List of Abbots 1325, in *Dipl. Isl.* II, p. 2.

[2] W. A. Craigie, *Icelandic Sagas*, p. 81. The king pays a tribute to Englishmen who had brought wheat, honey, flax, homespun and kettles, and denounces Germans for bringing wine and spirits in exchange for butter and fish. Sverrissaga trans. J. Sephton, London 1899.

[3] F. J. IV, pp. 44-5.

a remarkable paraphrase of the historical books of the Old Testament in Icelandic, later incorporated with an unfinished commentary ordered by Hakon V. This large compilation, called Stjörn *Foundation*, appeared at the beginning of the fourteenth century (*c.* 1310), at a time when monks were making translations of Lives of saints, but no one else appears to have tackled the Bible, so that Stjörn remained the only work until after the Reformation in which unlearned men could get any knowledge of the Old Testament.[1] This monastery housed an abbot and twelve monks in 1403, when half of the brothers died of the plague.[2]

A second Augustinian community was established in 1172 in Flatey in the north-west by Øgmund Kalfsson, who became its first abbot; but twelve years later, no doubt on account of the wind-swept nature of this small island, subject to earthquakes, the monastery dedicated to St Mary was transferred to Helgafell, formerly Gudrun's retreat, and originally the most famous of heathen sanctuaries. The learned Hall Gizurarson became abbot here (1221-5), after having served as Lawman. He was the author of *Flos Peregrinationis*, of which nothing but the title is known. That itself, like Abbot Nicolas' *Leidavisir*, indicates Icelandic interest in pilgrimages. Those to the Holy Land became a fashion of these centuries and gave a surname to more than one pilgrim (*e.g.*, Jórsala-Björn, *c.* 1225; Björn Jórsalafari, †1415). Helgafell was destined to become one of the most important monastic houses in Iceland, distinguished for its large library, vast estates, and scholastic enterprise.[3]

The third religious house inaugurated by Bishop Klaeng was established about the year 1166 at Hitardal, possibly as a memorial foundation, since it had been the scene of the fire in 1148 in which Bishop Magnus and seventy-two others were burnt to death. Its glebe remained in lay hands, an arrangement which was contested a hundred years later by the zealous Bishop Arni Thorlaksson, so that, after having five abbots, the monastery was dissolved and its goodwill passed to the Augustinian house on Videy Island.[4]

The attempt of the deacon-chieftain, Jón Loptsson, to found a monastery, for which he built a fine church at Keld in 1190, was quashed by Bishop Thorlak on account of what the Annals tersely

---

[1] E. Henderson, *Journal*, pp. 463 *sq.* As a colporteur Dr Henderson took a personal interest in this matter. The commentary covered Genesis to Exodus xxii. Gudrun, d. of Bp. Brand I., was grandmother of Bp. Brand II.

[2] Annals, *inf.*, p. 134.

[3] F. J. IV, pp. 65-77; *inf.*, p. 126.

[4] F. J. IV, pp. 24-6; J. H., p. 101.

call Ragnhildar mál—the trouble about Ragnhild, who was the bishop's sister.[1]

In 1226 the father of Jarl or Earl Gizur founded a monastery for Regular Austin Canons on Videy Island on Faxa Fjörd. Here the Jarl ended his days after a troublous life, but he died before he took the vows. Videy, like Helgafell and Thykkvabaer, acted as a school when the episcopal colleges lapsed, and acquired lands as a condition of teaching chieftains' sons. In the year 1518 the register of Skálholt was officially inspected by "brother Øgmund, by Divine tolerance, Abbot of Videy."[2]

This foundation, the richest monastery in the country, owning 131 farms, was the first to tempt the State raiders at the Reformation.[3] Much of the mediaeval building still remains, its strong basalt walls having weathered the hurricanes which sweep the island, now a sanctuary for eider duck. The church was restored in 1904 and preserves the old woodwork, including a well-carved confessional (skriftastöll). It is one of the few churches in Iceland with an ever-open door; here to let the birds fly in and out.

(d) Two nunneries found a place in the religious life of Iceland, one in each diocese. A Benedictine nunnery was established at Kirkjubaer, Thorlak's original retreat-house, the fourth religious house to be consecrated by Bishop Klaeng. This homestead in early days had been taken over as a Christian settlement from Irish monks by the line of Ketill, Christians from father to son for many generations. In 1188 the influential priest-owner Bjarnard presented it to be used as a nunnery, and so it continued with an abbess and thirteen sisters down to the time of the Reformation, when its thirty-six farms were confiscated by the Crown, and the place became a church-farm from that day to this. Its name Kirkjubaerklauster indicates its history.

The first and last and three others of its twelve abbesses were called Halldora. In 1343, according to the Annals, Sister Christina was burnt alive for promiscuous incontinence, on the ground that she had in writing given her body over to the Devil. But Annals, like newspapers, record the unusual. They make no mention of lives of quiet service and steady devotion. Kirkjubaer suffered terribly in the great plague. The abbess and seven sisters died, leaving six to run the nunnery and milk the cows, as all domestics died. So many bodies were brought for burial that they could not be counted.[4]

---

[1] Sup., p. 69; Annals 1164, Al. Ragnheid.
[2] Dipl. Isl., IV, pp. 170-1.   [3] F. J. IV, pp. 82-96; inf., pp. 145-6.
[4] Annals, sub anno 1403, inf., p. 134.

A nunnery, also following the rule of St Benedict, was consecrated in 1296 by Bishop Jörund at Reynistad in the fertile valley which leads into Skagafjörd, not far from Hólar. Of this cloister, dedicated to God and St Stephen, Bishop Audun's confirmation of the original deed, dated 1315, remains to this day. After the plague there is no mention of the nunnery for ten years, but in that period Hólar had no bishop for seventeen years. Except for the names of ten abbesses up to the time of the Reformation and of forty-five small farms, we know little about this nunnery, which thus possessed the happiness of having no history.[1]

About the same time Bishop Jörund established a monastery for Austin Canons at Mödruvellir on Eyjafjörd, reserving to the Bishop of Hólar the right of being abbot. The endowment for these two foundations came from the estate at Stad, given for the purpose by Jarl Gizur—after the bishopsteads, the best farm in Iceland. The joint rule of bishop-abbot and prior led to difficulties, which came to a head when Laurence was bishop, and led to an appeal to the primate at Trondhjem, who finally supported the bishop (*inf.*, p.123). The monastery was burnt down through carelessness in 1316, which gave Laurence an opportunity for a display of generosity in rebuilding the place. His church, with its delightfully named bells, was destroyed by a storm a century later, 1431. The fine library was frittered away before the Reformation, when the Crown confiscated its fifty-nine farms. However, Torfi, the son of the last prior, became a prestur under the new order.[2]

The last religious house to be built was an Augustinian priory, founded in 1493 by the learned Bishop Stefán Jónsson at Skrida, the only monastery in the eastern Quarter. The house, a local benefaction, was dedicated to God, the B.V.M., and the Sacred Blood, and its church to Corpus Christi. Some ruins of this cloister remain at the top of the beautiful valley of Lagarfljot. At the Reformation the thirty-seven monastic farms supported two monks under a prior, eighty-three years of age, who had three sons.[3]

The result of the impact of the Reformation on Icelandic monasteries was almost entirely destructive. King Christian III wrote on November 21, 1542, to the Abbot of Helgafell, and in the same year to the Prior of Skrida and to the Abbess of Kirkjubaer, asking them to remain at their posts and establish schools for teaching reading,

---

[1] F. J. IV, pp. 105-113.
[2] Annals; Lárentius S. 47, 52-61; F. J. IV, 96-105.
[3] F. J. II, pp. 492-3; IV, 113-121.

writing, and the principles of true religion; but this project came to nothing. The number of the "religious" had been much reduced by the beginning of the sixteenth century; so that Kirkjubaer had six, Thykkvabaer five, Videy four, and Helgafell and Skrida only two under vows. In spite of the unfeeling treatment meted out to his monastery, the Abbot of Videy adopted Lutheranism. At the confiscation of the monastic estates in the year 1551 all the religious were pensioned out of the spoils, and a few farms allotted or small payment made to pastors of the Reformed Church.

(e) All the Icelandic monasteries followed the Benedictine or Augustinian rule. No strict white-robed Cistercians settled in this stern country, nor did grey-habited Franciscans wander over its townless stretches. We meet only black-robed Benedictines with their rounds of services, and studious Austin Canons, whose reputation for learning was nobly upheld in their libraries painfully collected on the edge of the Arctic Circle. Thus these foundations made a conspicuous contribution to Icelandic life, offering Divine and human companionship to isolated and harassed souls.

Three characteristics of their work emerge:

1. Like the early Icelandic Church, they were intensely national. It was more than the time factor which prevented the early foundations of the foreigners Alskik and Bishop Rudolf from coming to anything. After the close of the thirteenth century, when Church and State fell under foreign domination, only one small monastery was founded. Abbots and monks continued to be natives of the country. Visitors from overseas came to admire, but were not encouraged to settle.

2. Most of the foundations became homes of learning and literature. It is chiefly to the Church that Iceland is indebted for her literature down the ages. This significant fact will be illustrated in the following chapter-section. Here it has been indicated that a large and valuable contribution was made by monasteries, not only in ecclesiastical writings, but also in historical research and the humanities.

3. Episcopal schools in south and north served the Church and the country well during the first two centuries of Christianity in Iceland. When foreign bishops neglected to maintain the schools, monasteries took their place as centres of teaching. In spite of the disintegration and decadence of the country, the general level of education in the later Middle Ages was higher than that of Norway and far higher than that of England[1]—as, indeed, it appears to be today.

[1] Gj., p. 253.

The intellectual spirit which animates Icelanders found a home and was fostered in the monasteries. Even though in the dark years of the fifteenth and sixteenth centuries the clear and sparkling stream of Icelandic literature ceased to flow, yet these communities never failed to offer draughts from the sacred fount of learning. *Hinc lucem et pocula sacra.*

(ii) ECCLESIASTICAL INFLUENCE IN ICELANDIC LITERATURE

The small sub-arctic Commonwealth of Iceland produced a literature which has won almost universal recognition, as it handed on a more complete and accurate account of the early history of Norway and Iceland than that produced by any other country in the world. Moreover, the saga masterpieces were written in the last fifty years of the Commonwealth, during the first half of the thirteenth century, thus constituting the noble Icelandic contribution to the contemporary emergence of Europe from the Dark Ages.

(*a*) Impetus to this great achievement was given by the adoption of Christianity, which led to the acquisition of writing. Hitherto runes incised on basalt rock had satisfied the needs of a people who cultivated the gift of memory and revelled in the art of recitation; but from the middle of the eleventh century the Church taught European script, first to its priests and soon afterwards to a larger proportion of laymen than other countries could boast. This enterprise resulted in the production of a native literature, for the genius of the country soon discarded Latin for the native tongue.

The historic Sturlunga Saga states that "all sagas were committed to writing before the death of Bishop Brand" (1201).[1] But this estimate seems to refer only to pre-Christian sagas (*i.e.*, before 1000); and even so, modern critics extend the period of their transcription another half-century. So that we may say that the ancient heroic sagas handed on by oral tradition were written down from about 1150 to 1250. The earliest of these prose epics have a straightforward, almost colloquial style—a prose so terse, clear, and picturesque as to make a reader wish all prose were spoken before being written down. Later compilations are romantically elaborated.[2] The heroic sagas compiled in Christian times faithfully retain an atmosphere of exuberant paganism. Professor Macalister points out that this

---

[1] Sturlunga S. I, 107.
[2] W. S. Craigie, *Icelandic Sagas*, pp. 30-1. Turville-Petre has shown (*History*, Sept., 1942) that some later recensions curbed the loquacity of some sagas orally handed down.

absence of expurgation of heathenisms indicates the strength of the Christian hold on Iceland in the days when the sagas were put into writing. The country could afford to be generous to the old faith because it had ceased to be dangerous. "It is needless to kill dead gods."[1] Some of the later sagas—e.g., two of the most famous and interesting, Njála and Laxdale—have interpolations of Christian details and incidents. Furthermore, this departure from the usual ecclesiastical editing of past records indicates the independence, nationalism, and devotion to accuracy inherent in the Icelandic Church.

(b) Before the sagas were committed to writing the initiative in Icelandic literature had been taken by Saemund (1056-1133) and Ari (1066-1148), priests designated as the "Wise," who specialised respectively in early Norwegian and Icelandic history. The work of these pioneers has already been described (sup., pp. 52-53), and also the notable and varied monastic contribution (V [i]).

The mantle of Saemund fell on his foster-son Snorri Sturluson (1178-1241), compiler of the renowned prose Edda and Heimskringla.[2] The Edda, together with some references in old Icelandic poems and sagas, preserve for the world almost all that is known of ancient Scandinavian mythology and Germanic religion (which is much the same today as it was in pre-Christian times). There is nothing particularly ecclesiastical in Snorri's work, but it was cradled in the school at Oddi, founded by Saemund and continued by his priestly descendants. Dr Bertha Philpotts suggests that the name Edda may mean "the book of Oddi."[3]

The work on Icelandic history initiated by Ari was carried on by many anonymous authors of Lives or Sagas of individuals. The large ecclesiastical element in Ari's Islendingábók found an expansion in Kristni Saga, based on his researches.

(c) The lives of the first five bishops of Skálholt are recounted in a homely and picturesque little book bearing the odd title Hungrvaka ("Hungerwaker"), which the anonymous author gave it because he hoped it might rouse the curiosity of his young people to learn more about the remarkable men whose careers it relates, and to learn in what manner and with what customs Christianity had spread in the country.

The writer compares his book to a horn-spoon, homely and useful,

---

[1] Archæology of Ireland, p. 232.
[2] And (it is now considered) of the outstanding Njál's Saga (Njála).
[3] Edda and Saga, p. 19.

and yet a thing which the user can carve into beauty. Thus he be-
speaks imagination in his readers. He expresses his indebtedness to
Gizur (1124-1206), a great-grandson of Isleif (the first bishop of Iceland), who knew five bishops of Skálholt. This reference, together
with other evidence, suggests that the *Hungrvaka* was compiled about
the year 1200.

Three characteristics of this attractive record emerge:

1. The *Hungrvaka* is no monkish chronicle. Its atmosphere is
refreshingly clearer than that of the saga of Thorvald and Bishop
Fridrek, Iceland's first missionaries, picturesquely recorded in Latin
by Gunnlaug, a monk of Thingeyrar († 1218) about the time when the
Hungrvaka was written "in the Norwegian tongue"—*i.e.*, in Icelandic.

2. The picture is given a national rather than a Catholic atmosphere. Bishops stand out as leaders of the people rather than
promoters of a system. The author prefers the type of Pál, with whom
he lived, rather than St Jón of Hólar or the Blessed Gudmund. His
indifference to monastic establishments is significant; he does not
use their foundation to add to the glory of his heroes such as Bishop
Klaeng, as if he felt them foreign to Icelandic churchmanship. For
this author, Catholic Christianity means that which touches life at all
its points in the spirit of his heroes, who were leaders in all social and
national concerns.

3. The author of the *Hungrvaka* is not a mere annalist. His book
would not come under Dr Johnson's ban "as a kind of almanack-
making." In the saga manner, by the selection and presentation of
facts, rather than by didactic abstractions or philosophising, he brings
home to his readers the spirit and complexion of the Church of his
country in the glowing first century of its growth. He is intensely
proud of the national existence of Iceland and its Church, and, like
Ari and other writers of his time, he is determined to hand down an
accurate account of their history and the principles of their development. As R. H. Gretton said of Macaulay, "The motive force in his
work is concern for the existing state of affairs, and an interest in the
conditions which produced it."[1]

(*d*) Pálssaga, the detailed life of Pál, seventh bishop of Skálholt
(1195-1211), seems to have been written by the same author, who
lived obviously in close touch with the bishop's circle. The required
conditions would fit Pál's wife's brother Thorlak or Gudlaug
Eyjolfsson, grandson of Saemund the Learned, the span of whose
lives covers the period of the first seven bishops.

[1] *History*, pp. 22-3, London, 1917.

The lives of the two episcopal saints were recorded in sagas of their own. An account of St Jón of Hólar has come down to us in two versions in Icelandic from a Latin original by the learned monk Gunnlaug.

We have also two editions of St Thorlak's Saga written by a contemporary, the second of which adds controversial matters, and a later Life embroidered with miracles. The original versions of the sagas of these two saints may well have been adapted from the eulogies read at the Althing before their canonisation.

Abundant interest of another kind fastened on the strange, turbulent life of Gudmund, Bishop of Hólar (1161-1237), which evoked four sagas: two by contemporaries—one about his popular priesthood, written by a companion called Hrafn, and the other describing his militant episcopate, written by Aron, one of his more respectable associates; a third and longer Life written after his death; and a later miraculous Latin Life by Abbot Arngrim Brandsson about 1345, existing in an Icelandic translation.[1]

Many passages in these sagas recall the spirit and stir, the violence and clash of character, which animate the old epic tales, and, indeed, their hero was himself a reversion, a viking of the Church.

Two other bishops deservedly were commemorated in sagas—Arni Thorlaksson, a vigorous bishop of Skálholt (1269-98), and Lárentius Kalfsson, a popular and pious bishop of Hólar (1323-31). Both these important Lives were written by contemporaries. The life of Bishop Arni was set down by his nephew and successor, Arni Helgason (1303/4-20). It fills a gap in historical records and throws searching light on the discreditable contest between Church and chieftains over ecclesiastical property. The Life of Bishop Laurence by his chaplain Einar Haflidason (1304-73) has the distinction of being the last historical work in old Icelandic literature.[2] It subtly reveals the complexity of character that marks even saintly lives.

(e) It may be argued that sagas deal with persons and periods, not with problems and principles, and so make poor history. But Iceland is an intensely individualistic country, and the problems of its Church and Commonwealth, largely the product of isolation and harsh natural conditions, have been personal in their essence and in their treatment. The Danish historian Saxo Grammaticus (c. 1200) well says: "The pains of the men of Thule may not be blotted in oblivion;

---

[1] Craigie, pp. 71-2, 75-6; Turville-Petre and Olszewska, *Life of G.*, pp. xxvi-vii.
[2] Gj., pp. 237-8.

for, though they lack all that can foster luxury (so naturally barren is their soil), yet they make up for their neediness by their wit."[1]

The particular genius of Icelandic literature lies in the story, with its details and pithy sayings and its play of character. Sagas, indeed, present no philosophies or academic abstractions, but they reveal the baffling crosslights, the heat of loves and hatreds, the intangible suspicions, and the equally intangible confidence and trust which make up much of the real moving forces of life.[2]

The classical sagas described heroic events which took place before the year 1030. Lives of bishops followed this "saga-age," as if their ecclesiastical authors were determined to make one fact plain to posterity (for, though remote and comparatively unimportant, they consciously wrote for all time)—the fact that the heroic spirit was not dead, but lived on in the achievements of leaders of their country's Church. These writers, almost all of them anonymous, may rest well content that they have succeeded in their high-hearted and altruistic enterprise.

(iii) CHURCH LAW, PROPERTY, AND PATRONAGE

The most remarkable feature of the Icelandic Church, at least until the Norwegian aggression in the thirteenth century, was its national character. The Church was not a separate self-governing corporation in the State, as in other countries, but it was bound up with the State so completely as to constitute the country on its religious side.[3] This nationalisation is apparent in the method of election of bishops, in the administration of the law, and in the private ownership of churches and glebes.

(a) The first native bishops were elected "by the whole commonwealth"—i.e., by the chieftains and other members of the Althing. Then they went to see the King of Norway and the Pope, and were consecrated by the Archbishop of Bremen, Primate of the north. Jón Øgmundsson, the first Bishop of Hólar, was chosen "by God and good men" (a method of appointment which preserved primitive tradition).[4] He then took Bishop Gizur's writ to the Pope before his consecration by the Archbishop of Lund. Gizur nominated his

---

[1] Cp. Phillpotts, *Edda and Saga*, p. 228.
[2] Cp. R. H. Gretton, *op. cit.*, p. 45.
[3] Aage Gregersen, *L'Islande . . . Son Statut à travers les âges*, p. 43.
[4] Elsewhere co-operation of the laity in elections, after becoming a formality, had lapsed, as elections were increasingly taken over by the bishops (Turner, *Cam. Med. Hist.*, I, pp. 152 *sq.*).

successor to the Althing, and on other occasions the assembly referred the choice to the bishop. When Klaeng's episcopate was drawing to its close, the Althing could not decide between three candidates, and entrusted the nomination to the dying bishop.

Bremen in Germany and Lund in Sweden proved to be too remote from Iceland for the primates to exercise full control over the independent Icelandic Church, so that in 1152, with a view to closer supervision, an archbishopric was established at Nidaros, the capital of Norway (afterwards called Trondhjem). The province consisted of Norway, Iceland, Greenland, and the Orkneys and Hebrides.[1] Nevertheless, the Icelandic Althing continued its ancient right of episcopal nomination until the death of Bishop Gudmund, which occurred in the same year as that of the southern bishop. The two bishops-elect went overseas for consecration in 1238, but were vetoed for political reasons, and substitutes were elected by the chapter of Nidaros.

Norway retained the initiative for two centuries, and foreign bishops, many of them unworthy, were foisted on the long-suffering country. After 1413, Iceland was left much to itself, but interest had been wellnigh killed, and bishops of varied origin followed in quick succession for a century.

In 1522 the Trondhjem chapter renounced electoral powers in favour of the Icelandic synod, who nominated two native bishops of the old type, destined to fall before Danish State aggression at the Reformation. Since then the State has always appointed Icelanders.

It is noteworthy that full and exact dates of the consecrations and deaths of early Icelandic bishops are preserved—a testimonial to their historians' detailed accuracy and appreciation of the importance of these prelates.

(b) The Church in Iceland obtained its first property when Bishop Gizur, on the death of his mother, inherited the ancestral estate at Skálholt and made it the bishopstead of the diocese (c. 1096).

It acquired its endowment on the passing of the Tithe Law in 1096 on the advice of Markus Skeggjason, the Law-speaker, in response to the advocacy of Gizur, supported by the priest, Saemund the Wise.

Bishop Gizur may be accounted the founder of the Icelandic Church. Before his day the bishop, like the Celtic bishops, was

---

[1] *Dipl. Isl.*, I, pp. 717-8. The Hebrides appear as "ecclesia Sancti Columbi [sic] de insula Hy [Iona] et Sudereiensis alias Manensi" [sic]; whence "Sodor and Man." Norway gave up the Hebrides and Man in 1268.

nomadic. As the *Hungrvaka* says, "the see was nowhere." Churches depended on the generosity of chieftains to found and maintain them and provide their priests. Encouraged by the bishop, chieftains took orders themselves, and served the churches which they built on their estates. State and Church were one, as in the days of the heathen godi, and as in the time of the Old Testament, when Israel became the People and the Church of God. So in Gizur's days, most of the leading men of the country were priests and at the same time chieftains (prestar tho at hofdingjar).

This is a high ideal. Human nature could not maintain it long. When bishops were humble and unacquisitive, and chieftain-priests loyal and devoted, the ideal worked. Gizur won allegiance as an almost perfect prelate, being "both king and bishop over the land as long as he lived." And all men regarded Saemund and Ari and Hall, son of Teit, and their successors in the next generation, as leaders of their country in things temporal as well as in things spiritual.

(c) A compendium of Church law, drawn up by Bishops Ketill and Thorlak I, on the advice of Ozur the Primate and Saemund, was approved by the Althing in the years 1122-33, and incorporated in the law of the land.[1]

It includes the following interesting regulations:

On Faith and Baptism.

"All men shall be Christian in this country and believe in One God, Father, Son, and Holy Ghost." And so, "every child shall go to baptism as soon as may be. The three men who bring the child to baptism shall be fed by the yeoman-farmer (responsible for the church). Every man and every woman that hath understanding thereto is bound to learn Paternoster and Credo on pain of a fine."

On Burial.

"Yeomen are instructed to feed bearers and horses. Graves shall be the same price whether near the church or away from it in the churchyard.[2] Ten (=12) ells of wadmal cloth shall be paid for adults, 5 ells for infants. The priests shall have 5 ells for the service.[3]

"Burial in the churchyard is forbidden for the unbaptised, for suicides and for outlaws, unless the bishop gives consent."

---

[1] *Ut sup.*, p. 50; Codex Regius Grágás, ed. Olason; *Islandica*, IV, pp. 12-15; Canon Law, collected by Gratian, c. 1140.

[2] English cemetery custom has not reached this Christian equality, even in the face of death, the great leveller.

[3] 100 = 120 ells = 1 cow = 6 sheep = 240 fish (Gj., p. 206).

On Priests.

"A yeoman is responsible for fostering and training a boy for the priesthood."

(This characteristic Icelandic custom has given the Church its most notable bishops, priests, and scholars, and was continued with effect after the Reformation.)

"A priest shall say mass, mattins, and evensong every holy day. At Long-fast and Yule-fast (Lent and Advent) he shall give public notice of his engagements. A priest shall not hire out his services, nor say more masses than two (daily)."[1]

"The bishop is bound to go round his diocese and visit each Quarter once a year for consecrations and confessions, and so that men may see him."

Holy Days.

The list of approved Mass-days includes: Jan. 21—Agnes, Feb. 1—Brigid, Mar. 12—Gregory, Mar. 21—Benedict (later), Apr. 23—Jón of Hólar, Apr. 25—first Gangday (Rogation), May 3— Cross-Mass, June 9—Columba, July 8—Seljamen's Mass, July 29— Olaf's Mass, Aug. 10—Lavran's Mass (St Lawrence), Sept. 14— Cross-Mass, Dec. 23 (afterwards July 3)—Thorlak's Mass (whose festival with the Church Day is among High Days to be kept). There were four Mary-Masses: in the sagas Aug. 15 and Sept. 8, and later also Feb. 2 and Mar. 25. The Arna-Magnean collection at Copenhagen shows that kalendars had found their way to Iceland early in the thirteenth century.[2]

Yule was hallowed for thirteen days, the first, eighth, and thirteenth day—*i.e.*, twelfth night—being kept as Easter Day. The great festivals were Yule, Easter, and Whit-Sunday, the last being specially used for baptisms and its octave known as Holy Week (the northern Dominica in albis).[3] St John the Apostle does not appear in this kalendar. For the early Icelandic Church St John means the Baptist, whose festival ranked among the High Days, being often used for consecrations. It fell during the Althing and was the day when Christianity was "taken into the Law." St John Baptist was a

[1] Later Canon Law restricted priests to one mass. Hence the addition of a second (anomalous) gospel to eke out the fee.

[2] *Icelandic Illuminated MSS*, pp. 10-11.

[3] *Lndbk* 40; *B.S.* I, 62. Easter = Paskar (plur.). Hvita-sunna, the name for Pentecost, as in old Norway, deriving from England, shows that our Whit-Sunday is not Pfingstenday, but White Sunday, so the ecclesiastical colour in the English Church should not be red (*Dic. C.V.*).

favourite saint with Bishop Thorlak, who appealed to him as "God's champion" . . . "wellnigh the most noble of all God's saints."[1] Of the 330 churches in the country, 150 were dedicated to B.V.M., 60 to St Peter, 52 to St Olaf, 40 to St John (probably the Baptist), 13 to St Andrew, and 3 to St Paul.[2]

Churches.

"A church burnt or destroyed (by storms) must be rebuilt by the landowner, who should endow it and arrange an Annual Church Day to be as holy as Pask-Day."

"The yeoman dwelling in the church estate is responsible for carrying fire into the church and for ringing the bells. The priest also may do this and light the candles."

"Men shall not bear weapons in church, and shall not set them against the walls on pain of fine. These were reckoned weapons under this head: axe, sword, spear, cutlass, and halberd." We found difficulty in meeting Lutheran feeling in this matter during the British occupation of 1940-42. Nehemiah iv, 14-21 suggests the answer.

"If a man go berserk (run amok), he shall pay a fine, and all bystanders, if they fail to stop him."

"If a man dwell on a glebe or church estate, he shall keep up the houses and garths. If the property be wasted, he shall make amends to the Church. If a man better church-land, he shall have God's thanks, but he shall not get amends therefor."[3]

(d) Charters were drawn up defining church rights and properties. Many copies have been preserved and are reprinted in the monumental *Diplomatarium Islandicum*.[4]

One original vellum broadsheet has survived fire, tempest, earthquake, robbers, and Reformation, and exists today after 800 years— the oldest Icelandic document extant. It is reproduced in Sir R. Burton's *Ultima Thule* (II, p. 70). This charter of Reykholt Church, started in the years 1178-95,was added to between 1204 and 1208, and again in 1224-41, and completed later.[5] History and graphology

---

[1] Sturlunga S. I, pp. 29 *sq.* (Vigfusson).
[2] Gj., pp. 279-80.
[3] Chiefly from *O.I.* I, pp. 616-24.
[4] Esp. Vols. II-IV; *O.I.* I, pp. 624-38. For specimens, see *infra*, pp. 90 *sq.*
[5] *Reykholt's Máldagi*, by B. Olsen and J. Hoffery, Cpn, 1883; art. on Graphological Aspect by G. Turville-Petre in *Vik. Soc. Saga*, Book XII, III, 1941, pp. 195 *sq.*

indicate that the first three owners were Pál, an easygoing, forgetful priest (†1135); his son Magnus, a simple, broadminded man who fell on evil days, and about the year 1206 handed over his estate to the historian Snorri Sturluson, whose script indicates a writer of an unbridled artistic nature with a remarkable memory and an urge for creation.[1]

In the Ketill-Thorlak codification of ecclesiastical law, as was customary then in north-west Europe, there is little questioning of lay ownership of churches, but the responsibility of chieftains and yeomen farmers (bondi) for priests, buildings, and land is clearly laid down.[2] This early Church code reflected Bishop Gizur's principles, and depended on an administrator of his character, firm but not aggressive, to maintain its basis. After his death some priests were inclined to act as petty chieftains, and many of the chieftains stretched their liberty into lawlessness. Some of them acted as secularised ecclesiastics ("half-priests" they were dubbed) and other chieftains insisted on appointing untrained private chaplains, responsible to no authority but their chieftain masters.

These irregularities provided occasion for bishops, jealous for the Church's rights, to ride roughshod over the hereditary claims of lay patrons, who took a native pride in the benefices they had founded and maintained at much sacrifice. After two centuries the apostolic comprehensiveness of early Icelandic Christianity hardened into rival secularities, political and ecclesiastical. Abp Eystein (1157-88), like his contemporary Grosseteste in England, set out to bring the north into line with later Canon Law, and instigated Bishop Thorlak's opposition to the chieftains' claims. The furious resistance this aroused has been illustrated in the section on the bishop's life. The matter was dropped by his successor Pál, with the result that his episcopate breathes a fragrant atmosphere reminiscent of the glowing epoch of the early Icelandic bishops.[3]

But his northern colleague Gudmund displayed a different spirit. Where Thorlak had threatened, Gudmund used force. He stalked up and down the country asserting his rights, backed by a band of outlaws and marauders.[4]

Such was the ignoble beginning of a long and bitter struggle, which played into the hands of external powers, leading to the degradation of the Church and the country. Norway, finally called

---

[1] Sturlunga S. I, pp. 25, 76, 141 sq., 152; II, pp. 17, 30.
[2] See Stutz, *Eigenkirke*; and ref. *inf.*, p. 228.
[3] *Inf.*, pp. 93-99.   [4] *Inf.*, pp. 99-105.

in to arbitrate, seized the chance to assert her domination over her "colony," and Rome was not slow in support of monarchy to appoint foreign bishops more amenable to her discipline, and thus to denationalise the Icelandic Church.

In this way the contest over ecclesiastical patronage and property, more than anything else, brought about the decadence of the Church, and, as we shall see, contributed largely to the fall of the Icelandic Commonwealth.

APPENDIX TO CHAPTER V (iii)

Some Church Charters preserved in "Dipl. Isl." I, No. 25 (Stafaholt 1140), III and IV, etc.

St Peter's, Reykholt, 1178.

To the church in Reykholt belongeth the home-land, with the profit of all the land that pertaineth thereto; 20 cows, a steer two winters old, 130 ewes (=156).

There pertaineth thereto five parts of all Grimsá, but three parts not, save what I will now count up—that is, all the flood fence and three parts of the river north of Mid-rock, but the fourth not. There pertaineth thereto also a fourth part of Harrow-pool, after the sixth part is excepted, and the fishing down at Redwater-oyce.[1]

There pertaineth thereto three horses no worse than fourteen ounces (worth apiece). There pertaineth thereto also a (mountain) sheepwalk at the Copses, with the river fishing, a half that pertaineth thereto, and commons in Ramfjörd heath, and the intakes (isolated spots) that she (the Church) hath in Faxdale and Goatland with the thicket; the thicket in Sanddale down from the rocks that are callen Cloven—they stand over against Sanddale-river, and thence up to the Fell-brow.[2]

There pertaineth thereto the wood or rushes on Thwartwater-lithe for wood for the shieling. A turbary in Steinthors-stead land; a measure of seed-corn sown. . . . (O. I.; Dipl. Isl. I, No. 120).

Videy Cloister.

This Charter was made at the Althing by the counsel of Bishop

---

[1] Grimsá, southern tributary of the Hvitá, still a good salmon river, and easily fished.

[2] Vigfusson likes translating place-names; Cloven rocks—*i.e.*, Skorradal, by the lake.

Magnus (1216-37) (of Skálholt); and Snorri Sturluson[1] brought it up at the Court of Law, and named witnesses.

That between Reykness and Boz-river there shall be paid by every homestead where cheese is made, such a loaf (of cheese) as is there made, to the church-estate of Videy every harvest, and in return all they that pay this homage to the church-estate share in the prayers of the brethren and clerks of the church-estate, as it is set in the rule, every day with all those that do good or pay rent to the church-estate for charity or the good of souls.

These are witnesses: Magnus Gudmundsson[2] and Asmund his brother; Arni Magnusson; Thorleif,[3] Bodvar and Marcus, sons of Thord; Teit Thorvaldsson;[4] Sigurd Jónsson;[5] Styrmir Karsson;[6] Ketill Thorlaksson;[7] Orm Kodransson;[8] Styrkar Sweynbjörnarson; Jerusalem-Björn;[9] Kodran Swartheadsson (*Dipl. Isl.* I, No. 124).

St Mary's, Hitarnes (c. 1180).

The church owneth Hitarnes land with all its profits. She hath 10 cows, and 100 ewe-worth sheep; 1,000 eils in farm-implements and house furniture; 20 weights of meal except of seals and fishes.

This is the outlay for this property: there shall be a priest domiciled to sing all the services, and every other day in the Long Fast (Lent), two masses; every day in the Yule-fast (Advent) a mass. . . . There shall be lights every night from the second Mary-Mass (Mar. 25) until Pask week is over.

There shall be two poor women of the kin of Thorhall and Steinunn that can help themselves.

Jörund shall be warden of this property, and his heirs, if the bishop think them fit, or else one of Thorhall's kin or Steinunn's.

The church has 3 altar-cloths; 2 candlesticks; 2 bells; 2 hand-basins, and a hanging to go round the church; 10 marks of wax. At four marks of wadmal the priest shall be fed.

Burial is allowed there (*O. I.* I, pp. 630-1; *Dipl. Isl.* I, No. 64).

Saurbaèr in Hvalfjörd (1352).

Kirkiu: Saurbae fylgia xi kyr. thriar oc xx aer. thrijr hestar. fimm

---

[1] The historian-statesman (†1241).
[2] Nephew of Bishop Pál, bishop-elect of Skálholt, drowned 1240.
[3] Protagonist in battle at Bae in 1237 *v.* Sturla Sighvatsson; thirty men killed († 1257).
[4] Leading priest, twice lawman—1219, 1236 († 1259).
[5] Grandson of Lopt, son of Saemund (p. 53).
[6] A remarkable man; priest, called the Prior and the Wise; Lawman 1210 († 1232) (F. J. IV, p. 123; J. H. I, pp. 146 *sq.*).
[7] Priest († 1273).   [8] Priest († 1253).   [9] A Pilgrim.

gelldfiár kugilldi. xx hundrad j metfie. threnn messuklaedi oc ij hokla lausa. iij sloppa. ij altaraklaedi. ij kantara kápu(r). krossar iij. mariu skript oc johannis baptiste og olafs skript. kerttistikur iij. vatzketill. glodaker. baksturjarnn. merki ij. xx baekur (*Dipl. Isl.* III, No. 26).

The church of Saurbaer possesses 11 cows, 23 (milch) ewes, 3 horses, 5 non-milch ewes, valued at one cow's value, 20 cows' value in prized living stock. Three sets of vestments (mass cloths) and 2 loose (separate) copes, 3 gowns, 2 altar-cloths, 2 chanting (choir) copes, 3 crucifixes, a picture of (St) Mary and of (St) John the Baptist and of (St) Olaf, 3 candlesticks, a water-kettle, a warming-pan, an iron plate for baking sacramental wafers, 2 banners, 20 books.

CHAPTER VI

THE LAST YEARS OF THE ICELANDIC COMMONWEALTH

(i) THE LAST OF THE PRINCE-BISHOPS—PÁL (1195-1211)

ICELANDIC history is concerned with persons rather than with movements; or, indeed, with principles dramatised through personality. This gives it vivid interest. Ideas are objectified. What chiefly counts is individual character, and in that ideals and movements are envisaged.

Thus the adoption of Christianity centres round the protagonists Hjalti and Gizur, Snorri and Thorgeir; the Reformation embodies what might well be a saga of the redoubtable Catholic champion, Bishop Jón Arason. So the end of the heroic period of the Icelandic Church emerges in the contrasting Lives of Bishops Pál and Gudmund.

The political and ecclesiastical causes which led to the collapse of the Commonwealth are involved in the character and exploits of bishops and chieftains, realistically described in contemporary sagas: Pálssaga, Gudmundssaga, and Sturlungasaga. The last forms a history of Iceland from *c.* 1100 to 1262, arranged round Lives of leading men in Church and State.

(*a*) The saintly Thorlak on his death-bed handed his episcopal ring to Pál, the illegitimate son of his sister. Pál was then forty years old, a deacon like his father, the powerful chieftain Jón Loptsson, and married to a priest's daughter. All that blazons forth the irregularities of the old régime, but its real greatness—such as the maintenance of peace and holding the country together—lies deeper.

Pál was a godi—a magistrate, almost a judge, acting as a chief in his countryside. In his youth he had been hirdman (retainer) to Harald, Earl of the Orkneys, and later went to England to be educated. On his return he acquired a reputation for skill in making verse, for general book-lore, and for his musical ability. In these respects he resembled his versatile father, as godi, deacon, scholar, singer; in his courtliness (kurteisi)[1] and piety we conclude he took after his mother.

These social and personal qualities marked him out as Thorlak's successor in the bishopric of Skálholt. The irregularity of his birth

---

[1] This is not a native word, nor a native grace, and his Saga states that it was in England Pál acquired his great learning and grace (kurteisi) of scholarship. No one learnt so much in so short a time (*B.S.* p. 127).

made some hesitance necessary.[1] The Althing naturally had much debate as to whether they should accept Thorlak's nomination, but finally referred the matter to Brand, Bishop of Hólar, who had no scruples about asking Pál to fare overseas to be consecrated. However, Pál himself felt some reluctance, until at his father's old home in Oddi at the church festival on Seljamen's-mass he felt moved to "put himself under the burden."

Eirik, the Archbishop of Nidaros, had been forced to flee from Norway, but King Sverrir received Pál with great honour, and he was ordained priest by the archbishop at Lund in the Lent Ember Days, and consecrated bishop "on St Jón of Hólar's day"—April 23, 1195. That the Pope resented the independence of the Icelandic Church and particularly the friendship of its bishops with King Sverrir, an opponent of ecclesiastical claims, is shown by a letter of Innocent III to Bishops Pál and Brand on July 30, 1198.[2]

At the start Pál won the hearts of his people by deferring his first mass as priest and bishop until he could celebrate it at his own cathedral. For this a great congregation assembled, including his father and brothers and the venerable churchman Gizur Hall's son, father of Magnus, who was to succeed Pál.

(b) Like most chieftain-bishops, Pál enriched his cathedral. He had brought from Norway "for his spiritual spouse" two windows of glass, the first mention of glazing in Icelandic history, windows hitherto being mere lattices to let out smoke.

He made another advance in ecclesiastical architecture in having a steeple (stöpul) erected to house the bells presented by his predecessor. To build this he imported wood from Norway, and entrusted the work to Amund Arnason, "the best carpenter in the country," and, as we shall see, a poet, though not the country's best. He made the upper storey of the belfry into a chapel dedicated to St Thorlak, with a crypt in which he placed an elaborate stone coffin to receive his body after death—a custom followed by priests down to modern times, for coffins are hard to get, and country churches are used as store-rooms. Pál translated the remains of Bishop Thorlak to his chapel in 1198, after obtaining the consent of the Althing and collecting offerings. Later he had a large shrine wrought in gold and gems and burnt silver by Thorstein, the most skilful metal-worker in the country.

[1] Corp. Iur. Canoni, c. 5; X, 1, 18 (Alex. III).
[2] Dipl. Isl. I, Nos. 75, 76. Innocent III was the pope who backed King John when Magna Carta was extorted from him.

A festival of St Thorlak on December 23 was established by law in 1199 throughout the land, with two days' fast preceding it. The Althing acted in this matter without any reference to Rome. But no ill effects appeared to follow from such ecclesiastical inadvertence, for we read that many pilgrims came, not only from all parts of Iceland, but also from overseas, "and carried away proofs of the saintliness of the blessed Bishop Thorlak and of the liberality and magnificence of Bishop Pál." "The glory was Thorlak's, the good hap was Pál's."

Better than this, many visitors noted that the new saint's nephew resembled him in character and devotion, and applied here in Icelandic fashion the local proverb: "A man takes after his mother's brother."[1] Pál lived for the most part ascetically, though given to hospitality, and became noted for his almsgiving, humility, and patience.

Moreover, his saga records "for the example of posterity" that Bishop Pál seldom preached, confining himself to four times a year—Christmas Day, Ash Wednesday, Maundy Thursday (Skirdagur), and Dedication Festival—and only otherwise when he had something special to say. The mediæval Book of Icelandic Homilies shows that most sermons were laudably concise, forcible and earnest, with their message brought home by means of popular proverbs, leading their hearers to make good resolutions.

(c) As the main object of this sketch of Pál's episcopate is to set out the contrast between a bishop of the old school and one of the new, and the changing temper of the times, the story would not be complete without some account of Pál's impressive family life.

His wife Herdis justified her upbringing as a priest's daughter, as she proved a skilful manager at the bishopstead, though there were one hundred persons on the estate, including seventy or eighty servants. As we have seen, the bishop maintained the reputation of an Icelandic chieftain. To celebrate his consecration he gave a feast to his northern colleague Brand and other friends, serving "wine and ale of the best." He commemorated similarly the translation of St Thorlak's relics.

A memorable visitor in 1203, welcomed with another feast, was Bishop Jón of Greenland, whose visit cemented the friendly relationship between the two Churches that had existed from the beginning.

---

[1] Cp. the attitude in ancient Germany—e.g., Tacitus, *Germania* 20: "Sororum filiis idem apud avunculum qui ad patrem honor. Quidem sanctiorem artioremque hunc nexum sanguinis arbitrantur."

The two bishops " laid wise plans, and hallowed much anointing oil." Bishop Jón produced a recipe given him by King Sweyn for making wine out of crowberries, which Pál used for the sacrament. The Annals note that this was the first occasion on which wine was so made in Iceland.

Pál and Herdis had four children, "the best brought up in all the countryside." Their several excellences are thus commemorated in a skaldic quatrain by the cathedral artificer Amund: "Lopt was growing up skilled in handicraft, Ketill in handwriting, Halla in book-learning and housecraft, Thora in obedience and love. . . . So it went with each of them, until the day on which they were visited with misfortune."

On May 17, 1207 (these exact details attest the attachment of the author of Pálssaga to the household), Herdis with her children Ketill and Halla went to the bishop's house at Skard to get servants and to see to affairs. They were accompanied by the bishop's chaplain, Björn, and Herdis' niece, Gudrun, and others. They had to cross the Thorsá, even in the height of summer a furious river, which they found on their return to be in flood, as the glaciers were melting. The ford was impassable, so that a boat was obtained and the horses towed across. Herdis' horse was washed away; nevertheless, she persisted in fulfilling her plan to get home that day. But the boat foundered, and Herdis, Halla, and Gudrun were drowned. When the bishop was told at midnight "it was plain to all that God had measured close what he could bear." But he faced up to the consequences, so that men learnt the truth of the proverb: "A deep plough stands stronger than a shallow one." The household management was taken over by Thora, a maiden fourteen years old, "with her father's loving supervision, and all who knew about it thought she managed very well."

Other personal losses shadowed Pál's episcopate. On November 1, 1197, his father Jón Loptsson died, aged about seventy-three. The saga calls Jón "the noblest chief in all Iceland," but the epithet in justice should apply to his status rather than to his character, in which the elements were so strangely mixed. But in spite of moral aberrations, even for those days excessive, in an age heading for disaster he devoted the strength of his wealth, position, and talents to the maintenance of peace and order. Having inherited the wisdom of Saemund his grandfather, he handed on the torch to his foster-son Snorri Sturluson (*1178), the leader of the next generation. Jón twice averted or postponed civil war, the second time, with the help of Bishop Pál, not long before he died. His mother was the illegitimate daughter of Magnus Bareleg, King of Norway, which added to Jón's prestige in that country and in his own. His personal qualities bore out this royal relationship, and such was the general deference to his judgment and aptitude for rule that he came to be regarded almost as "uncrowned king of Iceland."[1]

Towards the end of his life Jón Loptsson, the chieftain-deacon, built an elaborate church on his estate at Keld in the volcanic district of the south, and would have founded a monastery there if its dangerous situation or the scruples of Bishop Thorlak had not prevented it.[2] Jón was living at Keld when his last illness seized him, and had himself carried to the door to see his church for the last time, saying: "There standest thou, my church! Thou bewailest me, and I bewail thee."

Another remarkable leader died a few years later, on July 6, 1206, at the age of eighty-two—Gizur Hallsson, doyen of the Church, the most learned man of his day. Grandson of the first, and foster-son of the third, Bishop of Skálholt, he had proved the friend and counsellor of every bishop afterwards and the stabilising factor in their policy. The author of *Hungrvaka*, the homely account of these early bishops, expresses his indebtedness to Gizur's fund of information. Another side of his character, which illustrates the rest of it, is revealed in a footnote to his Life added by Bishop Pál's brother: "In any kind of company Gizur was the rook or captain of all merriment."[3]

(d) Bishop Pál was responsible for two effective measures, one ecclesiastical and the other civil.

In order to determine and meet parochial needs, he took a census of the priests in the three Quarters comprising his diocese, and found that there were 220 churches served by 290 priests. This does not

---

[1] *B.S.* I, pp. 83, 282-4; F. J. I, pp. 292 *sq.*, 331 *sq.*, *Islandica* XXII, pp. 10-12. Magnus was so called because he adopted the kilt.

[2] F. J. IV, pp. 27-8 (fatis impeditus); ct. Oddaverja S.

[3] hrókr, rook, remarkable as one of the earliest reference to chess, a game in which Icelanders have always excelled. Until the fifteenth century the queen could move only one square diagonally, so the rook, or chariot with driver, was the most important piece. (Rook ? from Arabic rukh =chariot.) When Icelanders used to make chessmen out of fishbones, rooks were represented as captains, called centurions, each carrying a sword and blowing a little horn. *Bp.* Bótólf of Hólar (1238-46) was rebuked for neglecting his sermon-preparation for chess (*B.S.*, p. 186). Anna Comnena (cp. *sup.* p. 72) notes the popularity of chess in Constantinople, so it may have been brought thence to Iceland by the Varings.

appear to include the four or five small monastic establishments then existing. The Bishop of Hólar at the time was so fully engaged in a militant crusade against his chieftains that no such survey can have been made in the north. But adding rather more than one-third for the largest Quarter to complete the total for the island, Bishop Helgason estimates that 330 churches with 440 priests would make the complement at this time (against 276 churches in 111 pastorates with 109 ministers, the total of today).[1]

Pál's other achievement shows the connection of the Church of his day with everyday life; for it dealt with the length of an ell in measuring wadmal, the local homespun, about which much loose dealing prevailed among Icelanders and traders from overseas.

In 1200 the bishop persuaded the Althing to fix this measurement. They laid down that all men had to carry yardsticks of 2 ells in length—i.e., about 36½ inches—and this statutory measurement had to be marked on the walls of all parish churches. Opportunity was then taken to introduce (approximately) the English yard, a fact which indicates the amount of traffic there was at this time between the two countries.[2]

(e) The appointment of Gudmund Arason to succeed Brand as Bishop of Hólar in the last part of Pál's episcopate let loose a tornado of civil war in the north, on which Pál attempted to exercise a moderating influence. Such an attitude must have been the outcome of conviction and strength rather than of irresolution, for he was pressed by letters from Archbishop Eirik to support his colleague in fighting the chieftains on behalf of ecclesiastical rights. When we come to consider Gudmund's extraordinary campaign, the justification of Pál's attitude will be apparent.

Humility, tolerance, and fellowship had always been among the highest ideals of the seven southern chieftain-bishops. In a land of arrogance, self-assertion, and individualism, they made good as conquering Christian qualities, and were never so "precious" (to use the saga word) as in the latter years of Bishop Pál.

This "model biography of a model bishop"[3] thus ends: "After governing God's Christendom in Iceland for sixteen winters with great temperance, Pál died on the Eve of St Andrew's-Mass, 1211." Amund, the episcopal laureate, confirmed the saga's judgment in a

---

[1] J. H. I, p. 109.
[2] B.S. I, p. 135. Thingvellir church (and St Mary's, Nottingham) once had yards marked on walls.
[3] Vigfusson, Sturlunga S., Introd., p. cxx.

poem which commends the bishop as "a maker of peace and lover of justice . . . in a time of war, rapine, and arson, and the death of men in many dreadful ways."

The golden day of Icelandic churchmanship was drawing to an end. As the sombre night of conflict began to close in on his country, Pál's gentle, loving character glowed with a steady light on the gathering clouds.

(ii) The Turbulent Crusade of Bishop Gudmund (1202-37)

Gudmund Arason, popularly known as the Good and later as the Blessed, inherited an obstinate and truculent spirit, and was given a harsh upbringing; and, though he showed himself a pious and gifted priest, his thirty-five years as a bishop, spent in recklessly championing ecclesiastical rights, brought nothing but strife to the diocese of Hólar and was largely responsible for the loss of independence which soon after his death befell his Church and country.

(*a*) Gudmund was the natural son of a famous warrior, Ari the Icelander, who died fighting in Norway when the boy was seven years old.[1] Thus he was brought up by his uncle Ingimund, "and the first compensations he got for the loss of his father were floggings to make him learn, for he was extremely obstinate." But Ingimund was a scholar and loved his ward, and his affection was returned, so that Gudmund became a changed man when, after his ordination as priest, he had to bid farewell to his guardian and to his best friend, Thorgeir, son of Bishop Brand.[2] Nevertheless, at first his character was deepened and his priesthood enriched. People credited him with unusual powers of exorcism, and though he had crushed his foot in a shipwreck as a young man, he travelled incessantly, blessing springs and healing the sick.[3] He acquired immense popularity for his asceticism (like Bishop Thorlak, he was celibate), his optimism, and his beneficence. "The common people showed their opinion of him by nicknaming him Gudmund the Good." In later lists of bishops he is less inappropriately termed godi—The Chieftain.[4]

An illustration of Gudmund's popularity appears in an incident

---

[1] Gudmund's S. in *B.S.* I, pp. 407-558; trans. G. Turville-Petre and E. S. Olszewska 1-4, 6. Also cp. Sturlunga S. and see p. 83 *sup.*

[2] *Loc. cit.* 13-4.

[3] Such consecrated wells were called Gvendarbrunnar and, later, biskups-brunnar or -vatn.

[4] *Dipl. Isl.* II: *c.* 1325 Bps of Hólar—"Gudmund godi Arason," 1494 in Will; "St Jón of Hólar and godi Gudmund bp."

which may well have proved a turning-point in his life. In 1195 he was asked by Halldora, Abbess of Kirkjubaer, a veritable mother in Israel, to help her in the supervision of her nunnery. Gudmund agreed to do this, and episcopal consent was given to him; but the churchpeople of Vellir were so much upset at the thought of their loss that they held a meeting and induced Bishop Brand to withdraw his approval. So Gudmund did not come under monastic discipline, but continued his itinerant mission as a priestly wonder-worker, until five years later, much against his will, he was elected bishop.[1] Bishop Pál's consent to this step was given after some hesitation, but Gudmund let his better judgment be overruled by his ambitious uncle and unbalanced women recluses.[2]

(b) Gudmund was consecrated in 1202, at the age of forty-one, by Eirik, Archbishop of Nidaros, a prelate with a mediæval mind, who instigated the new bishop to stand up for episcopal rights over ecclesiastical property and for exemption of priests from civil juris-diction. Thus his campaign had official prompting.

It was fostered also by the spirit of the age, always a deceptive counsellor. His episcopate opened in an epoch when anarchy was beginning to stalk the land. Gone was the old healthy balance of chieftain power, often preserved by merely personal feuds. Strife now grew almost into civil war. Estates were falling to fewer owners, who collected followers to oust their rivals and increase their domi-nation. These contests for pre-eminence form the theme of the Sturlunga Saga, called after the Sturla family, who gave their name to this disastrous period, 1200-65.

Part of the aggressiveness of Gudmund's campaign was due to the turbulence of the time; but more arose from the truculence of his own character, for his southern contemporaries, Pál and Magnus Gizurarson, in spite of personal appeal from Eirik, kept themselves free from strife and attempted a mediatory policy. The archbishop later played into Gudmund's hands by summoning Magnus to Norway on some obscure ceremonial question and keeping him there for some years, while Gudmund carried his campaign into the southern diocese.

Gudmund's spirit and methods chiefly reflected his own character and upbringing, but he derived his inspiration largely from the example of St Thomas Becket (†1170), sagas of whose life grew to popularity in Iceland at this time. Gudmund's antagonist Kolbein

---

[1] *Loc. cit.* 26; Bogi Th. Melsted; Isl. Saga III, p. 331.
[2] Gudmund's Saga 42-7.

complains in a poem that God made him a second Thomas for masterfulness (glikr Tomasi at riki).[1] Happily, Iceland was not so far provoked as to make Gudmund a martyr.

The connecting link with this English champion of the Church's rights appears to have been Hrafn Sveinbjarnarson, a great friend and adviser of Gudmund, and the author of the "youngest" biography about him. In 1195 Hrafn captured a walrus which proved difficult to land, so he made a vow to reward St Thomas if he would help him. In fulfilment of this promise, two years later he went on a pilgrimage to the shrine at Canterbury, taking the tusks of the walrus, and probably returned with a copy of the Life of St Thomas, then being propagated throughout the country.[2]

Hrafn accompanied Gudmund in 1202 when he went to be consecrated, and has vividly described how fierce tempests drove them through the Hebrides and round Ireland before they could make across to Norway.

(c) After his consecration, Gudmund found his chief antagonist in Kolbein Tumason, leading chieftain of the north, a man with a temper as aggressive as his own, who had been prime mover in securing Gudmund's nomination as bishop, and on the strength of that patronage had taken over the administration of the episcopal estate at Hólar.

At first Gudmund's use of his power of excommunication had a weighty effect on Kolbein and other chiefs, but this weapon was soon blunted and broken by arbitrary and excessive use. Erring priests fled to the bishop to escape the law, and he refused to give them up. Finally the chiefs besieged Hólar, but to avoid a fight the bishop rode out and away, supported by 360 retainers, headed by three abbots and a couple of monks with vagabonds and women tramps in the rear. Gudmund owed his band of followers to his former beneficence as priest. Afterwards his more reputable supporters fell away, and he was followed up and down the north by a ragged regiment whom he called "God's Almsfolk," though they included some doughty outlaws, who fell out among themselves over the spoils they wrested from a resentful countryside. On this occasion Kolbein pursued the bishop's band from Hólar until on September 9, 1208, he cut them off at Vidines, where a pitched battle was fought, in which Kolbein was killed and his followers fled. This death directly or indirectly led

---

[1] E. Magnusson, *Thómas Saga Erkibiskups*, Rolls S. 65.
[2] *B.S.* I, p. 641; Sturlunga S. II, 245, 277 *sq.* F. J. says Hrafn was a famous surgeon. He operated on one of his men for vesical calculus with success.

to the Sturlunga disasters and the break-up of the Commonwealth.

Light is thrown on the character of this protagonist of chieftain rights by a poem he composed; he was not irreligious, but fought against ecclesiastical aggression:

Heyr, himna smidur,	Hear, Lord of the sky,
hvers skáldid bidur;	the poet's cry;
komi mjúk til min	let Thy mercy free
miskunin thin;	reach even to me;
thvi heitk á thig,	I cry to Thee;
thu hefr skaptan mig;	Thou hast fashioned me,
ég em thraellinn thinn,	Thy slave am I now,
thú 'st drottin minn.	my master Thou.
Gud, heitk á thig,	God, I pray to Thee,
ath graedir mig;	O heal Thou me.
minnst mildingur min,	Thou, merciful, know'st
mest thurfum thin;	my need the most.
ryd thú rödla gramur,	O king of the sun,
riklyndur og framur,	most mighty one,
höld hverri sorg,	chase sorrow cold
úr hjarta borg.	from my heart's stronghold.[1]

In spite of Bishop Pál's intervention, the quarrel, in Icelandic fashion, was taken over by Kolbein's relatives, the Sturlunga clan, who brought about Gudmund's banishment for some years.

(d) On his return the old game reopened. The ragged regiment re-formed and harried the countryside, so that the people appealed to their chiefs, and active war was renewed. In 1221 Gudmund and his followers took refuge in Malmey, a little barren island off the north coast, while Kolbein's nephew occupied the bishopstead at Hólar. Here he was raided by Gudmund's needy gang, taken unawares by night, and killed—an act condemned by old heroic ideals unlearned in civilised warcraft. Then the bishop had to flee to Grimsey in the Arctic Circle, where he was attacked, and after desperate adventures his band was defeated and he was once more banished. When he returned in 1226, for two years he was kept prisoner in the bishopstead.

All these escapades make good stories in Gudmund's sagas and would be enlivening, if not inspiring, in the pages of ecclesiastical history, as the hero of them is a bishop.[2]

Bishop Pál again attempted mediation and offered to house Gudmund at Skálholt, but he preferred his independence, distrusting

---

[1] Trans. Beatrice Ellen Barmby.   [2] G. S. 84, 87-93.

his colleague's noble proclivities. On another occasion Pál sent his chaplain, offering to pay for any damage Gudmund might consider he had received. But naturally he refused to be bought off, and charged Pál with abetting the chieftains. An offer by Gudmund to refer the matter to the archbishop for arbitration was rejected by the chieftains, whose patriotic independence led them to foresee the outcome of bringing in external authority.

And so the childish campaign went on. Its ecclesiastical aims had long since merged into a clash of clans. Gudmund made himself in turns a popular hero and a public nuisance. We can discover few episcopal functions performed by him. On August 29, 1220, just before a battle in the churchyard, he consecrated a church at Helgastadir, and during the next Ember Days (September 16-18) held an ordination at Saudanes on the north-east coast. Once he celebrated mass on a rock on the precipitous Drangey islet, property of the Hólar see. It is clear that he allowed the cathedral school to lapse, for after a visit to Norway he returned at the archbishop's desire with a teacher. When he was kept out of the bishopstead he settled with his undisciplined band on some sympathetic farmer, until the neighbourhood grew tired of their maraudings. He spent three or four long periods overseas—outlawed, or escaping from chieftains' revenges, renewing his ecclesiastical zeal or doing penance at Rome.

The grievous effect on religion of all this is strikingly summed up in Gudmund's Saga (62). "Wretched and lamentable was the state of the Christian Faith there in those days. Some priests abandoned the celebration of Mass for fear of God" (i.e., of Gudmund, who had forbidden it); "but some performed it because of their fear of the chiefs, others by their own desire. The cathedral church, the mother, stood in sorrow and grief, as did some of her daughters too, but others exulted in her tribulation, and everyone lived just as he pleased, and no one dared to remonstrate."

Finally, in 1232, a new archbishop deprived Gudmund of his office, at the same time censuring the chieftains for their opposition.[1] However, the energies of the stalwart bishop by then were beginning to fail, and no steps were taken to elect a successor. In his few remaining years he regained some of the popularity of his priesthood, and happily, when at last the Pope issued a writ for his suspension for incapacity, Gudmund had died before it was signed.[2] His last

[1] Sturlunga S. I, p. 295.
[2] Dipl. Isl., No. 132, dated May 11, 1237. On the same day the Pope also directed the suspension of Bishop Magnus for infirmity. Gudmund died March 16, 1237.

gesture illustrates much of his character. From his death-bed, blind and feeble, he had himself carried out of the house, and, like an ancient hero, laid on a hurdle spread with ashes so that he should not die under a roof, but on the earth, beneath the open sky, with the feel of the wind on his face.

(e) Gudmund's unyielding struggle for ecclesiastical rights brought nothing but disaster to his diocese and nation.[1] But he was popular with the people, for they appreciated his priestly powers of healing and exorcism. He had proved himself a people's bishop, siding with them against feudal ideas in the country, as his bodyguard of "God's Almsfolk" made inconveniently plain. Men of a higher type, like Hrafn, Eyjolf, and Aron, also supported him, especially in his earlier campaigns, admiring his unsparing energy and relentless zeal.

Nearly a century after his death, one of Gudmund's successors at Hólar, a similar godi-bishop, the Norwegian Audun (1314-23), paid him the honour of beatification. His neglected grave was discovered with difficulty and his remains exhumed, being recognised by great knobs on his broken leg.[2] An elaborate tomb was prepared inside the cathedral, and Gudmund's day, March 16, was established as a holiday, being known by the homely name of Gvendar dagr. He owed this distinction partly to the admiration of King Hákon V, but chiefly to the desire of expressing official approval of his struggle for ecclesiastical rights, which Norwegian bishops in Iceland were then bringing to a successful conclusion.

Nevertheless, Gudmund's campaign defeated its own ends. His taking of the sword to exact by force the requirements of Canon Law and the privileges of the priesthood led to defeat by the sword. If victorious, he might have won (as did later ecclesiastical aggressors) material advantages, but only at the cost of losing the goodwill of those who had built up the Church in the country, and forfeiting spiritual leadership. It is significant that he was celibate. Had he obeyed the apostolic injunction in this matter, like almost all his brethren, he might have found that a wife would have given him a sense of proportion and kept him from eccentric aberrations.[3] Like Pál's wife, she might have ruled the bishopstead, obviating the intrusion of Kolbein Tumason, which greatly aggravated the contest at the outset, and she would have kept in order the bishop's rampageous crowd of pensioners. Had he remained a priest, especially if he had put himself under discipline in a monastery, his unusual

---

[1] Turville-Petre and Olszewska, l.c., p. xxiv.
[2] 1314, Lárentius S.   [3] 1 Timothy iii, 2-5.

powers might have been transmuted and have proved of positive value to the Church. As it was, his episcopate did his Church and country irreparable harm, for it proved the occasion, if not entirely the cause, of the loss of their liberty, as his wilful truculence played into the hands of external ecclesiastical and political authority.

Magnus Gizurarson, Bishop of Skálholt, an aristocratic prelate of the old school, died in the same year as Gudmund, so that the Althing, following their invariable custom, elected two priests, who went overseas for consecration. But Norway's opportunity had arrived. The nominations were ignored, and two Norwegians were sent as bishops to Iceland.

The independence of the Icelandic Church came to an end. Had it remained as strongly national as before, it might have held together the disintegrating Commonwealth. As it was, it hastened its collapse, and by the end of the next generation control of the country was assumed by Norway (1262-6).

(iii) END OF THE EPOCH (1238-62)

Bishop Gudmund's reckless truculence opened the door for direct papal action through the archbishop. This offered an opportunity for political intervention by the State, of which the astute King Hákon Hákonsson (1217-63) was not slow to take advantage.

Thus the ambitions of the King of Norway for overlordship of Iceland were furthered by external ecclesiastical aspirations, so that in this respect the subjugation of Iceland by Norway resembles the conquest of England 200 years earlier by their cousins from Normandy, in which ruler and Pope were allied against the people.

(a) In this anti-national move the Church took the lead and provided the protagonists. About the same time the Pope was getting into trouble for staffing English benefices with Italian priests, a proceeding which the Statute of Provisors attempted to restrict (1351).

By transferring the election of Icelandic bishops from the Althing to the Cathedral Chapter at Nidaros, the archbishop acted plainly contrary to the custom of the Icelandic Church. Had he desired only to remove the anomaly of lay patronage, he could have ordered canonical chapters to be formed at Skálholt and Hólar, though the chieftains would have contested the cession of their prerogative to priestly fellow-countrymen outside the Althing.[1] But he was well informed about the temper of the country. In spite of the equali-

[1] Gj., p. 183.

tarian principles of its government, the order of bishops met with more than mediæval deference. For notwithstanding Gudmund's secular activities, his office and person were treated with strangely patient consideration, so that even Norwegian bishops when consecrated and sent into the country were able to count on acceptance. Furthermore, as in the matter of the Icelandic adoption of Christianity, two and a half centuries earlier, the consciousness that the King of Norway was behind its protagonists considerably accelerated the proceeding, so now acceptance of a new régime in Church and State was stimulated by the recognition of foreign control.

(b) Gudmund's campaign, or the bankruptcy it showed in Icelandic Church leadership, was made the occasion for Norwegian interference, but it was not the only cause of it.

Persistent lawlessness in high places, which the patriarchal government proved too inefficient to control, broke up the aristocratic Commonwealth of Iceland. The balance of power among chieftains had collapsed in the growing dominance of one or two rival families, so that one or other sought to establish pre-eminence by soliciting outside aid. In the old days control was maintained by strong bishops like Gizur, son of Isleif, Magnus, Klaeng, and Pál, and by highborn ecclesiastics like Saemund and Jón Loptsson.

Family retainers had grown tired of being forced to act as pawns in their leaders' wearing struggle for pre-eminence, and looked for peace and stability and improved social conditions in a strong external government.

People's minds had become reconciled to the idea of royal rule. Popular sagas of King Olaf the Saint "had given kingship a special consecration."[1] *Heimskringla*, the famous contemporary work of Snorri Sturluson, had brought the attractive story of Norwegian kings to every winter fireside. Monks had popularised the life of Sverrir, though he was strongly anti-clerical. At this time Icelanders were reading with interest "an eloquent panegyric on royalty" called "the King's Mirror." The Church found this favourable regal atmosphere congenial, as it did in England in the seventeenth century. Cardinal William of Sabina, who crowned Hákon IV in 1246, went so far as to send a message to the people of Iceland commanding them to submit to King Hákon, "as it was improper for them not to be governed by a king, like all other nations."[2]

---

[1] Gj., p. 203; *e.g.*, Geisli (The Sunbeam), by Sira Einar Skulason (*c.* 1152), Christ being the Sun and Olaf the sunbeam. Such is the effect of time and partisanship.

[2] Hákonar Saga 257; Gj., pp. 193, 203; Craigie, *Icelandic Sagas*, pp. 51-2, 85.

Thus was the ground sedulously prepared by the Church for the acceptance in Iceland of external overlordship.

(c) The first Norwegian bishops appointed for Iceland by the Chapter of Nidaros openly acted as royal agents. Civil war had broken out, the Sturlung family in the north under the historian Snorri being opposed by Gizur Thorvaldsson, descendant of the early southern bishops. Gizur, who had been appointed the king's representative, ingratiated himself with Sigvard, the new Bishop of Skálholt, to such good effect that when he arranged the assassination of Snorri on the night of September 22, 1241, Sigvard protected him against the natural resentment which followed this treacherous deed and took an active part in the indecisive battle which followed.

The bishop further encouraged Gizur's ally Kolbein to resist Thord, the last of the Sturlungs, who came to Iceland to avenge his famous father, and allowed Kolbein and his band of 700 men to fortify the bishopstead at Skálholt against him.

The final battle actually took place at sea in Hunafloi Bay—the first Icelandic naval engagement. Kolbein proved victorious, but became ill and made an agreement that the matter should be referred to the king (1244).[1]

Kolbein died; Gizur was detained in Norway; Thord was appointed king's representative, and with Heinrik, the new Norwegian Bishop of Hólar, came with the cardinal's mandate to put the king's case to the people. The Bishop of Skálholt now gave his support to Thord as the king's representative, and, had it not been for Thord's ambition for personal domination, the matter might have been settled (1248).

Bishop Heinrik reported Thord to the king, who replaced him by Gizur, who in his turn allowed his desire for self-aggrandisement to revive. Thus Icelandic independence continually defeated itself.

(d) The family feud flared up again, and the Commonwealth, which deservedly had long survived internal disasters, finally succumbed after a glaring act of perfidy unsurpassed in its previous history.

The scene is vividly described in the monumental Sturlunga Saga, and may be summarised here, as it gives a picture of the inevitable end of the epoch, with its internecine quarrels of intransigent chieftains, the partisan intrigues of the Church, and the lack of authority.

Gizur drove from his settlement a certain Eyjolf, who plotted vengeance and enlisted the ready help of Bishop Heinrik and other northern leaders. They formed a conspiracy to attack Gizur during

[1] Sturlunga Saga II, 7, 61 sq., 83.

wedding festivities for his son Hall, who was marrying Ingibjörg, daughter of Sturla, thus joining the once rival houses.

Gizur welcomed 120 guests and expressed the hope that peace would now be kept between the families in accordance with the recent understanding and pledge. One of the guests, Hrafn, knew about Eyjolf's plot, and yet joined in the party, even drinking the loving cup, without revealing it.

On the night after the party broke up, Eyjolf and a band of fifty-two men attacked the house, but, failing to break in, they set it on fire in the pagan saga fashion of three hundred years before. Gizur's wife Groa and his two sons perished in the flames. The young bride, Ingibjörg, refused the assailants' offer of release, preferring to die with the others, but she was carried in her nightdress to the church for sanctuary. Her bridegroom tried to fight his way out, but was wounded and brought to the church to die. Twenty-five people were burnt to death, though Gizur managed to save himself in a remarkable way by escaping to the outer pantry and getting into a vat of whey, where his enemies could not find him. When they left, he crawled to the church, though nearly dead from shock, exposure, and grief. Eyjolf and his band, thinking Gizur was burnt, hastened to Hólar, where they were welcomed by Bishop Heinrik and given absolution.

There is satisfaction in recording that Gizur recovered and pursued the incendiaries relentlessly, putting twelve to death before the end of the year. This execution of justice was handicapped by Heinrik, who put him under the ban of the Church, so that he had to move to the south. However, the Althing outlawed Eyjolf and fifteen of his band. Then Gizur was summoned to Norway by the king, and, like his rival Thord, he was kept in that country.[1]

To promote his interests the king in 1256 sent out a Norwegian lay official who induced the people of the north, led by the bishop, to acknowledge the king's claims and pay him taxes.[2] And in 1262 the Althing of the country submitted, being finally persuaded by an earnest speech of Gizur, who had returned as the king's deputy or Jarl, and recognised that the day of independence was done.[3] It had been a great and glorious day, though clouded at its close.

---

[1] Sturlunga Saga II, p. 192.
[2] Gamli Sáttmáli in *Dipl. Isl.* I, pp. 661-716; VI, pp. 4-6.
[3] The district of the Side fell into line in 1264. The year that marks the loss of independence of the Althing (founded 930) saw the summoning of the first free Parliament in England; so that if Britain claims to have the Mother of Parliaments, Iceland can claim their grandmother.

CHAPTER VII

EXTERNAL DOMINANCE (1264-1380)

(i) CANON LAW

SUBMISSION to the King of Norway brought to an end the golden age of the Icelandic Commonwealth and closed an era of much splendour and intellectual eminence.

The gold was mixed with the alloy, but this rendered it the more serviceable for the hard conditions of sub-arctic existence.

The leaders of the Church in this small Commonwealth had proved also leaders of the people and had played a noble part in its history. Bishops often forgot that they were churchmen in the outstanding qualities they showed as chieftains. But most of them excelled as men of learning and character. The Church in its schools and monasteries and by its individual scholars had a distinguished share in Iceland's almost unique contribution to world literature.

The collapse of the chieftains opened the way for the ascendancy of the Church, which is the most conspicuous feature in the years following the Norwegian agreement.

An early period of constructive ecclesiastical development by chieftain-bishops had been succeeded by a period of rivalry between the leaders of Church and State, culminating in the submission of both to external control.

Chieftains were replaced by unpopular foreign officials, in conflict with whom the bishops gradually acquired the dominance formerly held by leading laymen.

In the gradual decay of independence in the country during the next century and a half, they frequently abused these powers by exploiting their right of excommunication and the weakness of the people, so that in turn they lost their authority, and Iceland in the century before the Reformation, socially, intellectually, and spiritually, sank to its lowest state.

(A) Denationalisation

For the period succeeding the union of Norway and Iceland we have two authoritative accounts—the Lives of the notable bishops, Arni of Skálholt (1269-98) and Lárentius of Hólar (1323-30), specially valuable at a time when there is little first-hand information about the history of the country. These two bishops had very different characters. Arni proved an able if aggressive administrator, whereas Laurence was a gentle teacher and a monk.

(a) Arni Thorlaksson interrupted the scheme for controlling the Icelandic Church by a Norwegian episcopate, for he was a native of the country, sprung from the illustrious episcopal family of Isleif and Gizur, and showed himself a worthy descendant of that line in his gifts of intellect and statesmanship. He had been a disciple of Brand, the learned Abbot of Thykkvabaer, and became expert not only in letters but in mechanical arts, and afterwards displayed leadership in public affairs. As a versatile skald he won the favour of King Magnus of Norway by his courtly poems and tales, and subsequently they helped one another in the process of denationalising the Icelandic Church and Commonwealth. As bishop, Arni proved a vigorous ruler, taking in hand two thorny outstanding problems. He revised ecclesiastical law and brought about a settlement, though itself a compromise, of the vexed question of Church property.

To bring Iceland into line with Norwegian jurisprudence, King Magnus VI, called Lagaböter—i.e., Lawreformer—in 1271 sent over a new code of laws, nicknamed not inaptly Jarnsida (Ironside). This was a contravention of the settlement of 1262, the Gamli Sáttmáli, and, although introduced by the Icelandic historian and Lawman Sturla, it met with considerable opposition. It rightly abolished personal requital for injuries, putting all punishment into the hands of the State, but its penalties were harsh and exacting, though it contained a saving clause: "We are to hate evil deeds, but love men as our fellow-Christians, and most of all their souls."[1] However, the opposition was so strong that the code had to be modified on Icelandic lines, and in 1281 a new code called Jón's Book was introduced by Jón Einarsson and adopted by the Althing.[2]

Soon after his consecration on June 21, 1269, Bishop Arni took steps to bring the Icelandic Church more completely under Canon Law. The existing ecclesiastical code was the Kristinrettr (summarised above, pp. 86-88), which had been compiled by Bishops Ketill and Thorlak in the years 1122-33, and incorporated in the Icelandic Law-book Grágás. Now the law-making king and bishop did their best to render Grágás out of date as a civil and ecclesiastical authority. Arni forwarded the king's new codes in Iceland, while Magnus backed the bishop's Canon Law reforms.

[1] Gj., pp. 215-6.
[2] Jón's Bók, facsimile and Introd. (Larusson).

Arni summoned a conference of his leading priests and laymen and proposed the addition of five new clauses:

1. That all worshippers should genuflect at the elevation of the Host.

2. That marriage should only be solemnised after publication of banns in church on three successive Sundays.

3. That concubines should be repudiated or married on penalty of excommunication.

4. That all churches and church estates should be transferred to the bishop.

5. That it should be forbidden to let (ecclesiastical) goods and chattels on hire (*Nemini res inanimatas elocare licitum esto*).[1]

The synod formally agreed to the first three of these additions, but boggled at the last two clauses.

(*b*) The first two regulations did little more than define existing regulations, but clause 3 caused many searchings of heart, especially among the clergy, against whom it was particularly directed. Many a chieftain kept a concubine whom he could marry if he had not already a wife; but according to Canon Law priests had no such remedy. From the beginning of Christianity in Iceland bishops and priests had married. The only celibate priests were Thorlak the Saint and Gudmund, later styled the Blessed. Even St Jón of Hólar was married, as was St Denys of France, who, however, was not in orders. Leading priests, as Ari and Saemund, were married, though latterly clergy had contracted lifelong unions with "help-meets" *extra ecclesiam*.

Bishop Arni attempted to enforce celibacy, and while his influence remained even sub-deacons with families were compelled to repudiate their consorts. But the regulation soon became a dead letter, and, as in mediæval England, concubinage of priests came to be tolerated as less ecclesiastically offensive than matrimony.[2] The effect of Arni's stringency was to make matters worse, for hitherto the apostolic independence of the Icelandic Church made such evasion of the issue unnecessary. Concubinage increased. Even the saintly Bishop Laurence in his early days had a son by a woman called Thurid, who afterwards bore a son to Sira Solomon, another priest.[3]

In addition to ensuring the publicity of marriage by ordering the

---

1 Arni Biskups S. 5; Annals 1271; *Dipl. Isl.* II, 23-52; F. J. II, pp. 3 *sq.*
2 G. G. Coulton, *Mediæval Panorama*, pp. 117-9.
3 Lárentius S. 16, *sub anno* 1304.

publication of banns, Arni enforced the exacting mediæval degrees of affinity and consanguinity. Prohibition was extended to such absurdly remote relationships as that of seventh cousin. This particularly hit an isolated island like Iceland, where there was much intermarrying, and almost everyone was descended from the first few settlers. Later the injunction provided an excuse for grasping prelates to extort large fines from rich men who had married such distant relatives as their third cousins.[1]

All this intensification of ecclesiastical law had ultimately little effect on the common practice of priests and laymen, while it created a cleavage between Church and people and weakened the influence of many clergy, whom it marked out as technical offenders.

(c) The last of the regulations proposed by Bishop Arni in 1269 is difficult to interpret. It appears to link up with the preceding order as to church buildings and estates, and the meeting objected to both alike. "Inanimate things" is a strange way of denoting church furniture. But *Thesaurus Linguæ Latinæ* gives instances of the use of the expression by Jerome of a statue, by Boëthius of furniture, and Novellus of vessels; so that it may cover all church property other than lands (and advowsons). If chieftain owners of farms had considered ecclesiastical buildings and their contents as part of their hereditary homesteads, their comprehensive view of religion would have led them to borrow church property for secular purposes, such as entertainment of guests. It is difficult otherwise to understand how provision was made for large parties which assembled for weddings, funerals, and special occasions.[2]

Until lately some pastors have used churches as storehouses and even as dormitories for stranded visitors.[3] This was due probably to an Icelandic rather than a Lutheran view of religion, and to the smallness and isolation of parsonages. When a pastor was asked by a surprised traveller if he did not think it irreverent to sleep in church, he replied: "No, except during the sermon." Some visitors who had availed themselves of such hospitality derided the custom in their reports when they got home; and some abused the privilege, desecrating even the altars, so that such use of churches is now forbidden. But *abusus non tollit usum*. During the recent British occupation some of our troops had only tents to live in, while snow lay on

---

[1] *E.g.*, Bp Gottskalk Nikolasson, *inf.*, p. 138.

[2] Laxdale S. 27; sons of Hjalti entertained 1,200 = 1,440, and Olaf the Peacock 900 = 1080. Cp. Bp Magnus, *ut sup.*, p. 57, Bp Klaeng, p. 61, Bp Pál, p. 95; and (later) Bp Wilkin, p. 133.

[3] Baring-Gould, *Iceland*, p. 357, etc.

the mountains above them and hurricanes blew in from the sea. They would have been in a bad way had not the local pastor offered them the time-honoured hospitality of his snug little parish church.

(*d*) Before passing to a consideration of Arni's claims on church buildings and estates, it should be noted that he issued many rulings in regard to baptism and confession, and introduced innovations in Iceland in regard to the Mass. Communion in one kind was imposed on the laity, and the dogma of transubstantiation was laid down.[1] The number of fasts and vigils was increased. On the other hand, an attempt was made to quicken the ministry of the Word, for in 1290 the Council of Bergen enjoined the preaching of a sermon every Sunday.[2]

Arni exacted tithes and church dues with the utmost rigour, and in 1275 even persuaded the people to pay an annual tax of one ell of wadmal for six years to support the last crusade, which he advocated in his sermons. "None took up the Cross, but many redeemed it." In connection with this, indulgences were first put on sale by the two bishops. On pain of excommunication they enforced Peter's Pence (Roma skattr), one ell of wadmal from each family which the king collected after Arni died.[3]

Like his forebear Bishop Gizur, Arni attained almost to a position of regent in Iceland, so that he was able to exercise the authority of the Church and Canon Law with energy and effect, and to demand exemption of the clergy from secular jurisdiction.

His assertion of the Church's claims to ownership of ecclesiastical estates requires a section to itself.

(*B*) *Stadarmál*

The strife between bishops and chieftains over ecclesiastical property—glebe and advowsons, conveniently called in Icelandic "stadarmál"—after persisting for over a century, was settled by a compromise in 1297, effected by the prelate known as "Stad-Arni."

The Ketill-Thorlak Code of Church Law appeared to assume lay ownership and advowsons of churches by laying down the responsibility of landlords for endowment and maintenance. Nevertheless, some bishops, especially Thorlak II (1176-93), attempted to claim

---

[1] F. J. I, pp. 551 *sq.* [2] *Homiliu-bók*, Introd.
[3] F. J. I, pp. 455 *sq.*, 571-5. Wadmal is the Icelandic homespun. House-holders paid 20 ells to the king under the agreement of 1262-4. 100 ells = 6 sheep = 1 cow (Gj., p. 206).

powers over Church estates and to forbid marriage of priests. But even the popularity and noble life of Thorlak failed to effect this, and matters went on as before. Archbishops appealed to the faithful in vain. Mediæval catholicity had much the same complaint against the Church of Iceland as it had against the English Church;[1] it always came up against an incorrigible insular independence, tenacious of the customs of their first fathers in the Faith. Chieftains successfully maintained their rights in the churches they had built and endowed. Opposition roused by Thorlak's attempt to assert the Church's claims and the disastrous result of Bishop Gudmund's militant campaign in the generation after Thorlak led to quiescence, even on the part of Norwegian bishops, who cared nothing for Icelandic traditions.

(a) But Arni's Icelandic nature was endowed with his country's intractable temper. As soon as he returned home as bishop in 1269, he summoned a general council at Skálholt and proposed that all churches should be handed over to the control of the bishops. In spite of all previous attempts to effect this, almost all churches still remained in private hands. But the time-spirit now discounted chieftains. The bishops had behind them the admitted power of the king, as whose agents they acted. As the king looked to bishops to further his cause (and taxes) in the country, so in return bishops calculated on royal assistance to reinforce their prerogatives. Arni also, like Gudmund, did not hesitate to unsheathe the ecclesiastical weapon of ban and excommunication, which always affected Icelanders like a sorcerer's spell.

In order to bring the chieftains to heel, Archbishop Jón and Arni induced King Magnus to hold a council at Bergen in 1273. The king's disposition was placid and kindly, and he wished no severe action to be taken against the laity, but he was overruled by the prelates and handed the matter over to the archbishop, who proceeded to hear the two most important cases brought by Bishop Arni—Oddi and Vatnsfjörd.

The advowson and rich benefice of St Nicolas at Oddi was withheld by Sighvat Halfdansson on the ground that the benefice had always been in the wardship of the Oddi family since the great days of Saemund and Jón Loptsson. Nevertheless, the archbishop gave the case in favour of the bishop. At the same time he made the same award in regard to St Olaf's, Vatnsfjörd, though its lay-

---

[1] As it had against the "private" churches in Germany, Switzerland, and elsewhere, though these on the whole were given up earlier (see ref., p. 228).

rector claimed that his great-grandfather built and endowed the church on condition that his heirs should retain the administration of it.[1]

(b) As we have seen, Arni included a general injunction for surrendering churches in a new ecclesiastical code which in 1275 was provisionally adopted by the Althing. His influence there was paramount, but, although the code was passed, the chieftains managed to get a proviso inserted making its sanction depend on ratification by the king and archbishop, which shrewdly provided an opportunity for them to temporise. When King Magnus VI was succeeded in 1280 by his son Eirik, aged 12, whose regents lost no time in taking steps to curb the Church's aggressiveness, the chieftains seized the occasion to appeal to the Crown. For ecclesiastical affairs in Norway had taken a turn unfavourable to Arni's overweening claims. The arrogance of Archbishop Jón had become so intolerable that he was banished from Norway in 1281. This encouraged the chieftains to stand out once more for their church estates, and as Arni would not yield the conflict came to such a pass that he too was threatened with banishment and had to agree to leave the decision to the king.[2]

Two commissioners were sent to the country, one of whom was Sighvat Halfdansson, and laid down that matters should revert to the old state until the case was decided. Arni remained intransigent; but the Bishop of Hólar, Jörund, desiring peace for his diocese, wrote to the king promising full obedience. This compliance led to a gracious acknowledgment which provides a link at this time between our own country and Iceland. King Eirik's first wife, Margaret, daughter of King Alexander of Scotland, sent to Bishop Jörund a valuable royal cloak which the bishop turned into a cope, afterwards called "Drottingr naut" (Queen's Bounty).[3]

Arni finally agreed to go to Norway to state his case, and was detained there for three years, after which he returned home with the case unheard and renewed the controversy. But meanwhile the northern bishop, Jörund, had successfully inaugurated a compromise by buying out owners' rights in glebe farms.[4] At Mödruvellir, thus redeemed, he established a monastery in 1297, and about the same time he founded a nunnery on a valuable estate at Reynistad, given

---

[1] F. J. II, pp. 7-8; O. I. I, pp. 637 sq. (O. I. makes the Abbot of Videy the judge, but his statement is that made as Visitor in 1518; see F. J., II, p. 41.)

[2] Arni Biskups S. 14, 19.

[3] Camb. Mod. Hist. II, p. 546; F. J. II, 146-7. Eirik's second wife was a daughter of Robert Bruce. When he married Margaret, he was 13, she 20.

[4] Arni B. S. 53; Lárentius S. 6.

him for the purpose by the unpopular jarl and chieftain Gizur Thorvaldsson.

In spite of the official pronouncement enjoining the *status quo*, Arni forced twelve representatives of the landowners to agree to hand over all churches in the diocese. But the king was on guard against further episcopal acquisitiveness, and though he refrained from directly attacking Arni the subservient twelve were summoned to Norway to be tried for disobedience to the royal order.

Arni went with them, and on September 14, 1297, the whole matter was decided by a compromise. Rights of lay owners were to be retained in all churches of which they owned at least half the glebe; the other churches were to be handed over to the bishops.[1]

The result of this decision held good up to the last century. Some farmers then still owned churches or glebes and were responsible for the upkeep of the buildings, though they were empowered to collect small dues from parishioners.

For other churches, presumably those surrendered to the bishops in 1297, the congregations were responsible and collected dues through trustees. A few of the larger and anciently more important churches had become "Crown livings," having been taken over from monasteries or chieftains at the Reformation. These included Hitardal, Helgafell, Stadarstad, Kirkjubaer, and others. Latterly the prestar, ministers rather than farmers by training, let these large farms deteriorate.

(c) After the decision of 1297, which finally defeated one of the greatest ambitions of his episcopate, Bishop Arni remained in Norway, and died there the following year, aged sixty-two. Nearly six years elapsed before his successor was appointed. That Arni's perennial conflicts and final disappointment shortened his life is suggested by the fact that his more facile colleague Jörund died at a great age after an episcopate of forty-six years (1267-1313).

It would be unfair to leave Arni's life and work without noting a reference to him in Lárentius Saga which epitomises his two-sided character. When Laurence, a poor but promising young priest, went in 1294 to see Arni at Skálholt, the bishop received him graciously and gave him this advice: "If thou hast not yet mastered Canon Law, that must be thy business henceforth." Laurence later, when he had become a learned bishop and a holy man, emphasised a forgotten element in his patron's character; he used to say he had seen the face of a saint on two men only—on Arni Thorlaksson, Bishop of

[1] Arni, B. S. 79; Gj., pp. 221-5.

Skálholt, and on Björn, Abbot of Thingeyrar, at whose death, according to the Annals, the monastery bells tolled of themselves.[1]

(ii) BISHOPS AND CLERGY IN THE FOURTEENTH CENTURY

The fourteenth century in Iceland forms a transition between the robust individualism of the earlier period and the inanition of the century which followed. The Church still produced some vigorous prelates, and the people showed a measure of opposition to external aggression which decreased as the century wore on. There was more system and less personality.

This period is fortunate in being illuminated by a first-hand authority—the last historic work for 150 years—the Lárentius Saga by Einar Haflidason (1304-93). This is written in direct and unstudied style, after the manner of the earlier Lives of bishops, and, like them, by an intimate of the subject of the biography. It gives an account not only of Laurence's training and episcopate, but also of the episcopate of the princely Audun and the redoubtable Jörund; and, supplemented by the Annals of the same author, throws a light on education and the monastic and social life of the century.

The Latinisation of the Church in Iceland is shown by the fact that, although this Life retains most of the unsophistication which gives earlier sagas the fragrance of open country rather than the mustiness of the study, its hero Lafranz or Lavrans is always called Lárentius or even, as bishop, Lord Lárentius. A priest is entitled Sira (Jón), and a highly placed woman The Lady (Thurid).[2]

And yet this outward courtliness does not extend to manners, for, although we find less barbaric violence than in ancient sagas, rudeness and quarrels abound, as well as the slights that Icelanders are prone to give and quick to resent.

(A) Prelacy

(a) Laurence was the son of a priest, but as a votary of Canon Law was himself never married. As a poor boy he was adopted as foster-son by Bishop Jörund at Hólar, and brought up in the episcopal school. He had a hard struggle throughout his life, and his learned and imperious pronouncements gave offence to those in high place and created jealous enemies.

[1] Lárentius S. 7; Ann., sub anno 1299.
[2] Sira in Iceland appears at the end of the twelfth century. It is only applied to priests, and used only with the Christian name, a custom still continued (inf. p. 161). For Thurid see pp. 111, 118.

His skill at Latin was such that he could turn out Latin verses "as fast as men could speak"; and in pursuance of Bishop Arni's advice to study Canon Law he went to Norway, where he became a favourite of the archbishop, after an unpromising beginning, described in the saga in a characteristic story:

Sira Lárentius came to the archbishop holding a scroll. The archbishop looked at it, praised the handwriting, and said: "Read before us that thou hast written."

So Laurence read from it verses he had made in praise of the Lady Hallbera, Abbess of Stad (*i.e.*, Reynistad).

"Is she a good woman," asked the archbishop, "since thou hast praised her so much?"

"People in Iceland," replied Laurence, "count that certain."

"Cease verse-writing henceforth," said the archbishop, "and study Canon Law instead. Knowest thou not: Versificatura nihil est nisi falsa figura?"

"You must also know," retorted Laurence, "versificatura nihil est nisi maxima cura."

"Why do you wear red clothes," asked the archbishop, "which it is forbidden priests to wear?"

He replied, "Because I have no others."

Then the archbishop whispered to one of his pages, who went out and brought back some fine brown clothes of the archbishop's, which he gave Laurence to wear on festivals, and ordered his steward to buy some black clothing for everyday use.

Laurence was soon able to give shrewd and skilful help to the archbishop in his dealings with his disloyal and obstreperous Chapter, which led to his unpopularity with the canons.

After a visitation which he conducted for the archbishop on the Church of Iceland in 1307/8, when his strictness offended the bishops, his slacker colleague on his return to Nidaros slandered him to such an extent that the Chapter were able to seize on the occasion to throw him into a foul dungeon called Gulskitni, where he would have starved but for food handed him through a grating by Thurid, mother of his son. Finally, after seizing all his books and goods, the canons sent him back in chains to Iceland, where Bishop Jörund appointed him a monastic teacher. On account of the aged bishop's fear of the Chapter he was hounded from monastery to monastery, from Ver to Munkathvera and finally to Thingeyrar.

In the year 1317 Laurence and his son Arni, then thirteen years of age, took monastic vows at Thingeyrar. There we leave him for seven years faithfully keeping the rule of St Benedict and humbly teaching and studying. He took in hand the education of his son, who became an accomplished Latin scholar and a fine writer and versifier. Notwithstanding this "religious" bringing up, the priest's motherless son did not turn out well. Arni as a priest became a victim to drink "and other iniquity, and the Church got no good of his parts."[1] However, he is best remembered as the author of a Saga of St Dunstan, one of the extensive collection of saints' Lives which formed the popular reading of the day.[2]

(b) In the winter of 1313-14—a hard season nicknamed "horse-death winter"—Jörund, Bishop of Hólar, died. Latterly he acquired much power; in the saga phrase, "all men rose up and sat down at his bidding."[3] His episcopate of forty-six years created a pre-Reformation record.

In his place the archbishop consecrated Audun the Red, head of the Nidaros Chapter, a rich man of high standing, who had been priest of Trondenes parish on Lofoten Island in Halogoland, where the lofty church built in his day may still be seen below the mountains by the fjord approaching Harstad.

Audun was received with little ceremony when he arrived at Hólar, "though he was stiff with riding, being an old man." Sira Kodran and Sira Snjolf, leading priests, "did nothing but mock him; but scant heed he paid it."

Audun's episcopate (1313-22) was notable for his large expenditure on the bishopstead and cathedral. He brought over a stonemason and made an innovation by putting a stone chimney to his wooden Great Hall. In the cathedral he placed stone steps and pillars and a stone altar containing a fireproof safe. This may be the mediæval stone altar seen at Hólar by Baring-Gould in 1860 (5 feet 9 inches by 3 feet) with a frontal of five panels—the Blessed Gudmund, St Jón, and St Thorlak flanked by angels.[4] Audun's building was wrecked in a storm, 1393. Audun beautified the sanctuary and presented a fine cope called Skarmande—a touch of the biographer which indicates his acquaintance with *Hungrvaka*.[5]

[1] Lár. Saga 33 and 64.
[2] W. A. Craigie, *Icelandic Sagas*, pp. 107-8.
[3] Cp. *Hv.* about Bp Gizur, quoted *sup.*, p. 46.
[4] *Iceland : its Scenes and Sagas*, p. 295, London, 1863. Cp. the will of Rd. Russell, merchant of York, 1485, which provided for the erection of two altars, each to contain a cupboard for books and vestments (Frere, *Essays*, p. 147).
[5] Of Bishop Magnus Einarsson, *ut sup.*, p. 57.

It is significant that Audun revived interest in the sainted native bishops. He appointed as feasts the day of St Jón of Hólar's translation and the day of the Blessed Gudmund, whose neglected relics he found with difficulty and placed in a shrine.[1]

He lived in such great magnificence that his lavishness exhausted his private fortune, so he tried to extort heavier taxes and take over some glebes. This revived the old controversy, though a bishop's opponents now included not only chieftains but leading priests, whose goodwill Audun tried to win by giving dispensation to their sons to take orders. "Many cases brought before him he could not settle, as he did not know the ways of the country." In the end leading northern laymen pledged themselves at the Moot to suffer no innovations at his hands.

Bishop Audun carried on his Chapter's strained relations with Laurence until Egil Eyjolfsson, his schoolmaster at Hólar, persuaded the bishop to abandon the feud in 1319, when he appointed him tutor to his grandson Eystein, who became a noted priest of St Mary's, Trondhjem.[2]

The bishop needed all the support he could win, for the official opposition of leading priests and laymen made the glebe controversy take its old course and led to the customary summons of the protagonists to Norway.

Audun spent the winter with the archbishop at Nidaros, and "feasted deep at Yule and so took gout, which daily grew worse. So stout a fellow was he that he sat up with his mates making them as merry as though he had not a pang."

The archbishop asked who should succeed him at Hólar. Audun replied: "No man is more fitted than Brother Laurence. He is the best scholar, and skilled in Canon Law; and, further, he is bold and trusty in lawsuits and in the defence of Holy Church. For the men of North Iceland need to have as bishop over them, one who is both a great scholar and strong enough to chastise all the perverseness and disobedience of the place."[3]

(c) Perversity is often the reaction of a native independence provoked or wrongly led. It is significant that Bishop Audun's colleague in the south, Arni Helgason, did not meet with opposition. This

---

[1] Lár. Saga 33. March 3rd and March 16th—still in the Kalendar.
[2] Lár. Saga 35. Eystein, like his father, was also called Rauda = Red, a surname in its early stage. Trondhjem is the later name of Nidaros, though the old name was officially restored in January, 1930.
[3] Lár. Saga 36.

Bishop of Skálholt was a nephew of the great Bishop Arni, and from his birth knew the ways of the country. He did not overpress the claims of Canon Law and external churchmanship, being careful to preserve the patriarchal relations which from the first in Iceland had signalised dealings of bishops with their people.

Three features of Arni's considerate episcopate emerge (1303-20):

1. He wrote a saga on his uncle, Arni Thorlaksson, learning by contrast the better part.

2. Skálholt church was struck by lightning and burnt down on Saturday, January 24, 1309, "as swiftly as men swallow meat and drink at a meal."[1] Next year the bishop, having collected subscriptions throughout Iceland, went to Norway to get timber to rebuild it, and returned with many valuable gifts presented by King Hákon and his queen and many leading men, so that (according to the Annals) "it was a common opinion that no one had ever made a more successful trip to Norway since Iceland adopted Christianity."

3. King Hákon V, the last of the Norwegian line, died in 1319 and was succeeded by Magnus Smek, the infant son of his daughter Ingibjörg, who had married Duke Eirik of Sweden. Thus Iceland with Norway for some years came under Sweden, and disturbances arose.[2] The occasion was shrewdly seized by the Althing to set out their grievance under the settlement of 1262. Their spirited manifesto shows signs of episcopal influence, at least in its conclusion: "May the Lord Jesus Christ grant that you may take such steps as may redound to the benefit of the blessed king's soul, the honour and glory of Junker Magnus, and the peace and joy of us all, now and for ever. Amen."[3]

The bishops and leading laymen set out for Bergen to press their claims,[4] though Bishop Arni died after the voyage, and Bishop Audun was driven back by storms. The conference evidently succeeded, for in the following year the Althing agreed to take the oath of allegiance to the new king.

(d) Arni's successor, Grim Skútuson, spent only three months in the country. In that short time he squandered 300 hundrads,

---

[1] Annals. Thunderstorms are rare in Iceland and usually come in winter.

[2] *Væ terræ ubi puer rex est*, or, as the homely Icelandic has it: "No resting o' nights, for rats in the house, when the cat is a kitten." Quoted Sigrid Unset, *Kristin Lavransdottir*, p. 170, from Eccles. x, 16.

[3] Gj., pp. 235-6.

[4] The rights demanded by Iceland were: 1. Six ships to traffic from Norway yearly. 2. No exportation of cod in seasons of famine. 3. All magistrates to be Icelanders. 4. Cases to be tried at home.

equivalent to the value of 300 cows. The Annals point out that this
extravagance occurred during a period of famine when a number of
people died of hunger.

From the Norwegian settlement in 1262 to the Danish amalgama-
tion in 1380, all but three of the ten bishops of Skálholt were foreigners. The Grim episode is typical of the callous indifference with
which they normally treated the people and of the greed and grasp of
power too often manifested, with the result that they created a growing opposition to ecclesiastical officialism, which became characteristic of Icelandic churchmanship in the centuries before the
Reformation.[1]

Here, as in England, the foisting of foreign prelates on the Church
and ecclesiastical acquisitiveness largely helped to prepare the way
for the restoration of a more apostolic method and spirit of Church
government.[2]

(B) Apostle Bells and Singing Maids

When the election of Laurence to the bishopric of Hólar was
announced in Iceland, many could not imagine who this Laurence
could be; nor could Laurence himself believe it of his old enemies
the Chapter of Nidaros. The Governor of Iceland, Lord Ketill
Thorlaksson, announced the election on St Laurence's Day from the
Quire of the cathedral. The Te Deum was sung, followed by the
ringing of bells, during which the bishop-elect was conducted to
his seat.

The ship *Krafs* which took Laurence to his consecration was
wrecked as it approached Norway and he lost most of his stores and
all his money; but no one was drowned except Thordis, known as
"Blossom-cheek." The Bishops of Bergen and the Orkneys joined
the archbishop in his consecration on St John Baptist's Day, 1324.[3]

(*a*) Laurence's episcopate was comparatively uneventful. Provi-
dential flotsam of a whale helped the see's impoverished finances at
the start and enhanced the bishop's reputation,[4] so that he was able

---

[1] J. H. I, pp. 189-90; Gj., p. 237.

[2] Cp. G. Barraclough, *Papal Provisions*, pp. viii, 174 *sq.*, Oxford, 1935;
Maitland, *Constitutional Hist. of England*, p. 172.

[3] Lár. Saga 39-41. The diocese of the Orkneys was under the supervision
of the Archbishop of Nidaros until 1472, when it came into the province of
St Andrews. During the recent war the Bishop of Aberdeen and the
Orkneys took Confirmations for the British Force in Iceland, 1940-1.

[4] The Iceland phrase for godsend is hval-reki—*i.e.*, the drifting ashore of
a whale.

to tackle with a firm hand the grievances he inherited, which had long been nursed by Thingeyrar and Munkathvera monasteries. Thingeyrar he knew from inside. Its tithes had been taken since Bishop Jörund's day for the bishopric of Hólar. To settle this, Laurence bought out a layman who owned the rich glebe of Hvamm, ancient home of the Sturlungs, and gave the benefice to the monastery.

Another northern monastery, Mödruvellir, had almost ceased to exist, since it had been burnt down some years before owing to the carelessness of tipsy monks. This he rebuilt, providing for its church "Apostle" bells and five "singing-maids" (probably deep-toned bells and trebles); but in accordance with its foundation charter he only appointed a prior, making himself abbot. The monks appealed against this, and the Bishop of Skálholt and the Abbot of Ver (formerly Thykkvabaer), acting for the archbishop, decided against Laurence. Then Laurence in his turn appealed to the archbishop, who reversed the decision and presented Laurence's able emissary Egil "with a fair silver bason and the canon-law book called Tancred."[1]

To Munkathvera, whose abbot Thorir had been deposed by Bishop Audun, Laurence appointed Berg Sokkason, an old pupil of his, "a most accomplished scholar, a fine chanter and orator," and, as we shall see, a popular writer. Berg died in 1345.

Bishop Laurence, having been monk and teacher himself, and being an Icelander, proved an able administrator of the schools and monasteries.

(b) Nevertheless, his greatest contribution to the Church of his time lay in his personal life—a humble walk with God. He turned the bishopstead at Holár into a sort of monastery and himself dressed and lived as a monk. But he kept up the Icelandic episcopal reputation for hospitality, for "he maintained a good table and laid in drinkables from wherever in the country he could get them, and always had shares in two or three ships coming to Iceland."

He established twelve almsmen at Hólar and gave much to the poor. In particular in this respect it is noteworthy that he founded an infirmary for aged and retired priests, to which all clergy in the diocese subscribed half a mark a year for three years.[2]

He kept a notably good school, always having fifteen or more scholars, who presumably formed the cathedral choir. "He would never allow singing in two or three parts, which he called fiddling folly. No, they were to chant plainsong just as it was set in the choir books." He rebuked deacons for not taking off their coats

[1] Lár. Saga 52-61.   [2] Op. cit., 50.

before putting on their cassocks (a northern choir failing)—"that was how the stuff got torn."[1]

Laurence's sermons were notable, and Gamli, one of his priests, is called "a glorious preacher."[2]

At Mass, which he celebrated with heartfelt piety and tears, he would always have as server his friend and future biographer, the deacon Einar Haflidason, who in the long winter evenings from dusk at two or three o'clock till the vesper bell read him Norse Lives of the saints or Latin stories. This serviceable deacon, Einar, took a Boswellian interest in his master and deserves well of posterity.

He advanced the churchmanship of his day by introducing, in conjunction with Bishop Jón of Skálholt, the observance of Corpus Christi—a feast made law by the Althing in 1325.

One Easter evening of 1331, after a severe Lent, Laurence was taken ill. He sent his chaplain out to see how high the star had climbed up the sky. (For then, as now, Icelanders told the time in winter by the Pleiades).[3] Afterwards he took to his bed, and, knowing his end was approaching, wrote to the archbishop asking that his successor should be an Icelander, for "such could better serve the Church in Hólar, as he would have an understanding of the people's character."

A few days afterwards he bade his chaplains read the Office of the Holy Spirit which he had said daily since his early troubles. The Mass was celebrated, at which he died during the blessing (April 16, 1331).

(c) Laurence was succeeded by Egil Eyjolfsson, his most brilliant pupil, to whom he had given his episcopal ring on his death-bed. After an uneventful episcopate of ten years—probably the happiest kind—a Norwegian called Orm was sent over as his successor. He treated the people harshly, as did the Icelandic Bishop of Skálholt. Orm had twice to flee the country, and some time elapsed before anyone was officially appointed. A bishop going to take up his work in Greenland found this vacancy at Hólar and stopped there—preferring, no doubt, the green valleys of Iceland to the country-wide ice-cap of Greenland. However, priests and people would not receive him until he could show the Pope's sanction, which he was unable to obtain until fifteen years later.

As the century drew to its close the Church in Iceland appears to have got along more comfortably without bishops.[4] Certainly foreign-

---

[1] Lár. Saga 44.   [2] Homiliu-bók, Introd., inf. p. 212 .
[3] Cp. Ljosvet. Saga 43: "Keep to the Star"—i.e., be in good time.
[4] J. H. I, pp. 181 sq. Gj., pp. 238-9.

born and foreign-minded prelates proved of no real use. The detailed accounts of Arni and Laurence show what greater response Icelanders gave to their own native leaders. After these capable administrators no bishop had any influence in the country until Iceland, with its ecclesiastical affairs in confusion, came, with Norway, under Danish rule in 1380.

(iii) LEARNING AND LETTERS

In the realm of the arts the fourteenth century saw the culmination of Icelandic craftsmanship, especially in calligraphy, illumination of manuscripts, and carving. Manuscripts preserved in the Arna-Magnean Collection at Copenhagen, particularly the manuscripts of Bishop Brand Jónsson's Biblical Stjörn (c. 1310), show workmanship of a high degree of skill.[1]

Bishop Laurence of Hólar in his care for churches proved a patron of the arts. He entrusted Stefán Hauksson, "master of many crafts," with the beautifying of the famous cup of St Jón of Hólar.[2] Thorarinn 'the painter" (probably a layman) figures in correspondence in 1338 between the Bishops of Bergen and Skálholt;[3] and the Annals praise Thorstein Illugason, priest of Grenjadarstadir (†1334), for skill in calligraphy, painting, and cross-carving.

But mediæval art in Iceland was derivative and flourished when continental ecclesiasticism developed, while the country's original literature declined.

(a) In literature and education the fourteenth century witnessed a middle stage between the glowing enterprise of the first three centuries of Icelandic civilisation and the general decay during the 150 years which preceded the Reformation.

Great schools like Oddi and Haukadal had gone, but individual priests still showed readiness to act as teachers, and the bishopsteads and monasteries, such as Helgafell, Thingeyrar, and Munkathvera, remained for a time centres of learning.

The golden age of saga-writing went down in a blaze of splendour in Njála about the middle of the thirteenth century. After that Icelandic literature took on a twilight mood and became imitative, and finally writers turned mere copyists or scribes. The mediæval genius for abstractions and allegory found no place for the vivid and objective saga-presentation of truth.[4]

[1] *Icelandic MSS of the Middle Ages*, pp. 12 sq.
[2] *B. S.* I, p. 843. *Inf.* p. 212. [3] *Dipl. Isl.* II, pp. 723-4.
[4] Cp. H. O. Taylor, *The Mediæval Mind*, II, p. 280.

Cession of the larger glebes to the Church—*i.e.*, to the bishops—meant the extinction of traditional seats of learning maintained by leading families. There were no successors to Hall and Saemund and Jón Loptsson, whose schools produced the sound scholarship and achievements of Ari, Gizur, and Snorri Sturluson. But some notable instances of fosterage remained. Arni Thorlaksson, Bishop of Skálholt (1269-98), was trained by the priest Grim Holmsteinsson at the historic prestsetar of Kirkjubaer. Bishop Laurence's great-uncle kept a similar school, and Laurence himself was adopted as a poor boy by Bishop Jörund and educated for the priesthood.

The episcopal school at Hólar, neglected since the troubled days of Gudmund, was reopened by Jörund (1267-1313). Laurence himself taught there as a priest, and during his episcopate maintained it with never fewer than fifteen pupils. Some of these he induced to become teachers, notably his son Arni, Einar Haflidason, his biographer, Berg Sokkason, the hagiographer, and Egil Eyjolfsson, who succeeded him as bishop and doubtless carried on this traditional episcopal enterprise. In the latter half of the century foreign bishops who were appointed to the see apparently took no interest in education and the schools lapsed. We hear nothing about the school at Skálholt from the arrival of the first Norwegian bishop in 1236 until the end of the fifteenth century.

(*b*) Nevertheless, some monasteries maintained their love of learning and literature, and took over the work of the cathedral schools, training future clergy and sons of chieftains. Under Abbot Thorstein Snorrason (1322-51) and his successor, Asgrim (1352-79), Helgafell became one of the chief centres of learning in the country and possessed one of the largest libraries. According to an inventory dated 1397, it owned 35 Icelandic and nearly one hundred Latin books. It was also unusually rich in lands, owning 96 farms.[1] Another comprehensive library was owned by Mödruvellir, also in the north. An inventory made in 1461 shows that it contained 39 sagas, more than 30 writings in Latin, and no fewer than 70 service books. A later inventory (1525) indicates that the library was dispersed in the dark period before the Reformation.[2]

To further the work of education chieftains gave some of their lands. In the middle of the century Einar Thorlaksson handed over two estates to the monastery of Helgafell on condition that Abbot Asgrim instructed his son. Another landowner in 1377 gave half his

---

[1] *Dipl. Isl.*, IV., pp. 65-77, 170-1.
[2] *Dipl. Isl.* IV, pp. 286-90; *Islandica* IX, pp. 317-8.

estate to the same monastery so that his son could be trained to become a sub-deacon. Videy also received some lands with the proviso that the donor's son should be educated there for six years.[1]

Latin became the language of culture and the law, the general ecclesiastical speech; so much so that it was not until over a century after the Reformation that it ceased to be the language of the Church. Nevertheless, the people still used the vernacular, for when Jón Halldorsson, Bishop of Skálholt (1325-39), addressed a meeting of chieftains in Latin, Laurence said: "We all know, Lord Jón, that you have as fine a flow of Latin as of your mother tongue. But it is not understanded of the people. Therefore let us talk clearly that all may understand." Afterwards, when the archbishop sent over a ruling, Laurence had it translated "into Norse" (*i.e.*, Icelandic).[2]

(*c*) Lives of the saints constituted the popular reading of the day. The era of simple direct story had passed; these are veritable monkish productions, most of them translations from Latin into the vernacular. Runolf Sigmundsson (1307), Abbot of Thykkvabaer, now being called Ver, produced a Life of St Austin. About the same time another monk embellished an earlier Life of St Jón of Hólar with miracles. Arni Lafransson made a saga on St Dunstan. Arngrim Brandsson, Abbot of Thingeyrar in 1345, was responsible for a Latin Life of Gudmund, which has come down to us in an Icelandic version. The cult of the northern saints was blossoming in those days. Another abbot, Arni Jónsson, composed a popular hymn in honour of the Blessed Gudmund. Berg Sokkason translated Lives of St Michael and St Nicolas of Bari, which showed no sign of losing their popularity fifty years after they were translated.[3] Other popular subjects were Edward the Confessor, St Oswald, St Thomas of Canterbury, Peter the Hermit, and Legends of the Cross. Forty-five sagas of this kind are in existence, and there is a collection of Mary-sagas.[4] Someone should have translated Adamnan's Life of Columba, but, as in England, a luxuriant exotic growth overlaid the rock from which they were hewn, and early history was given a southern twist.

Some table-talk of Bishop Jón Halldorsson has come down to us which does not fulfil the expectations raised by its title, as it merely contains fables such as Bishop Abraham and the Pheasant. Jón Halldorsson acquired a doubtful reputation for enlivening his sermons with "worldly stories."[5]

---

[1] Gj., pp. 252-4.   [2] Lár. Saga, 55, 62.
[3] Lár. Saga, 33 and 47; Vigfusson, *Sturlunga S.*, Prolegom., lxxxiii *sq.*
[4] Craigie, *Icelandic Sagas*, p. 107.
[5] *B. S.* II, p. 221-230; *Homiliu-bók*, Paasche, Cpn, 1935.

But these *réchauffés* did not fully satisfy the Icelanders' appetite for history. Early in the century, when most men were paraphrasing, some were copying, and it is to this period that we owe Hauk's Book, the earliest surviving edition of *Landnámabók* and *Kristnisaga*, which was edited by Haukur Erlendssön[1] (†1334), one of the Lawmen of the country.

Another valuable compilation is the massive *Flateybook*, a collection of ancient sagas made by the priests Jón Thordarson and Magnus Thorhallson, 1387-95, which contains some new matter chiefly about the bringing of Christianity to the Faroes.[2]

Mention has been made of Bishop Brand's O.T. paraphrase called Stjörn (*c.* 1310), a unique work of its kind (p. 76).

(*d*) The most striking and famous religious work produced in the later Middle Ages in Iceland was *Lilja*, an encomiastic poem on the Blessed Virgin Mary, which was the work of a monk of Thykkvabaer, Eystein Asgrimsson, whose only other appearances in the Annals are disreputable. In 1342 he assaulted his abbot and was imprisoned for immorality. When released and readmitted as a monk at Helgafell, he lampooned Gyrd, Bishop of Skálholt. However, he was soon restored to favour, for he was appointed officialis or bishop's deputy in one of the numerous vacancies (1349-51). In 1356 the archbishop sent him to hold a visitation in Iceland to try to extort more tithes, which, like the two other recorded visitations (1307 and 1340), led to much recrimination. Afterwards Eystein sailed to Norway and was tempest-tossed throughout the winter, until at last he effected a landing in North Norway, then called Halogoland, where he died soon afterwards (1361).[3]

It is difficult to find a place for the writing of *Lilja* in the varied ecclesiastical and temperamental life of the author. The Annals say that it was composed after the libel on the bishop. But legend or tradition tells how Eystein wrote it in prison in deep penitence, and as the poem lengthened and his devotion deepened he found himself lifted out of his cell. Figuratively this may well express the truth. Some marked sign of repentance would be needed to restore this renegade monk to favour. Even though incontinence in a priest was not then regarded as a heinous offence, he had caused his superior to flee for his life. And the poem displays a mood of fervent penitence culminating in a personal prayer for grace and pardon.

---

[1] Presumably sön as his father was Norwegian.
[2] Craigie, *Ice. Sag.*, pp. 87-9; *Flateyjar-bók*, ed. Finnur Jónsson, Cpn, 1930.
[3] Annals; F. J. IV, p. 60 *sq.*; E. Magnusson, *Lilja*, pp. viii *sq.*

Lilja consists of 100 8-line stanzas, replete with Icelandic assonance and alliteration and interior rhymes; yet all through this intricate device it presents the unity of a lofty aim, and must have proved sonorous and stately in recital.

The poem contains three main sections, the central portion comprising half the matter and the last forming a practical conclusion.

I. Deals with the Creation and Fall, like Caedmon's prototype.

II. Redemption through Christ: (i) His Life on Earth; (ii) His After-work; (iii) Hell and Heaven.

III. Prayers to God and Christ (ten verses); to the B.V.M. (ten verses); Exhortation to the Reader (five verses).

The poem opens and closes with the same stanza, addressing the Almighty, and the parts are marked and held together by a similar refrain, like Passion music with chorales.

Thus the *Lilja* formed a valuable compendium of religious teaching, though distorting biblical proportions in its over-emphasis on the B.V.M. and Rewards and Punishments. It deserved its firm place in the memories and hearts of many generations of Icelanders. A similar poem would be useful in England today.

How highly Iceland, at least in those centuries, thought of this poem, which has been called "the most skilled and artistic poem of the Middle Ages," is expressed in the saying: "Oll skald vildu Lilja kvedid hafa" (All poets would fain have written *Lilja*).[1]

---

[1] J. H., I, pp. 212 *sq.*; F. J. II, 398 *sq.* (gives the poem in full in original with Latin translation).

CHAPTER VIII

DECADENCE OF CHURCH AND NATION (1380-1550)

(i) FURY OF THE ELEMENTS

MOST modern accounts of Iceland are written by tourists who have spent there a few midsummer weeks and paint a distorted picture of the country and its people. They touch up the climate and terrain and caricature the inhabitants. The British Force who protected Iceland in the World War at least wintered and summered in that apparently ungracious and unfinished land and found it a country of strange contrasts. They wandered through the small hours of its lovely nightless June, when mountains and sky take on a glory of translucent colour; in the long dark hours of its winter evenings they stood beneath the Polar Star to gaze at brilliant skies shot through with Northern Lights; they endured its isolation and made their way by stony or snowbound tracks to cover its incredible distances; they traversed its savage seas and gave lives to its storms and hurricanes; and they came to marvel at the fortitude of that imperturbable little race that has fought its way down a thousand years of history to maintain its home and its national existence against the fury of the elements.

(*a*) Iceland has been called the land of ice and fire, and that describes the people no less than the country. Most of them are a mixture, hiding a warm heart beneath a forbidding exterior; a few, perhaps those of distant Celtic ancestry, seem excitable and volcanic; some present a cold, silent, sluggish nature inherited from Norse forebears and moulded by their grim environment.[1]

The opinion of their character held by King Eirik of Norway at the end of the thirteenth century is expressed in a story giving reasons or his devotion to St Jón of Hólar. After praying in vain in a storm to other saints, he was advised by an Icelandic sailor to try St Jón. The king agreed to do so, adding: "Let him show that he is no sluggard, as Icelanders usually are."[2]

Without going into the vexed question of heredity and environment, it may be noted that the melancholy grandeur of their country and its hard conditions have profoundly influenced the character of Icelanders and the spirit and methods of their Church. Isolation and long winters hardened their native independence; grim surroundings

---

[1] Cp. Olive Murray Chapman, *Across Iceland*, pp. 154-5.
[2] Lár. Saga 5.

and the reaction they provoked intensified their stubbornness; the rock entered into their soul. This intransigence prolonged their resistance to papal claims on glebes and benefices and to papal demands for full acceptance of Canon Law. In neither respect up to the Reformation did they yield completely.

Their character, like their country, resembles the stern hill country of Judæa rather than the soft sylvan stretches of the Campagna. Preceding chapters (it is hoped) have afforded ample evidence that Iceland's forbidding land and fierce seas produced tough bodies; and as Thomas Aquinas observes, "A tough body means normally a tough soul."

(b) Early Icelandic writers take no notice of the "wonders of nature" in their accounts. The first description of the country's natural features is that of Bishop Gisli Jónsson in the sixteenth century. Though Haukadal, where Ari the Learned was brought up, is within sight of the famous Geysir, neither he nor any other local writer makes any reference to it. The learned Bishop Brynjolf (1639-75), also a neighbour, is the first to mention it. Adam of Bremen (1068 sq.) says, "Icelanders have their springs for their delights," presumably for warm baths, in the classic manner of the historian Snorri, who used to meet his friends for discussion sitting at his bath, the remains of which may be seen at Reykholt.

Saxo Grammaticus, who wrote in Denmark a century after Adam of Bremen, observes that "Iceland is a squalid country to live in (obsoletæ admodum habitationis tellus), but it is noteworthy for marvels," of which he singles out Geysir and Hekla. "There is a spring which turns all to stone with its reeking fumes, and casts a mass of spray upwards; and there is a mountain which belches out floods of incessant fires in an everlasting blaze."[1] He also mentions mineral springs (near Hitardal) "whose waters resemble the bowl of Ceres"—i.e., beer. The *Royal Mirror* (c. 1250) refers to them, noting their possession of the admirable property of losing their effect if not consumed on the spot. The pious Henderson viewed them with misgiving in 1814;[2] but our soldiers failed to find them. Icelanders call them ölkeldur. The Geysir stopped itself up with silica in 1916, but science came to the rescue in 1935, and operated on its lip, and by the help of soft soap a patient visitor may now see a fountain shoot up 150 to 200 feet.[3] Smaller geysirs and hot springs

[1] *Hist. of Denmark*, Pref., 6, trans. O Elton, London, 1894. Ed. by Olrik and Raeder, 1931.   [2] *Iceland*, p. 307.
[3] See *The Midnight Sun*, No. 51, Aug. 15, 1941.

appear in many parts of Iceland, some owing their origin and disappearance to earthquakes. Perhaps the second recorded eruption of
Hekla in 1157 brought the great Geysir into action, which would
account for the silence of Ari and its mention soon afterwards by
Saxo Grammaticus. But it is more likely that local writers took such
phenomena for granted, as they did their unrivalled waterfalls,
colossal glaciers, and aurora borealis.

The hot springs have two special ecclesiastical connections. St
Martin's bath near Haukadal was used by many in the Middle Ages
to cure diseases. Being but twenty-five miles north of Skálholt, it
was easy for the faithful to take a cure at the baths in connection with
their attendance at the Dedication Festival at the cathedral. *Hungrvaka* records that the aged Bishop Ketill lost his life in 1145 after
bathing in a hot spring after supper while staying with his friend
Bishop Magnus for the Church Day.[1]

The other connection is mercenary rather than religious. Many of
the springs are sulphurous, and the first speculator to see commercial
possibilities in this seems to have been the Archbishop of Trondhjem,
who held a monopoly of the Icelandic sulphur trade in the fifteenth
century.

(c) Sagas take for granted the normal hardships of Icelandic life.
They note exceptional outbursts of natural forces, which appear to
have increased towards the end of the Middle Ages, though Annals,
which form our authority for that period, emphasise, like journalists,
the abnormal. Abbot Arngrim ([†]1361) devotes a short section to the
wonders of his country as a background for his Life of the turbulent
Bishop Gudmund.[2]

The first three records that "fire came up out of Hekla" occur in
the series of *Hungrvaka* writings 1029, 1157, and 1206.[3] But these
eruptions appear to have been episodes, and it was not until after the
fourteenth and fifteenth centuries that an epidemic of volcanic
disasters befell. The Annals state that on July 13, 1300, the sixth
eruption of Hekla was so violent "that the mountain was cloven, as
will be there to see while Iceland is dwelt in." (This characteristic
prophecy has turned out to be more accurate than many made about
permanence of bishoprics and reputations.) A dark pall covered the
land for two days and violent earthquakes destroyed local farms and
cattle, followed by an epidemic which carried off 500 people.[4] Storms

---

[1] *Ut sup.*, p. 57.   [2] *B.S.* II, pp. 5-6.   [3] *Hv.* 2-20; 5, 13; Pálssaga 7-6.
[4] For list of twenty-three eruptions, see Henderson, *Iceland*, p. 267, from
Van Troil, and W. G. Lock's *Guide*, 1882; Baring-Gould, *Iceland*, pp. xxi-xxiii.

in 1326 and 1350 prevented any ships coming, with the unusual result (recorded in the Annals) that some churches, owing to the shortage of wine in the diocese of Skálholt, had no Masses that year.

Frequent volcanic outbursts are recorded during the century, with many severe winters, followed by floods, causing widespread damage and deaths of people and cattle, especially in the south-east. Floods swept off sheep and cattle, avalanches destroyed houses, pastures, and woods, and famine and disease completed the devastation.

These calamities wrought widespread havoc on the economic and social life of the country; and it is a remarkable tribute to the dogged character of the people that so small and scattered a community survived at all.[1]

Conditions of Church life became confused, as lack of supervision increased and general sickness was intensified. No attempt at betterment was made until the end of the century, when Wilkin, a Dane, was appointed Bishop of Skálholt (1394-1405). His able administration was abruptly terminated by the arrival of the Black Death, which had swept Norway in the middle of the fourteenth century and was brought across to Iceland during its second visitation fifty years later.

(d) We owe the account of this period to the "New Annals" (1392-1430), the last authoritative records for a century and a half. Annals had long been a characteristic feature of Icelandic historical expression, largely fostered by the Church, and though, like diaries, they make poor history by over-emphasising details and idiosyncrasies, and obscuring tendencies and movements, they vividly illuminate these dark years.

1392. Lord Peter (Bishop of Hólar) arrived in *Petersbowl*, which was dashed to pieces between Krisuvik and Grindavik (S.W.). All money was lost, but the crew were saved. Great storms and wrecks.

1393. On the 4th day of Yule, Hólar church and steeple fell.

1394. Lord Wilkin came out (to Iceland). He gave a great feast at Skálholt for seven days, during which nothing was drunk but German ale, and then more costly ale. Such lavish hospitality was shown that all might drink as much as they wished, both early and late.

1402. The Plague (brada-sott), brought by a ship. At Skálholt everyone died except the bishop and two laymen.

---

[1] Annals record devastating earthquakes in 1300, 1308, -11, -13, -39, -70, -90, -91 (E. H., p. 451).

1403. Many died in I., including the Lord Abbots of Videy and Helgafell. At Thykkvabaer the abbot and six out of twelve monks died. At Kirkjubaer the Abbess Halldora and seven sisters died, leaving six. This nunnery was thrice desolated of all menservants, so that the sisters had to milk the cows. 640 bodies came here to be buried at the first counting; then so many that a count could not be kept. Thykkvabaer also lost all its menservants thrice.

1404. "Men's death-winter." Skálholt thrice lost all menservants. Three more priests died, leaving the bishop and his chaplain.

1405. "Great snow-winter," with great loss of cattle. Of 300 horses at Skálholt, only 35 were left with the bishop's 24. Bishop Wilkin went to Bergen and died there. He had been a great benefactor to Skálholt church, building a steeple and paying all its debts to Kirkjubaer. He enshrined St Thorlak's head in silver.

1406. Björn Einarsson made a pilgrimage to Rome and Palestine, and came back by Canterbury.[1]

1415. Arni Olafsson became Bishop of Skálholt, and was appointed by King Eirik to be Governor of Iceland.

1419. A great gale on Maundy Thursday wrecked 25 ships chaffering (chapfaring, trading) from England.

1420-21. Great sickness. . . . A storm destroyed Mödruvellir (monastery).

1425. Helgafell monastery attacked and destroyed.

1429. Munkathvera church and monastery burnt down in an hour and a half.

1430. A good "un-snowsome" (osnjosamur) winter. Einar Hauksson died, sixteen and a half years manager at Skálholt—a well beloved man.[2]

Thus pestilence completed the onslaught of fire, earthquakes, and floods, and resulted in the depopulation of whole districts and the impoverishment of the people who survived. Small-holders were unable to carry on, and their farms fell into the hands of the Church or of a few rich landlords such as Björn Jorsalafari.

Indirect effects appear in the lessening of public spirit in the people and in the weakening of their higher aspirations.[3] They were ready to respond to the least sign of leadership, but leadership at home and abroad was far to seek.

[1] Like his namesake in the previous century, he was known as Jorsalafari = Jerusalem-pilgrim. He became a great church benefactor. *Sup.*, p. 76.
[2] Rolls Series 88, 4, pp. 421 *sq.*, abstract from trans. G. W. Dasent.
[3] Gj., p. 245.

Calamities befell earlier generations, though we hear less of them, as in those days there were more stirring events to write about. Furthermore, then the race and the individual were stronger. Their natural pride and independence of spirit showed at its best in tackling adversity and making nothing of it. The early national churchmanship developed and deepened those qualities; but they wilted under the dominance of later mediævalism. For a stereotyped system is the graveyard of personality.

(e) Mediæval Icelanders proved the truth of Homer's saying that the gods take away half of man's manhood when he loses his freedom. As happened after the fall of ancient Greece, the country's literature became feeble and imitative; history and biography frittered away into Annals and religious romances; education almost died out, and enterprising sea voyages and travels almost ceased.

So in the matter of the Church, its machinery remained and even improved, but hard ecclesiastical legalism and biting officialdom well-nigh destroyed the native sovereignty of the Icelander's soul and the apostolic simplicity of his churchmanship. He was called on to practise obedience, exhausting almsgiving, patience in the Latin sense of resignation rather than endurance—the qualities of a subject.[1]

But seeds of resilience remained to spring up and blossom when the inevitable Reformation gave them opportunity. In the Annals, quoted above, it is remarkable that in two or three years of plague two religious houses and a nunnery each thrice lost their superiors, almost all their staff and all their domestics. Yet after each devastation the stricken community picked itself up and started all over again.

(ii) Mediæval Medley

Strange figures strut across the Icelandic stage in the fifteenth century, appearing like caricatures rather than characters. The external power, now Denmark-Norway, seems not to have adopted any settled policy for Iceland, provided that dues were paid and that any trouble was confined to its much harassed island partner. It was a period of foreign contacts. Bishops from overseas, most of them indifferent or tyrannous and acquisitive, increased the dissatisfaction with ecclesiastical dominance; growing trade, chiefly in stockfish,[2] led to inequalities of wealth at home but provided inter-

---

[1] Cp. W. R. Inge (of the Greeks), *The Church and the World*, p. 54.
[2] Cp. Hakluyt, *Voyages* II, 136 (1437): "Of Island to write is little nede/ save of stockfish."

course with European renewal of knowledge. These conditions opened the way for religious, political, and economic change.

(a) That bishops were acquiring more authority and wealth is shown in the record of Arni Olafsson, Bishop of Skálholt (1415-9). The king appointed him Governor of Iceland; the archbishop made him visitor of its two dioceses, and the absentee Bishop of Hólar gave him authority over his northern see. Thus Arni "had such great power as no man before him, either clerk or layman."[1] In his visitations over the whole island he acquired much wealth, some of which he devoted to enriching his cathedral, adding four altars and presenting a silver bowl and a monstrance. A large part of these exactions was due to Hólar, but when its bishop Jón finally came out to his diocese Arni merely gave him the cross called "Dazzle," and Jón "felt it was a sorry recompense for the loss of his dues."

This ecclesiastical aggrandisement was displayed in a period visited by volcanic outbursts (as shown in the Annals quoted above), with long, hard winters marked by gales, floods, and shipwrecks, followed by much distress, sickness, and scarcity. That considerable feeling was roused against the Church is indicated by the attack on Helgafell monastery in 1425, which left it despoiled and desolate for four years.[2] Such outbreaks would account for the fact that many of the great monastic collections of manuscripts, such as that at Helgafell, were largely scattered before the Reformation.[3]

Arni was the only native bishop appointed until the end of the century. Skálholt had five Danes, one Englishman (Craxton, translated from Hólar), a Dutchman, and an absentee German, Marcellus (a favourite of the king, rejected for the archbishopric of Nidaros), who appointed a vicarius to collect his revenues (1148-60). Hólar had three Norwegians, two Danes, and three Englishmen: John Williamson Craxton (1426-35)[4]—the only instance of the characteristically English custom of translation to be found in the long list of Icelandic bishops; John Bloxwich, a Carmelite (1436-40); and Robert Wodeburn, an Augustinian (1441).[5] This episcopal invasion occurred (as we shall see) in a period of English trading, but the Icelandic Church never responded much to advances on the international front.

---

[1] Annals *sub anno* 1415, Rolls Series 88, 4, p. 433. Arni died 1425.
[2] Annals, *l.c.*, pp. 435-7.   [3] Hermannsson in *Islandica* XIX.
[4] Surely the first recorded instance of an Englishman with two Christian names. Probably his name was John and his father's William, and Iceland characteristically retained the patronymic.
[5] J H., *Biskupatal* I, p. 265.

When vacancies occurred in bishoprics there were often considerable intervals before a new appointment was made, and once or twice the country had no bishops for some years.[1] The short tenure of their sees by many of the bishops suggests that old men were appointed, and it was doubtless salutary that not much more than their names has found a place in history, for the records of all those who figure prominently are unsatisfactory.

(b) The most notorious of these foreign bishops was Jón Gereksson, Bishop of Skálholt (1426-33). He had been Archbishop of Upsala, but owing to his vicious life had been tried and ejected. Nevertheless, he remained a favourite of the king, a patron of wayward ecclesiastics, who had him elected Bishop of Skálholt. He did not take up his work until three years after his appointment, having stayed a winter in England and collected a body of retainers, "most of whom were little good to the land." The Annals add another cautious criticism: "The bishop sent back much stockfish to England, for he was a great gatherer of fish and other things."

The bishop's exploits are elaborated in Jón Egilsson's Annals, compiled about the year 1600. With his bodyguard of Irish rowdies, he rode about the countryside doing much mischief in the fashion of Bishop Gudmund two centuries earlier. He carried two opponents, Teit Gunnlaugsson and Thorvald Loptsson, prisoner to Skálholt and put them in irons, in which they languished for some months, until they found means to escape on an occasion when their guards got drunk.

The vengeance they justifiably planned received fresh provocation from the ambition of the bishop's illegitimate son Magnus to marry Margaret Vigfusdóttir, who was of the same high standing as Teit and Thorvald and would have nothing to do with him. Then Magnus set fire to her home at Kirkjubol and killed her brother. Margaret escaped "through an oven, in which she made a hole with her scissors," and vowed she would marry the man who avenged her brother. Thorvald came forward as her champion, and with his friends advanced on Skálholt bishopstead at Thorlaksmas (July 2-10), taking cover behind the tents of those who had come for the Patronal Festival. The bishop got wind of this ambush, and, rushing into the church with his gang, put on his vestments, barred the door, and started Mass.

However, Thorvald and Teit levered up the doorpost and got in.

[1] Vacancies at Skálholt, 1406-8, 1420-26, 1446-62, 1465-7, 1518-21; at Hólar, 1423-6, 1457-60, 1495-8, 1520-4.

The bishop held the consecrated wafer in his hand, hoping thus to escape as sacrosanct, but he was seized and dragged out of the church, carried to the rushing waters of Brúará, put in a sack weighed down with stones, and thrown in. The bishop's men clambered up on the church rafters, from which they were despatched with bows and spears, and their bodies were buried in the "Irish yard."

The story ends in the approved manner. Thorvald married Margaret, and both he and Teit lived long and enjoyed the people's highest esteem.[1]

This incident indicates that Icelanders were ready to hold that the inviolability of bishops depended on more than their consecration, and to regard even the Host itself, put to an unworthy use, as not sacrosanct.

Two other bishops helped to undermine the foundations of prelacy: the litigious and grasping Olaf Rogvaldsson, Bishop of Hólar (1460-95), and his successor Gottskalk Nikolasson (1498-1520), known as "the Cruel," owner of over 100 farms.[2] The latter, though he lived in concubinage, extorted such heavy fines from the Lawman Jón Sigmundsson, who in marrying a third cousin had broken the ecclesiastical code of prohibited degrees, that he finally left him penniless, as well as depriving him of his wife.

Such hierarchical tyranny and rapaciousness helped to prepare the minds of people to welcome some measure of reform, already gathering momentum over a wide area of Northern Europe. They held with the expressed protest of the English Parliament that "God gave His sheep to be pastured, and not shaven and shorn."[3]

(c) In the social and economic spheres also influences were making for a change. The Jerusalem pilgrim Björn mentioned in the contemporary Annals already quoted was a member of one of the few rich and prominent families, who, like the Church, in a period of famine and loss of cattle and property, accumulated most of the farms, to the social and economic disadvantage of the mass of the people.

Such magnates kept up the old chieftain customs of foreign travel and of giving large feasts. Björn also endowed many churches with lands and gave money for Masses. Inequalities multiplied and the people failed to get real leadership from bishops and chieftains.

---

[1] Jón Egilsson; Biskúpa Annalar 1603; Björn of Skardsá, Annals, c. 1639, Rolls Series 88, 4.
[2] F. J. II, pp. 590-644.
[3] J. R. Green, Hist. of Eng. People, p. 230.

Money rather than character or prowess began to be reckoned the measure of a man's greatness and brought him into favour in Church and State.

Not all pilgrims were rich. We read of "Wytfrid, a pilgrim of the island of Ysland," who claimed to be a relative of St Thomas of Canterbury and so received from the Chapter there on October 7, 1415, a commendatory letter.[1] Thus travel and pilgrimages promoted Icelandic intercourse with the larger world overseas.

In creating an atmosphere favourable to reform economics played both a direct and an indirect part. Trade with England and Germany in the fifteenth century provided Iceland with contacts with national aspirations which were beginning to assert themselves in Europe and fostered a new economic outlook and restlessness.

Traffic with England in fish had begun many years earlier. On August 23, 1224, King Henry III wrote to the harbour-master of Yarmouth ordering him to afford access to merchants from Iceland.[2] Leland records that Kingston-upon-Hull, soon after its foundation in 1299, sprang into importance owing to commerce with Iceland in stockfish.[3] The Sweden-Norway régime, commercially dominated by the Hanseatic League, regarded English trade with Iceland as piracy, so that at first it was accompanied by violence. For instance, in 1422 English merchants, failing to meet with a welcome on the northern coasts, raided the islands of Hrisey and Grimsey and the ancient port of Húsavik, and robbed churches.[4] Such violence was no part of the official English policy in this matter, for Henry V (1387-1422) turned his attention from his French wars in order to forward this expedition and sent with it a letter to the principal men in Iceland asking permission to trade in fish. Unofficially the people welcomed this trade as time went on, and in 1440, when it was forbidden by their king, Henry VI of England evaded the ban by granting a licence to barter fish for goods to the Bishop of Skálholt, who had two boats in the traffic. In exchange for the best fish in Europe, Icelanders too often received wine and spirits, for the bishop's chief need for himself and his friends was for something stronger to drink than Icelandic beer. Owing to this traffic, an

[1] Rolls Series 85, 3, p. 137. Wytfrid had eight children.
[2] *Dipl. Isl.* I, No. 121—De navibus deliberandis.   Cp. X., No 4,
[3] *Itin.* I, 51. In 1303 Commissioners met in Hull to consider how the new roads should be made. Leland adds that stones from Iceland brought back as ballast were used for paving. Cp. Dipl. Isl. VI, Nos. 66, 426.
[4] At Húsavik a small British garrison in 1940-2 were freely granted the use of the church, where an English officer was married to an Icelandic girl.

ineffective state of war existed in 1469-74 between England and Sweden-Norway.

The most interesting illustration of the intercourse between Iceland and the rest of Europe at this period appears in a note in the Journal of Christopher Columbus: "In February 1477 I sailed beyond the island of Tile (*i.e.*, Iceland) . . . an island as large as England, where English merchants, especially those of Bristol, have commercial relations."[1] Columbus is said to have visited Hafnarfjördur at this time, and it is possible that he heard there of the Icelandic discovery of "Vinland" across the Atlantic, while he was feeling the urge for exploration, before he himself set out and rediscovered America.[2]

Towards the end of the century Germany commenced trading, and some conflict developed between England and Germany over the use of harbours. Eventually the English concentrated on Rif, near Snaefellsnes, and the Germans monopolised Hafnarfjördur, where they built a church for their seamen and merchants. This indicates that the religion which they held in common with the Icelanders was not as international as is often assumed. Commercial relations with Germany, as we shall see, provided for Icelanders a contact with the growing continental dissatisfaction with the spirit and methods which had come to dominate official Christianity.

That their intercourse with England was also extensive is shown by numerous official records preserved in *Diplomatarium Islandicum* (vols. V-X). At the end of the fifteenth century King John of Denmark and King Henry VII gave permission for English fishermen "to fish and trade in the island of Tyle" (VIII, No. 72). English broadcloth was exchanged for Icelandic fish. It appears that John Cabot went to Newfoundland via Iceland (VII, No. 491, December 18, 1497). As they speeded him on his historic journey Icelanders little thought that the Newfoundland cod was to become a formidable rival of Icelandic stockfish. This international trade grew as the next century opened. The rulers concerned exchanged letters and many licences were granted. On August 15, 1523, King Christian II sent a brief about the matter to King Henry VIII (IX, No. 138).

The importance of this traffic for our purpose is its indication that Iceland in the years before the Reformation was by no means in a backwater. Its relations with the continent, especially with England and Germany, provided abundant opportunities for contact with the progressive tendencies then spreading over Western Europe.

---

[1] Salvador de Madariaga, *Chr. Col.*, London, 1939, p. 81.
[2] Monsen, *Heimskringla*, p. 202 *n.* Cp. *sup.*, p. 47.

(*d*) By the latter part of the fifteenth century Iceland had recovered from the ravages of plague and devastation by the elements, and secured a measure of its old independence in nominating native bishops of some education and character.

Sveinn Pétursson, Bishop of Skálholt (1467-75), graduated abroad as Master of Arts and was known as spaki—learned. His successors were also Icelanders. Stefán Jónsson (1491-1518), the ablest of the later mediæval bishops, restored to the Church in his diocese much of its former order and spiritual leadership. He reopened the episcopal school, and in 1493 founded an Augustinian priory at Skrida in the eastern district—the first religious house to be founded for two hundred years, and the last to be established in Iceland. He revised many church charters and inventories, which indicates a general quickening of ecclesiastical life.[1]

The cult of the Blessed Virgin flourished at this time, about half of the churches in the country being dedicated to her. Traditional verse-making and folk-songs had lapsed or been driven underground under the dominance of external ecclesiasticism. Poetry took a religious form and began to show a revival towards the end of the century, chiefly under the inspiration of Jón Pálsson, priest of Grenjadarstadir (†1472), who became known as Mariúskald—poet-laureate of the Virgin.

Monasteries, such as Helgafell and Munkathvera, enjoyed some revival of learning. The episcopal school at Hólar also was reopened by Gottskalk Nikolasson (1498-1520). This revival proved to be a final flicker, for afterwards obscurantism, aggressiveness, and lack of spirituality once more prevailed. But the reawakening of national aspirations in ecclesiastical government and in education prepared the way for the wave of independence in political and religious life about to sweep the Continent and ultimately reach the naturally free and rugged shores of Iceland.

In moral, social, economic, and intellectual fields the rising waters of reformation were being fed through many inlets. It remains to be seen into what channel they ultimately converged.

[1] For Bp Stefán, see F. J. II, pp. 491-521; *Dipl. Isl.* VII.

CHAPTER IX

REFORMATION

THE years 1540-51 saw the passing of the Icelandic Church from the Roman obedience and its adoption of Lutheran reforms in religion, forcibly sponsored by the Danish administration. This political and ecclesiastical change took effect in the southern and northern dioceses in successive stages and was followed by a period of religious reconstruction latent in the earlier stages.

(i) The first phase concerns the application of the reforming movement to the southern diocese of Skálholt, which, being easier of access to the Continent, was earliest to be influenced by the new teaching and was first tackled by King Christian III's aggressive representatives. The monastery of Videy was seized, so that Bishop Øgmund's friends were provoked to slay the Danish official responsible, which led to the bishop's supersession and capture, and, as he was blind and aged, to his speedy death in 1541.

(ii) The second phase concerns the northern diocese of Hólar, whose fighting bishop, Jón Arason, took ten years to subdue. He was put to death in 1550, more as a victim of his factiousness than as a martyr for his faith.

(iii) But the reformation of the Church was not complete without its third and positive phase, in which the inherent individualism and independence of Icelanders, so long repressed, began to respond to evangelical principles and to recover their intellectual and moral vigour.

(i) FIRST PHASE—SKÁLHOLT (1526-41)

At the beginning of the second quarter of the sixteenth century the stage was set for the "Change of Fashion" (sidaskipti), as Icelanders term their ecclesiastical reformation.

The Icelandic stage was very small, but the principles at issue were those which were convulsing the countries of Europe at the time and finding this or that occasion for working themselves out. In Iceland, as usual more than elsewhere, the issue hinged on a few outstanding characters.

Masterful men who might have stepped out of the old sagas held the two episcopal sees: at Skálholt, Øgmund Pálsson (1521-41), and at Hólar, Jón Arason (1524-50). Øgmund was tall, blunt, and homely; Jón was dignified, witty, and debonair. Øgmund did his best to keep Jón from being elected to Hólar, and, when, after four years, he was consecrated, clashes arose between the two arrogant and vigorous prelates.

At their first meeting at the Althing in 1526, Øgmund attended with 1,300 retainers, Jón had an escort of 900, and a battle was averted by abbots and priests, on condition that the quarrel should be settled by a fight between two selected champions. The story of these years is recorded in his Annals by Jón Egilsson, grandson of one of the spectators. The duel was fought in the traditional, but long-since illegal, fashion on an island in the Oxará in the presence of the rival parties, headed by the bishops. Øgmund's representative succeeded in throwing his opponent, but Jón Arason refused to accept this as final, and both bishops went home in cantankerous mood.

Øgmund returned to Skálholt to find that the cathedral had been burnt to the ground, with all its fittings, which he regarded as a sign of Divine displeasure, and in much distress took measures to rebuild it and to make peace with his colleague in face of larger issues beginning to threaten their common churchmanship. Superstitious people looked on the catastrophe as a sign that the old régime was doomed.[1]

(a) Martin Luther, having denounced the papal traffic in indulgences, had faced the Diet of Worms in 1521 on a moral issue with his: "Here I stand: I can no other." But Luther's moral reforms became entangled in politics, and the double issue reached the north. The kingdom of Denmark-Norway was in the throes of party strife over the royal succession, a conflict which involved Iceland. For in 1533 the Althing, encouraged by the two bishops, passed a decree to support the King of Norway and the Catholic Church. The latter allegiance made it plain that the catholic Christian II was their choice. But he was defeated by Christian III, the Lutheran; so that the Archbishop of Trondhjem fled, and in 1536 Bishop Øgmund had to take the oath to Christian III.[2]

On December 12 of that year Luther wrote to the new king approving the suppression of episcopacy, but urging that confiscated Church property should be used to establish schools.[3]

It was natural that the South of Iceland should first feel the political weight of the "Change of Fashion," for the Danish Governor

---

[1] F. J. II, p. 527: "causa aut casu," cp. Oswald, *By Fell and Fjord*, p. 241, for the "old wives'" amazement.

[2] Jón Espolin, *Arbaekur* III, 79. The Annals state that Christian II appealed to Henry VIII for help, offering him Iceland in return.

[3] For Reformation in Denmark, see Kurtz, *Church Hist.*, 139, 2.

lived at Bessastadir, on the peninsula just south of Hafnarfjördur, then the chief port for the Continent. Claus van Merwitz, the Governor, and his deputy Didrek von Minden (both German adventurers, though Claus was of Dutch extraction), proved inconsiderate and grasping administrators. Bessastadir was exposed to all the gales that blew, while round the corner in Faxafjörd nestled Videy Island with its tempting rich monastic farm.

(b) Meanwhile the inward and spiritual side of the Reformation had been making headway in the country. German merchants had brought Lutheran books in their ships from Hamburg. Young ecclesiastics, travelling to improve their education in Denmark and Germany, returned with the new teaching; and, despite the bishops, spread it surreptitiously even in the cathedral precincts.

One of the Skálholt priests, Jón Einarsson, was moved by Lutheran writings to preach a sermon at Candlemas urging that the veneration of saints was idolatrous. This would have been a thankless task, for the cult of Icelandic saints was very popular. At the beginning of the century pilgrimages were so thronged that sixty pilgrims had been drowned on Holy Cross Day in passing over the bridge to the Cross at Kaldadarnes. Jón Einarsson was reprimanded by the bishop, but he continued his ecclesiastical polemic on ground congenial to Icelandic practice by claiming the authority of St Paul for the marriage of priests. A young priest, Gisli Jónsson, destined to be a future bishop and rebuilder of the Church, was caught studying Luther's translation of St Luke's Gospel.[1] More influential was the work of Odd and Gissur, both foster-sons of Bishop Øgmund, whose training he had undertaken, in the admirable Icelandic manner, with a view to their future usefulness in the Church.

Odd Gottskalksson, son of a former bishop of Hólar, studied in Norway, where he wrestled with the new doctrine in the watches of the night, getting out of bed to engage in fervent prayer, and after three days embraced Lutheranism. On his return home in 1533, the summer of the Althing's manifesto on behalf of Catholicism, he became secretary to the aging Bishop Øgmund. Nevertheless, he started to translate the New Testament into Icelandic. After discovery by the bishop, he carried on this epoch-making work in a cow-byre, saying that "as the original Incarnation of the Word of God took place in a stable at Bethlehem, so in similar surroundings the Icelandic Word of God was brought to light." Odd's translation, published in 1540 at the Royal Danish Press at Roskilde, is the earliest existing

[1] F. J. II, p. 539.

book printed in Icelandic. It became the basis of the noble Icelandic Bible, which did much to stabilise the old Norwegian language and set the standard of literary revival in the country.[1] To help clergy to face the new demands for evangelical preaching and teaching, Odd also translated Corvinus' *Sermons* (1546), Bugenhagen's *Passion and Resurrection* (1558), and (? Luther's) *Catechism*, printed in Iceland in 1562. Odd subsequently became Lawman, and was drowned in 1556 while crossing the Laxá on his pony. Rightly recognised as one of the chief benefactors of his country, his body was buried in the mother-church at Skálholt.

The bishop, at this time failing to see the growing strength of the new teaching, sent Gissur Einarsson to be trained in Germany with a view to nominating him as his successor at Skálholt. The young man was a nephew of the Abbess of Kirkjubaer, who had taught him as a boy. But in spite of his patron and his upbringing, Gissur was greatly impressed by the preaching of Luther and Melanchthon in Wittenberg, and returned a convert. When the new Church code was sent to Iceland by Dr Pétur Palladius, the Lutheran administrator in Denmark, although it was ignored by Bishop Øgmund, Gissur translated it into the vernacular.[2]

Øgmund by then had grown old and feeble. He was riding in the sunshine one day with some retainers, when his sight suddenly went from him. He was told that the sun was still shining brightly; then he said: "Farewell, world! Thou hast served me long enough."[3] He decided on a plan, unusual in Iceland, of appointing an assistant; and, probably suspicious of the Lutheran proclivities of his fostersons, sent his nephew Sigmund to Trondhjem to be consecrated. But Sigmund died soon afterwards, and in 1538 the bishop, with the assent of the clergy, chose his able and astute protégé Gissur, whose real opinions by then can hardly have been concealed. It is certainly significant that the bishop-elect went, not to Norway, whose archbishop was strongly anti-Lutheran, but to Denmark, where Bugenhagen and Palladius were violently promoting Lutheranism under the ægis of King Christian III.

(c) After Gissur set off, the deputy-governor Didrek took action. On the plea that the king had granted to the governor the monastery of Videy, he attacked the island on Whit-Sunday, 1539, rowing

---

[1] *B.S.* II, pp. 76-7; F. J. III, pp. 202 *sq.;* Haraldur Neilsson, *Studier*, pp. 182-4.
[2] *Dipl. Isl.* X, No. 95, 2 Sept., 1537, Latin and Icelandic.
[3] *B.S.* II, pp. 267 *sq.;* W. P. Ker, art. on Jón Arason.

across the bay with thirteen retainers, and drove out the monks. He seized the place for the governor with its 20 cows, 120 sheep, and 620 stockfish.[1] At the ensuing meeting of the Althing the blind old bishop bravely demanded Didrek's authority for this outrage, only to receive an insulting reply, which aggravated popular dissatisfaction and bade fair to undo such spiritual and intellectual work as had been achieved for the reformed Faith.

Didrek went from the Althing to seize the monasteries of Thykk-vabaer and Kirkjubaer in the south-east, staying on the way at the bishopstead at Skálholt, where he was hospitably received by Øgmund, though he again questioned him as to his authority. The bishop was met with further abuse, and replied with the warning that, although he himself was blind and useless, he would not answer for his people if they were further provoked. At that, the cathedral treasurer sent word round the countryside, and a band of yeoman farmers marched on the bishopstead and slew Didrek and his followers.[2] These franklins were subsequently exonerated by a local jury of twelve men on the ground that they had executed criminals, but the governor ignored this finding and denounced Bishop Øgmund to the king.

(d) On March 15, 1540, Gissur was commissioned by the king as superintendent of Skálholt, and returned soon afterwards to take over the bishopstead and diocese, though on account of his youth he did not receive the Royal sanction for his consecration as bishop until 1542.[3] He was welcomed by the Althing, and laid before them the new Church ordinance, with a letter from the king demanding its adoption and blaming Øgmund for Didrek's death. After heated discussion, dominated by Bishop Jón, the code was rejected—a rebuff which the bishop rubbed in with a letter he sent the king from the twenty-four Hólar members. The Althing added a petition asking for a new governor in place of "one who does not know or keep the law of the land and is not of the old Norse tongue" (i.e., Icelandic). To this the king and his council agreed; Van Merwitz was recalled and imprisoned, and it seemed as if the first round of the political and ecclesiastical struggle had been won by the old Icelandic Church.

But the new governor, Christopher Huitfeldt, ominously arrived

[1] F. J. IV, p. 92.
[2] B.S. II, pp. 27 sq.; Jón Egilsson, Annals, p. 70.
[3] Dipl. Isl. X, No. 228, June 29, 1540: "Eg Gizur Einarsson, Sup. Schal-holltz stiklis. . . ." For ordinance, see Appendix, p. 148.

next spring in a Danish warship, having the king's authority to seize the bishops and their extensive property. Soon after his arrival Huitfeldt ordered the arrest of Bishop Øgmund, probably with the connivance of Gissur, who shows up badly at this juncture. The bishop, blind and eighty years of age, was dragged from his bed by night—an ignoble stratagem which would not have been tolerated in heroic days. He was carried off to the official residence at Bessastadir, and all his property was confiscated.

That Gissur was implicated in this sorry and unnecessary episode is indicated by a letter written in Low German on Whit-Sunday, 1541, evangelical in language but not in spirit, urging the "Good Christopher" . . . "not to let the old fox loose on land again . . ., lest the people raise an uproar." The letter is headed "Jhesus," and signed "Gissurus Einari, Superintendens Skálholt."[1] Huitfeldt then put the aged bishop on a ship bound for Denmark, an ordeal which he did not long survive. On a pretext of ransom the governor secured all the bishop's silver and valuables, even to his sister's brooch, and persuaded him to hand over all the episcopal estate, which included about 120 farms—enough to tempt the avarice of an unscrupulous reformer. Gissur had already moved into the bishop-stead at Skálholt after the Althing accepted his appointment as superintendent of the see, when Øgmund retired to Haukadal. The subsequent Althing in the summer of 1541 met in the presence of the governor and a Danish force, and so at last the new Church ordinance was adopted, though the Hólar members did not vote.

Thus was completed the first phase of the Icelandic Reformation, and no further opposition was encountered from the south. The relative contributions of force and persuasion in this first stage should be fairly borne in mind. Though the result was finally effected by political aggression, in which the new bishop was involved, the ground had been prepared morally and intellectually by the work of Gisli and Odd. The Reformation was much more than an external State imposition. The partisan and political intrigues, scandals, and extortions were but by-products of a deep, widespread spiritual movement in the hearts and minds of ordinary men and women groping after real personal religion.

[1] *Dipl. Isl.* X, 618; Ker, art. on Jón Arason, p. 15.

SUMMARY OF THE NEW CHURCH ORDER, SEPTEMBER 2, 1537

(*Dipl. Isl.* X, No. 95, pp. 117-328, in Icelandic and Latin.)
Adopted: Skálholt, 1541; Hólar, 1551.

1. *Doctrine.* . . . *e.g.*, "This sacrament to be the Body and Blood
of Christ to those Christians who eat and drink (the same); and the
Body and indeed the Blood of Christ to be solely for eating and
drinking in memory of Christ."

2. *Education.* "There shall be masters in each city and town to
ground the youth in reliable teaching."

3. *Ceremonial.* "Useful and uniform rites to be adopted, so that
lower differing rites be not followed."

4. *Sustentation.* Provision to be made for clergy and poor.

5. *Superintendents and their Provosts* (Superattendentes). Fol. 46,
"Superintendents, who are true bishops or archbishops of the
Churches . . ."

Ordination of Supt. Fol. 62, Some Preacher or Provost to be
ordainer. . . . Supt. to be ordained in his see-town, in church before
the altar (ad altare) by a Provost and five or six neighbouring pastors.

Status of Supt. "The Supt. with an honest wife and children shall
have two maids for domestic purposes, a notary, a groom and four-
horsed carriage, a page and foster-son, with a view to being trained
for ordination."

Ordination of Prestur. To be conducted at the altar. After Veni
Creator the Bishop—*i.e.*, Superintendent (episcopus sive superat-
tendens)—with presbyters lay their hands on the ordinand with Pater
noster (vulgariter) and prayer, to which all add Amen; followed by
the Holy Communion.

6. *Books.* Bible. Luther's Sermons and Lesser Catechism;
Apologies of Philip (Melanchthon); and The New Order-Book.[1]

(ii) SECOND PHASE—HÓLAR (1542-51)

In the diocese of Hólar transition to the new order proved a much
slower and more desperate business than in the south. In the north
social and economic causes were not so clamant and foreign commerce
was less flourishing. Men fished and farmed as of old, and so remained independent and conservative. Hólar, too, had made little
recovery from its fifteenth-century deadness of scholarship. Bishop

[1] *Docts. of the Chr. Church*, pp. 283-94.

Gottskalk, who saw the fourteenth century in, spent his energies in extortion and excess, showing none of the humane graces of his southern brother. His successor, Jón Arason (1524-50), like the soldier and chieftain he was at heart, made light of any Latin he had learnt as a poor boy from the Abbot of Munkathvera.[1]

But it was Jón Arason's character and conduct rather than any lack of intellectual powers that hindered reformation in the north. He turned his native combativeness and his long-standing family feud into a crusade on behalf of the old order. His final attack on his chief antagonist, Dadi Gudmundsson, brother-in-law of Martein, Lutheran Bishop of Skálholt, led to his defeat, capture, and death in 1550, and the compulsory adherence of his diocese to the new Church ordinance.

(a) Jón Arason, as was shrewdly said by one of his biographers, had the misfortune to be born out of due time.[2] He was a prelate of the turbulent type, like his predecessor and namesake, Gudmund Arason (1203-37), who had a better excuse by three centuries for his buccaneering episcopate. Bishop Jón lived as an old-fashioned chieftain delighting in wealth and dominance. He married *extra ecclesiam*, taking a concubina, like a Roman general, in the semi-official way. His helpmeet, Helga, a Church provost's daughter, was a strong-minded woman, and they had a large family. Of the three sons, Ari became Lawman and Sigurd and Björn became priests. All supported their father's Catholic campaign, though at least two of them had other inclinations. A daughter, Thorunn, married a priest, Isleif Sigurdsson, but after her husband's death she was known from her property as Thorunn of Grund, one of the first instances of a topographical surname. Her signature has survived to the present day, as she inscribed it on the flyleaf of a noble copy of Grágás—the "grey-goose" Law Book, which was inherited by the antiquarian bishop Brynjolf and given by him in 1656 to the King of Denmark.[3]

Like an ancient chieftain, Jón Arason cherished a family feud, which the spirit of the times and himself exalted or debased into a religious conflict. It began in 1523, the year before he was consecrated bishop, as part of the protracted lawsuit of Glaumbaer, coming to a head in a rivalry with Dadi Gudmundsson, and finished,

---

[1] *B.S.* II, p. 326; J. H. II, p. 12.

[2] Adeo miserum est, infelici tempore natum est. Jón Egilsson, *Memoirs*; Björn of Skardsá, Annals; W. P. Ker, art. on J. A., p. 10.

[3] Hence called Codex Regius. See Cod. Reg. Grágás, Introd. Páll Olason. The Victoria and Albert Museum preserves a fine chalice from Grund church.

as far as the bishop was concerned, with his capture in 1550 at the hands of Dadi, who handed him over to his allies, the State promoters of the Reformation.

The story is told that Jón's mitre fell off as he was coming from the cathedral after his consecration, a mishap which he at once accepted as an omen indicating that his episcopate would be forcibly terminated.[1] Certainly the incident provides an illustration of his reckless haughtiness. And for the first twenty years of his life he worked chiefly for worldly ends, using worldly means to attain them—legal craft, guile, and violence. He exploited his position to exact fines and confiscated the property of those who could not or would not pay them. With his sons he made forays on the lands of his rival Dadi, whose claims are extant for various petty larcenies.[2] When Jón succeeded as bishop to the Hólar estates they had been swelled by 109 farms left to the Church by Olaf Rögnvaldsson († c. 1495) "for the good of his soul." By the time Jón had finished his accumulations the property had been doubled. From a lowly origin and poor upbringing he had grown to be the richest man in the country, surrounded always by a bodyguard of sons and retainers.

The statement in travellers' tales that Jón Arason was "illiterate" and "extremely ignorant" is unsupported.[3] It may have arisen from Danish or German self-justification or more probably from a characteristically flippant remark of the bishop himself in one of his poems. He was no student or man of letters in the best post-Reformation sense, but he was a wit and a poet, maintaining in this way the more graceful traditions of the chieftains of his land. Fishermen in the Faroes long used his poem *Ljómur* (The Light of the World) as a charm.[4] He must be given credit for bringing over to Iceland its first printing press, which he set up in Hólar with a Swedish priest, Jón Matthiasson, in charge; but the inventory made at the bishop's death indicates that no more than a breviary was printed on it before 1550.[5] However, it was destined to become a mighty instrument of evangelical propaganda. But Jón Arason held that the sword was mightier than the pen.

[1] F. J. II, p. 655.
[2] *E.g.*, mustard and pepper mills (W. P. Ker, *l.c.*, pp. 4, 17).
[3] von Troil, *Letters on Iceland* (1772), p. 181; Mackenzie, *Travels* (1811), p. 57, contrast J. H. II, p. 12; Gj., p. 282.
[4] Finnur Jónsson: *J. A.'s Religious Poetry*, Cpn, 1918.
[5] *B.S.* II, p. 377; *Gudspjallabók*, Introd. Halldor Hermannsson. But Sigfus Blöndal (*Islandske Kulturbilleder*, p. 15) suggests that Arason's Gospels, etc., were destroyed by Puritan zealots. The last copy of the breviary perished in the fire of Cpn (1728).

(*b*) The brunt of the first phase of the Reformation fell on the south. Nevertheless, the Bishop of Hólar joined his old opponent, Bishop Øgmund, and "the best men in Iceland" in 1533 in pledging their allegiance to the King of Norway (as they still called the ruler of the united kingdom) and to the Catholic faith. As we have seen, he led the Althing to reject the new ordinance in 1540 and followed up the accompanying protest of the Hólar members with a dignified remonstrance to the Royal Commissioner against the high-handed capture of his fellow-bishop,[1] though he discreetly kept away from next year's assembly. When the State had replaced Øgmund by Gissur in 1542, the two bishops were summoned to Denmark, but Jón evaded this trap by pleading his age and sending three deputies— his son Sigurd, his son-in-law Isleif, and Olaf Hjaltason. All of them signed the new Church ordinance, and Olaf on his return preached the new doctrine—the only one of the Hólar priests who appears to have taken any active part in the promotion of Lutheranism.[2]

Bishop Jón for some years did not interfere with Olaf's preaching, and his diocese, at least up to 1545, paid the king's new taxes; but he ignored the new Church order, maintaining his religious practices (as the historian Finnur Jónsson says) *more papistico*. With Bishop Gissur, who was a friend of his son Ari, his relations appear to have been non-committal in Church matters, though characteristically he seized an estate which he claimed in the diocese of Skálholt without waiting for arbitration.[3]

Gissur died in 1548, when only thirty-three years of age. Had he fulfilled the usual span of life, or had Jón Arason died instead, the further course of the Reformation in Iceland might have proceeded peacefully. Except in relation to Bishop Øgmund, Gissur proved an able diplomat and a considerate administrator, tempering the harsh wind of State Lutheranism to the shorn lambs (and pastors) of the old régime. On Gissur's death, Jón Arason took action. He came south and announced that he would assume the administration of the diocese of Skálholt, probably with a view to getting his son Björn elected bishop. But Jón was not popular with the clergy, especially in the south, and Björn, who had all his father's haughtiness without his bonhomie, was actively disliked. Moreover, seven years of steady, quiet propaganda had put Lutherans in a majority, and when leading priests and laymen met to elect a bishop, though the Catholic party nominated the Abbot of Thykkvabaer, they were outvoted, and

[1] F. J. II, p. 566; Gj., pp. 288, 290-1.　　　[2] J. H. II, p. 57.
[3] Sigfus Blöndal, *l.c.*, p. 15; Gj., p. 292.

Martein Einarsson, nephew of the able bishop Stefán Jónsson, was elected.

Martein had worked for nine years with English traders, sailing with them to England, where he went to school and learnt to be a painter. Then he lived as a merchant at Grindavik until he was twenty years old, when he was brought to the notice of Bishop Øgmund and was ordained, though, like most of Øgmund's protégés, he came to favour the new teaching, probably under the influence of Odd.[1] After his election he spent a winter in Copenhagen studying evangelical theology under John MacAlpine, sometime Prior of Blackfriars in Perth, who had become Dr Hans Machabeus, professor of divinity in Denmark.[2]

Jón Arason persuaded the Althing to appoint him to the charge of Skálholt diocese during the interregnum, but Martein's deputies in the see proved strong enough to prevent this, so that Jón had to retire to Hólar. Some months later he sallied forth with 100 men, a significant diminution of his earlier force of 900, and marched on Skálholt. But the news got out, and under the direction of Martein's brother, who had studied strategy abroad, the bishopstead was fortified with redoubts and guns and manned by Dadi's bodyguard and neighbouring supporters. Bishop Jón demanded their surrender, but was met with jeers and taunts, so the stalwart prelate attacked. However, his efforts failed, and he was forced again to withdraw to Hólar, where, reading the signs of the times, he prepared himself a fortified retreat to the mountains, of which traces remain to this day.[3] Personal point was given to Jón's opposition, as the new bishop was Dadi's son-in-law.

(c) Martein was consecrated (using the word in its new sense) by Palladius, King Christian's Lutheran primate, in 1549. His rival the abbot, at the suggestion of Jón Arason, had also gone to see the king, but when his claim was unheard he turned Lutheran, and died in Denmark two years afterwards.[4] Martein returned in the spring of 1549, with a letter from the king which he read at the Althing, proclaiming Jón Arason an outlaw: "He has treated us with disrespect, and not regarded our letters in no wise." The bishop's old rival, the chieftain Dadi, was instructed to arrest him and his sons— a task which was all the more congenial as a few months before Jón had sacked three of Dadi's estates and put him under the ban of the Church.

---

[1] Jón Gizurarson's Annals, Rolls S. 88, 4, p. 447.
[2] W. P. Ker, l.c., pp. 17-8.   [3] Cp. E. H., p. 101.   [4] Gj., p. 295.

As an experienced warrior, Jón held that the best defence was to
attack. He kept away from the Althing, but on receipt of a letter
from the Pope commending his loyalty and urging him to continue
his resistance he called together his clergy, read them the Pope's
letter, and before the altar of his cathedral made a vow to die rather
than be unfaithful. Jón's son Ari did his best to dissuade his father
from further violence, and had to be shamed into co-operation by the
time-honoured method of a present of a woman's skirt.

On learning that Bishop Martein was travelling on a diocesan
visitation in the west, Jón sent his sons, Ari and Björn, with 100
retainers to capture him at the parsonage at Stadarstad beneath
Snaefellsjökul. The plan was successful, and the unsuspecting
bishop with his chaplain Arni was carried off. Arni had been
officialis during the interregnum and had led the Skálholt opposition
to Jón, so the vindictive bishop for a time put him in a privy and made
scurrilous rhymes about him. Martein was confined in the monastery
at Mödruvellir and set to help in the unsavoury job of drying cod.

It was at this time that Jón took notice of the Lutheran teaching of
Olaf Hjaltason and deprived him of his orders. Olaf went to Denmark
and reported the situation to the king, who sent a letter to Hólar,
again declaring Jón an outlaw and announcing the selection of Gisli
Jonsson for the bishopric. Whereupon Bishop Jón excommunicated
Gisli and seized his benefice and property, so that he had to flee to
Palladius.[1]

Then the redoubtable old prelate rose to the occasion and with
great courage and resource carried the attack into the enemy's camp.
In the summer of 1550 he rode to the Althing with a bodyguard of
200 men, followed by his sons, Ari and Björn, each with a force of
100. The King's Commissioner was unable to face such opposition,
and could offer no resistance. Jón compelled the Lutheran State
Lawman to resign, and reinstated his son Ari. Then, with Bishop
Martein in tow, he marched in triumph to Skálholt, which surrendered to him. He left Martein there under guard in his own
bishopstead, and, continuing his victorious march to Faxafjörd, he
crossed to Videy, where the monastery had been turned into a State
residence for the royal commandant and his staff. The Danes no
doubt considered themselves safe on an island; nevertheless they
were captured and driven into a boat back to where they belonged.
Jón exacerbated their discomfiture in his usual manner with barbed
verses. Then the bishop reconsecrated the building and reinstated

[1] F. J. III, pp. 300-1.

the abbot, Alexius Pálsson. The hearts of all Icelanders, whatever
their shade of belief, must have warmed at this patriotic act of
justice against foreign tyranny.

Afterwards the bishop rode up the west coast to Helgafell and
restored the abbot and the old régime. Then he returned again to
Hólar. At this juncture, on August 10, 1550, the bishop's family
wrote to the king professing the readiness of their father and themselves to "keep the holy Evangelium the king enjoined." It is doubtful if Jón Arason concurred in this offer, which reflects the spirit of
his son Ari, who at this time counselled the bishop to stay quietly at
Hólar. Had he done so, content with his admirable retaliation at
Videy, he would no doubt have been supplanted by the king's
nominee, but probably he would have been allowed to escape (as was
the Archbishop of Trondhjem) and have ended his days, like most
of the abbots, in pensioned retirement. But Jón Arason was not made
like that, and would have considered it dishonourable thus to retire
from "God's Battle." More than that, his old rival Dadi Gudmundsson was still at large, and, with his native arrogance, Jón thought
that his recent successes would carry him through to victory over his
real foe. But overwhelming audacity proved no match for much-
tried craftiness. Jón set out again with his two sons and a force of
150 men, with a view to taking over the estate of Saudafell, which
both he and Dadi claimed. Dadi lay in wait for him, camouflaging
his men in grey to match the rocks and misty atmosphere, and made
a surprise attack. The bishop's force gave in. Jón and his sons
retreated to the church, where they were taken prisoner.[1]

Dadi escorted them to Bessastadir, where he handed them over to
the only remaining Danish official, a clerk called Christian (the)
Skriver, who felt himself unequal to the task of guarding such a
famous group of prisoners with so many resourceful friends.[2] So
they were sent to Skálholt, where a priest ignobly suggested that an
axe and the earth would keep them best, thus putting his party in the
wrong and conferring on the bishop the semblance of martyrdom.
It must be recorded that Dadi strongly opposed this course, though
he gave way when it was supported by the Lutheran bishop Martein.

(d) Jón Arason and his sons Ari and Björn were beheaded on
November 7, 1550. The bishop met his death as a soldier and a wit,
with a final bequest to the poor, a skittish remark to the pastor in

---

[1] A full account of the Battle of Saudafell (proelium Saudafellense) is
given by F. J. II, pp. 708-12, and Dadi's *Apologia*, pp. 745-54.
[2] *B.S.* II, pp. 488 *sq.*

attendance, and a last epigram on his lips, thus translated by Professor
Ker:

> What is the world? A bitter cheat,
> If Danes must sit on the judgment seat,
> When I step forth my death to meet
> And lay my head at the king's feet.

Ari, as he went to his execution, remarked that he had gone into
the game unwillingly, and now willingly left it. When he saw the
block and axe he cried out: "Lord, is this to be borne?" When
Christian nodded his head, he added: "Confound you, blind idiot!
I was not addressing you, but my Lord God." Then, without
flinching or closing his eyes, he knelt at the block and commended
his soul to God.[1]

This summary execution was ill received by the bulk of the people,
especially in the diocese of Hólar, where such resentment was aroused
that when men came down for the winter fishing a band of them, at
the instigation of Thorunn, the bishop's daughter, marched on
Bessastadir and slew Christian Skriver with his son and Danish
assistants.

After Easter, the priest Sigurd, son of the bishop, sent a company of men to Skálholt to bring back the three bodies buried in its
churchyard. Bells were fastened beneath the biers, and as the procession passed along, headed by three priests, church bells tolled and
the people came out to pay all due reverence. A great concourse
assembled at Hólar, where their bodies were buried in the cathedral
with the utmost honour.

Sigurd was elected bishop by the clergy, and Jón Arason's vast
estate was divided between his descendants and the Church. But
King Christian III had by now initiated vigorous measures to enforce
allegiance, and four warships were already approaching Iceland from
Denmark. Two of them went to the south, where the new governor
summoned the Althing, which met in the presence of 200 soldiers
and thus took the oath of allegiance. Two ships sailed north, where
a special thing was called to take the oath and hear the royal deci-
sions on the Church question. Olaf Hjaltason was appointed bishop;
Jón Arason and his sons were pronounced traitors and their property
confiscated, including the 300 farms belonging to the see, with their
pasturage for 15,000 cows.[2] The slayers of Christian Skriver were to

[1] B.S. II, pp. 450, 719-20.
[2] Dipl. Isl. XII, pp. 361-70; Lists of Hólar property, 1553; cp. IX,
pp. 293 sq., Skálholt, pp. 371-425.

be punished. Nothing was said of the execution of the bishop without a trial, though it could have been argued that an outlaw might thus be put to death. Hólar Church property and treasures were seized, together with the local monasteries at Mödruvellir and Thvera.

In neither south nor north did the people offer any resistance or make any disturbance, so the Danish force returned before the summer broke.

Thus before the end of 1551 the Reformation was launched in Iceland, or rather all external opposition and obstruction to such launching had been removed. The State contribution had been negative and destructive, and the use of material force had hindered rather than helped the movement of the spirit, except that it was given an opportunity for freely getting under way, though in an atmosphere clouded with apathy and sullen ill-will.

(iii) THIRD PHASE—CONSTRUCTIVE (1551-1630)

Danish aggressions have always been felt by Icelanders to be more intolerable than similar tendencies on the part of Norway, their ancient mother. And at the adoption of Christianity, King Olaf of Norway, respecting Icelandic independence, mediated his authority through native agents, so that strong local opposition could be co-opted on a common front. Thus it is not surprising that the immediate general reaction in Iceland to direct foreign interference with the course of reformation took the form of a wave of non-co-operation.

The spiritual influence of intellectual reformers in the country received a damaging setback by the intrusion of political violence and acquisitiveness. During the era of reformation political antagonisms overlay the spirit of reconstruction and renewal, as a devastating flood of lava, pouring down from some volcano from time to time, buried a fertile tract of crops and meadowland. Only after the withdrawal of Danish officials with their booty did the essential character of the Reformation resume its growth in a renewal of Christianity, and in a generation "a flowery crop of knowledge and new light sprang up."[1]

(a) The new life flowed through the historic channels of ecclesiastical order and Christian faith, the Church and individual salvation. The Government dealt with bureaucratic centralising of administration, so that the Crown arrogated to itself or to its servants the

---

[1] Milton, *Areopagitica*, 1644.

aggressiveness and greed of the pre-Reformation prelates, and in the Reformed Church there was little danger of autocracy in its new superintendents, whom Icelanders almost from the start called bishops. Religious houses (five at Skálholt and four at Hólar) were dissolved and their extensive property was confiscated. The original suggestion of King Christian III and Bishop Gissur to use them for scholastic purposes was foiled by both religious parties for opposite reasons, but their chapels became parish churches, receiving a portion of their endowments.[1] Such farms as remained to the benefices pastors had to cultivate themselves in order to augment their sadly reduced stipends, for the grants made by the Crown from confiscated Church lands proved hopelessly inadequate. However, from henceforth the standard of clerical life in Iceland was much on the level of that of their people, and never afterwards were they tempted to become wealthy landlords.

The Augsburg Confession, promulgated in 1530 and adopted at Skálholt in 1541, gave only vague directions on the constitution and discipline of the Church, as being matters of secondary importance. "The Church is the congregation of saints, in which the gospel is rightly taught and the sacraments rightly administered." The one indispensable ministry is the ministry of the word and sacraments. Thus episcopacy is not of the *esse* of the Church; ubi Christus, ibi ecclesia.[2] Therefore, on this premiss, what the State made of the Church constitution did not fundamentally matter. In Iceland, happily, it worked out that when the State had finished its work and done its worst, then the real business of the Reformation began, the "saints" being "rightly" taught the gospel, and having the sacraments "rightly" administered.

Consequently it is unfair to regard the Reformation merely as a political measure, without considering its doctrinal and moral implications. Excesses and scandals formed but the ugly by-products of a deep intellectual and spiritual movement. But its essential character took some time to develop. Iceland, like England, was "slow to imbibe the food of her revived life." Just as, after the adoption of Christianity, the conservative folk of Iceland clung to some comparatively harmless customs, so after the Reformation, in the privacy of their homes, many people, though outwardly conforming, continued mediæval practices, such as the cult of the saints with its con-

[1] F. J. III, pp. 96-7.
[2] Kidd, *Documents of the Continental Refn*, 116; J. Mackinnon, *Luther and the Refn*, II, pp. 280 *sq.*

sequent burning of candles and visits to sacred sites. In neither case for some time were any strong measures taken to curb this survival, though the popular cross at Kaldadarnes, removed by Bishop Gissur Einarsson in 1548, was broken up by Bishop Gisli Jónsson in 1560. About the same time Bishop Olaf destroyed the northern crosses and the famous Hofstad Virgin's shrine, the name of which indicates that it stood on the site of a pagan high place. Hofstad was on Skago-fjord, provokingly near the bishopstead of Hólar.[1]

Gisli Jónsson was the third Lutheran bishop of Skálholt. He had been elected in place of the gentle Bishop Martein, who "solemnly abdicated" in 1557. Martein, who lacked the courage of his German namesake, felt the strain of his office to be intolerable in the face of the rapacity of the political promoters of the Reformation, the hostility of Bishop Jón Arason's family and supporters, and the stubborn ignorance and indifference of the people.[2] Gisli Jónsson proved an able and vigorous administrator during an episcopate of nearly thirty years (1558-87). In his constructive evangelical work he was ably backed by two conscientious governors, Paul Stigsson and John Buckholt; but their ecclesiastical zeal was considerably dis-counted, as the Crown further robbed the Church in 1556 by extorting a quarter of the tithe.[3]

Bishop Gisli, of practical rather than intellectual ability, took pains to direct his clergy to visit their people to see that they knew the catechism. With the help of Paul Stigsson, he tried to deal with widespread sexual irregularities, the difficulty here (as the historian Finnur Jónsson points out) being that the reformed religion held as a crime what under the old régime (sub papatu) was hardly regarded as a misdeed, even if committed by a priest; though it is only fair to add that Lutheran clergy (even such a leader as Gudbrand) were not blameless in this respect. Gisli led no mere institutional life. Just before his death he recited the catechism and eight psalms, with an invocation to the Holy Spirit and the Holy Cross. Then he went into his historic cathedral and read the Song of Solomon and one of Havermann's Books of Prayers.[4]

(b) After the negative political and ecclesiastical steps had been taken, positive reformation began its task as essentially a movement for helping the individual to a "closer walk with God."

[1] F. J. III, pp. 305, 361; II, p. 365.
[2] F. J. III, pp. 295-6.
[3] Ibid., pp. 5-11; Arngrim Jónsson, Crymogæa III, p. 145.
[4] F. J. III, pp. 109, 297-332; B.S. II, pp. 629-54.

Papal supremacy was abolished, together with traffic in indulgences and benefices, a prime cause of the Reformation. Permission was given to the clergy to marry in a straightforward way, thus regularising the custom of Iceland from the first, openly followed in the early days, latterly practised unofficially. "There be some priests," writes an English observer in 1542, "the which be beggars, yet they will have concubines."[1]

In the realm of worship the time-honoured outward signs were largely preserved in Iceland. Clergy retained the old orders and titles of bishop and prestur, though, as in Sweden, the order of deacon dropped out. As already noted, a break was made in apostolic succession according to a modern theory of tactual transmission of episcopacy, although the Icelandic Church retained the spiritual inheritance of bishops receiving their appointment and consecration from the Church. In this matter Luther followed St Ignatius and St Augustine.[2] Continuity also was preserved in vestments and in altars, which with their fittings remained in the accustomed places in churches, unobscured by central pulpits. The mediæval form of the Eucharist was retained, with its title hámessa, but the language of the people was reinstated and the cup restored to the laity. The doctrine of the Real Presence was preserved, though officially "transubstantiation" was rejected for "consubstantiation." Auricular confession was retained and was in use to modern times.[3] Unlike the Church of England at this time, Iceland continued to commemorate her national saints.[4] Thus the Icelandic Church's severance from Rome did not involve abolition of Catholic faith, sacraments, or customs. It retained its emotional heritage.

After the people had recovered from the shock of the accompanying political dislocation, with their love of nationalism and independence, and their stress on individual worth and learning, they responded readily to the offer of intellectual and moral regeneration.

(c) The Church became a preaching and teaching body, relying on the open Bible and the Catechism. For the Bible was by no means the only book of Lutherans, nor was it left to stand alone as its own interpreter without instruction or prayer and praise. Every leading reformer became a teacher, beginning with Odd Gottskalksson with

---

[1] Andrew Boorde; cp. Seaton, *Literary Relations of England and Scandinavia*, p. 13.
[2] Ep. liii, 2; cp. Headlam, *Reunion*, pp. 160-1; Turner, *Church and Ministry*, pp. 192 *sq.*; R. H. Malden, *Church Quarterly Review*, Oct.-Dec., 1943—"Potestas Ordinis." [3] Baring-Gould, *Iceland*, p. 295.
[4] "Thorlak's Chapel" in Skalholt Cathedral was preserved.

his vernacular New Testament, issued in the first phase of the movement, and his subsequent helps for the clergy in translated sermons
and catechism. The chief contribution made by Bishop Martein, as
became his nature, was a manual of collects and hymns, which he
published in Copenhagen in 1555. The latter section consisted of
some robust hymns, composed by Luther as a feature of his reforms,
which Martein inadequately translated into Icelandic.[1] The collects
remained unchanged until 1852.

In the north, Bishop Olaf Hjaltason (1552-69) used Jón Arason's
printing press for propagating the reformed teaching, and in 1562
published a Gospel Book printed by the converted Jón Matthiasson,
one copy of which is still extant.[2] A year or two before this he translated and issued the evangelical sermons of Corvinus on the Passion
and Justus Jonas' Catechism. Olaf also circulated a practical guide
for the clergy, with directions for pastoral visitation and conduct of
services, including marriages and observation of holy days.[3] A real
effort was made by leaders of the reformed Church to develop in the
clergy a sense of ministerial and parochial responsibility, so that their
people should learn that the "change of fashion" in religion made for
moral, intellectual, and devotional advance, and should turn to
positive and practical value in their lives.

Gisli's successor at Skálholt was Odd Einarsson, whose episcopate
lasted forty-one years (1589-1630).[4] He was one of three post-
Reformation bishops whose fathers were named Einar, without any
connection between them except that all were Catholic priests (Odd's
father being a monk)—a sufficient indication of the glaring need for
regularising clerical marriages.

As a student at Hólar, where the Latin school had been re-
established, Odd showed such keenness and ability that by the help
of Bishop Gudbrand, the successor of Olaf, he was sent to Copenhagen, where Icelandic students were educated free, and read classics
and theology, finishing up with mathematics under the famous
astronomer Tycho Brahe. After graduating B.A., he returned home
to become Rector of his old school at Hólar, the forerunner of many
students who turned the educational opportunities of their day to

[1] F. J. III, p. 292.
[2] *Ut sup.*, p. 150; E. H., p. 473. This *Gudspjallabók* was reprinted twice
in the sixteenth century, five times in the seventeenth and thrice in the
eighteenth, and recently, with an Introduction by Halldor Hermannsson, at
Cpn in 1933.
[3] F. J. III, pp. 361-2; *B.S.* II, pp. 679-82.
[4] *B.S.* II, pp. 655-78; F. J. III, pp. 332-356; J. H. II, pp. 122-9, etc.

the benefit of their country. In this way Odd followed the example
of the magnanimous early bishops, Gizur, Thorlak, Pál, and the
like.

Odd's long episcopate was characterised chiefly by his pastoral
benevolence and his devotion to scholarship. The country at the
time was going through a period of distress on account of ravages by
English pirates and loss of trade,[1] and the bishop's activities were
directed to the support of his destitute clergy and people in the
infancy of their evangelical faith. In this he received no help from
his wife, who had the reputation of being a virago; so that the saying
went round: "The bishop can keep his diocese in order, but not his
wife." An instance of her callousness is given in her destruction of a
natural rock bridge over the Thorsá, so as to prevent vagrants from
crossing to the bishopstead to ask alms. But Odd is particularly
memorable as a lifelong student and collector of a large library of
inventories and deeds, with a view to the reconstruction of historical
studies on the foundations of the Icelandic Church. He wrote a
description of the country, and translated Danish and German works
into Icelandic. Most of his library perished in one of the disastrous
fires from which Skálholt suffered down the ages. Nevertheless, his
work for revival of letters in his country was permanent, especially as
he inspired a band of students to undertake similar research. His
son and successor, Gisli Oddsson, wrote the first treatise extant on
the geography and natural history of Iceland.

Sira Arngrim Jónsson[2] (1567-1648) followed Odd's example in his
scholastic career at Copenhagen and Hólar and in promoting
historical study. He was the proud owner of twenty-six codices. He
wrote in Latin an epitome of Icelandic history which he called *Crymogœa*, printed in Hamburg in 1609/10, and other books in Latin
forming an Apologia for his country to combat foreign ignorance and
misrepresentations. This able prestur, known as "the Learned," the
best scholar of his day, deserves commemoration as the restorer of
Icelandic learning.[3]

[1] *Inf.*, pp. 165-7.
[2] Iceland has happily retained for the clergy the title of Sira, used only (as
Reverend should be) with Christian names: Sira Jón, etc. ? = Latin dominus
for priest under degree of M.A. J. H. uses Meistari (not Sira) for Brynjolf
(Sveinsson, M.A.). Cp. Chaucer (1386), *Cant. Tales*, Persones T. Prologe
1, 22: "Sir preest, quod he, artow a vicary, Or art a person?"; Paston Letters
(1450), Sir John Bukk, parson of Stratford; Garstang Register, May 24,
1592, Sir Wyllm Horne, parson of Corwell in Oxfurthshyre (Rector of
Cornwell 1559-92).
[3] J. H. II, pp. 130-1; *Islandica* XIX, pp. 40 *sq.*, IX, 43-4.

A similarly erudite pastor, Magnus Olafsson (1574-1631), devoted his attention to compiling the first Icelandic dictionary—Lexicon Runicon, and in his lighter moments composed poems and hymns.[1]

This period saw also the production of Annals, valuable as a link with the past, covering the Reformation era and disclosing the various causes which led up to it. The Annals of Björn of Skardsá comprise the years 1400-1645. He was a self-educated farmer, pioneer of many such homestead students who spent the long winter nights in diligent reading and in copying old sagas.

Two other pastors helped to restore the national consciousness and historic sense, lost for almost two centuries: Jón Gizurarson (1589-1648) and his contemporary Jón Egilsson. At this time the attractive Saga of Pál, Bishop of Skálholt 1195-1211, came to light, and Bishop Odd suggested to Jón Egilsson that he should make that appealing Life a model for accounts of later prelates, thus clothing the dry bones of annalistic chronicles. In this way was started the second series of Biskupa Sögur, which contains a valuable account of the redoubtable Jón Arason, taken down from the lips of the bishop's grandson. Jón Gizurarson actually copied out Pálssaga, and as the original manuscript was subsequently lost, perhaps burnt with Bishop Odd's library, his copy proved the only means by which the most detailed history of that time was handed down to posterity.[2]

(d) The historical and literary foundations of Icelandic national life being now re-established on the old lines, chiefly by the inspiration of Bishop Odd and through the labours in various fields of his associates, the course was clear for the essential constructive work of the Reformation. The Bible and books of devotion were made available for all, so that a religious and moral regeneration was effected in the nation.

This was in particular the great achievement of Bishop Gudbrand Thorlaksson, who held the see of Hólar for the record period of fifty-six years (1570-1627). He was born in 1542, son of a priest, and was nominated as bishop by the king, who set aside the choice of the clergy. His strenuous and memorable episcopate justified the royal discernment. By his achievement the art of printing was glorified. He purchased the printing press at Hólar, and with the help of the son of Jón Matthiasson, the original printer (†1567), he made it a real power-house of evangelism. He published a Lutheran hymn-

---

[1] J. H. II, pp. 135-6. He sent the learned Ole Worm a set of chessmen with a poem in Latin.

[2] Vigfusson, Sturlunga S., pp. cxli sq.

book in 1589, designed to replace what he called the nonsensical
poetry of the popular *rimur*. This collection so improved the rudi-
mentary efforts of Bishops Olaf, Martein, and Gisli that it lasted for
200 years. In 1594, assisted by Bishop Odd, he issued a tune-book for
the hymns, called Grallarinn, and in 1598 published a Passional, a
type of devotion suited to the Icelandic temperament and destined
to become of great service in the country.

As the groundwork of these helps to worship, Gudbrand published
in 1584 the Bible in Icelandic. He incorporated the vernacular New
Testament of Odd Gottskalksson, and used, after considerable
revision, Gisli Jónsson's translation of the Prophets and 1 and 2
Maccabees, "written at Skálholt; begun September 23, 1574, ended
March 10, 1575,"[1]—a noble employment for long winter evenings.
Gudbrand not only welded the whole version into a literary master-
piece, but he also assisted with the type, and procured twenty-nine
woodcuts, carrying the work through in a space of ten years. Finnur
Jónsson praises his style as being "pure, simple, and free from
ornament: the words admirably adapted to the ideas they are designed to express." This Bible, like Odd's New Testament in its
degree, was long regarded as setting a standard on which every
translation should be modelled.[2]

As has been truly pointed out, "The literature of the Reformation
in Iceland was a battle for language. Was the Old Norse to survive,
or was it to be merged, like Norwegian, in the Danish literary
language?"[3] The Old Norse won. Owing to the definitive work of
Odd Gottskalksson and Gudbrand, the noble ancient language of
Scandinavia, our original mother-tongue, which had been im-
mortalised in the sagas, was preserved as the language of Iceland.
With little change, it remains the vernacular today.

By the aid of a royal grant and a tax of about 4s. on each church,
Gudbrand issued 1,000 copies of his Bible, and then set himself the
task of distributing them in the parishes at a nominal charge.[4] In
1609 he published a revised edition of the New Testament for poor
people. In addition to his *magnum opus*, during a space of over fifty
years the bishop published Catechisms long and short, books of
Prayers, Psalms, Meditations, Sermons, and an Icelandic revised

---

[1] E. H., pp. 477-8, correcting F. J. III, p. 376.
[2] F. J. III, p. 376; E. H., p. 479. Rvk Museum treasures a copy.
[3] Sigurdur Nordal, *Odd's N.T.*, Introd.
[4] The English A.V. of 1611, which every parish had to buy, cost 10s. (or
12s. bound), and thirty years later editions cost 30s. and 40s. (A. W. Pollard,
Records of Engl. Bible, pp. 65 *sq.*)

Kalendar. He did not confine himself to Lutheran productions, for he or Arngrim translated Savonarola's *Speculum Peccatoris* and St Bernard's *Hymn of the Cross*. Furthermore, this master printer made the first map of his country. The list of Gudbrand's publications fills four pages of Finnur Jónsson's great History, amounting to what may properly be styled the grand total of eighty-five works. "His memory will not die," wrote a contemporary, " while the country is inhabited and Icelandic remains the language of its people."

To complement the sedulous toil he spent until well past the age of eighty in making his press a sword of the Spirit, this "firebrand of God"[1] was indefatigable in seeing that his clergy and people acquired and practised the discipline, devotion, and good life he thus irradiated. Everyone had to learn the catechism, prayers, and hymns if he wished to be confirmed and receive the sacrament. Gudmund was ably seconded in these scholarly pursuits and pastoral activities by his colleague, Odd Einarsson. Thus immersed, they let Danish clergy in 1607 draw up for King Christian IV (1588-1648) a new Church code, in which Icelandic ecclesiastical order and administration were further subordinated to the royal supremacy, paving the way for the proclamation of absolutism in 1661-2.

Nevertheless, Gudbrand stands out in Iceland as the leading man of his generation, or rather of two generations. It was chiefly due to his zealous and untiring labours that by the close of the first quarter of the seventeenth century evangelical Christianity became a living force in the lives of the people.[2] As the chieftain-bishop Gizur in the twelfth century may be called the founder of the Icelandic Church, so 500 years later Gudbrand emerges as its second founder. His work has remained to this day. As his fellow-labourer Arngrim predicted, "His glory, recognised in his own age, will adorn years to come."[3]

Thus, with few national resources, deprived of all but the bare necessities of life, in face of inroads by volcanoes, earthquakes, and pirates, these champions of Christ and the naked Gospel, by unremitting exertion and dogged perseverance, rebuilt on the old foundations the walls of their Zion.

[1] Cp. Arngrim Jónsson:
        Miles eras Domini, multis versatus in armis,
          Gudbrande, et ratio nominis inde tui.
[2] Gj., pp. 305-8, 331-4.
[3] Ille non modo suæ ætatis sed et posteritatis ornamentum (Brev. Comm.).

CHAPTER X

FIGHTINGS AND FEARS (1630-1720)

(i) PIRATES, WITCHES, GHOSTS, AND LEPERS

NEITHER pirates nor witches would be expected to come into the purview of ecclesiastical interest, though lepers from the days of Christ Himself have been considered objects for compassionate care. However, in Iceland clergy were more directly involved in combating piracy and witchcraft than leprosy.

(*a*) In 1579 a shipload of English marauders landed on the north-west coast, and, finding the few inhabitants unarmed and helpless, they committed outrages which have marked piracy down the ages. They sacked churches, robbed houses and barns, ravished women, killed indiscriminately, and seized the richest inhabitants for ransom. All this appears sordid and barbarous, and it cannot be pretended that it was British retaliation on the Icelanders for what their ancestors had inflicted on our northern coasts 1,000 years before, when Scandinavian pirates were dignified by the name of vikings.

Icelanders were completely helpless, as the carrying of arms had been forbidden by the Danish State, though it failed to provide any military protection.[1] Suggestions to remedy this unpreparedness came to nothing, perhaps because no further raids occurred for a generation.

The same coastal district was raided in 1614 by Spaniards, who carried off cattle, sheep, and money. About the same time English pirates landed in the Westman Islands off the south coast. They sailed "under the command of one John, commonly called Gentleman from the softness of his manners." They committed every outrage except murder, taking particular delight in wanton indignities. "They seized the church bell and fastened it to the mast of their ship . . . they terrified people by pointing muskets at their hearts with laughter and ridicule." However, on their return, the church bell gave them away. King James had them punished and the Church property was returned.[2] Probably this wanton ill-treatment was largely due to disappointment of the pirates at the small results of their pains. Henry Hudson reported in 1610, as other voyagers might have done, that "the people are very poor and live miserably."[3]

---

[1] Espolin IV, 55, pp. 39 *sq.*; Gj., p. 304.
[2] Espolin, V, 14, pp. 133, 156.
[3] *Ap.* Purchas, *Pilgrimes*; *ap.* Seaton, *Lit. Relations*, p. 8.

In the following year more Spanish buccaneers came in three ships, committing robbery and violence. On this occasion the Icelandic elements fought against them. One of their ships was wrecked, and eighty Spaniards who got to land were attacked under Danish direction, and all of them were eventually slain.

At this stage Denmark woke up to the fact that Iceland was being neglected, so King Christian IV sent over warships and two commissioners with wide powers to deal, not only with the growing threats of buccaneers, but with outstanding questions of Church and State.[1] They put into action harsh laws of 1558-65, which remained at least on the statute book until 1838, prescribing hanging for men guilty of adultery and drowning for women.[2] Capital punishment also was inflicted without mercy for theft, witchcraft, and other crimes. This indicates that the Church failed to show any moral or social leadership, though it must be added that during the seventeenth century the same slackness prevailed in the rest of Europe.

In spite of Danish counter-measures, the worst (and final) piratical raid was made by Algerians in 1627 on the east coast of Iceland, from which they carried off 110 captives, some sheep, and much church plate. Then they went on to the Westman Islands. "Arriving there with three ships and 300 men, the pirates overran the whole island of Heimaey with loud yells, massacring (most of) the terror-stricken and helpless inhabitants."[3] The rest they drove into a large Danish storehouse, which they set on fire with the people inside, after carrying off the young and strong. Then they rang the church bells, put on clerical vestments, and fired the church. The chief prestur, Jón Thorsteinsson (a versifier of the Psalms and the Book of Genesis), was struck down before his family and friends, whom he had hidden in a cave. His wife and children, together with his junior colleague Olaf Egilsson, were put on board with about 400 captives and carried off to the Barbary coasts, where they were sold as slaves, as had happened there to St Vincent of Paul twenty years earlier. Olaf was released two years later, and wrote an account of the raid. Most of the captives died. Thirty-seven who survived seven years later sent a piteous appeal to the King of Denmark dated "Algiers, 1635."

---

[1] Björn of Skardsá, *Annals* II, p. 92.
[2] Cp. *Constitutio Criminalis Carolina*, 1532, art. 159, 162; Grimm, *Deutsche Rechtsaltertümer* (4th ed., 1899) II, p. 264; "Den Dieb soll man henken und die Hur ertränken."
[3] Gj., pp. 319-20.

A large ransom was raised, but only twenty-eight reached home, mental and physical wrecks.[1]

One minister acquired a reputation for going into action, as Algerian pirates approached his coastal parish near Kirkjubaer, by singing an incantation against them, his Tyrkjasvœfa, after which (*post hoc*, if not *propter hoc*) their ships collided with one another and all capsized.[2]

(b) The Icelandic mind has always had to face "terrors of the night," both physical and non-material—"Hekla, witches selling wind, family ghosts." Europe rather than Iceland regarded Hekla as the mouth of hell. Icelanders faced volcanoes and earthquakes with comparative equanimity, but what disturbed their mental balance down the ages was their obsession with sorcery and the powers of darkness, which was a grim inheritance from their pagan days. Early settlers were careful to propitiate the autochthonous deities, known as Asir. Sorcerers share with ghosts the murky background of the sagas. We read how the witch Thorbjörg Katla—the "kettle" —by waving her wand brought over Hvalfjörd sudden squalls of the kind which still beset that enchanted region. Laxdale Saga (c. 30) tells of men reciting "crooked verses" when their enemies put out to sea, so that storms arose and drowned them. The famous outlaw Grettir the Strong owed his death in 1031 primarily to the spell of an aged sorceress, Thurid. For "although the land was Christian, many sparks of heathendom remained. It was not illegal to conduct . . . pagan rites in private, but their public performance might lead to short outlawry." Thurid found a jetsam tree-stump on which she cut runes and reddened them with her blood, muttering spells as she walked backwards against the sun. Then the log drifted against the wind to Grettir's retreat on Drangey, and when he began to chop it up for firewood his axe slipped and cut deep into his knee, so that he fell at last a victim to his enemies.[3]

Early missionaries had to face the machinations of spámen, magician-prophets, who regarded them as their rivals. As Thang-brand rode across a fissured lava-field the earth opened up and swallowed his pony, as he just managed to throw himself free. In such a weird countryside something uncanny might happen any moment. A spáman's calling was held to qualify him "to sit outside

[1] F. J. III, pp. 80-83, 138 (with captives' letter); Espolin V, 49, p. 35; E. H., p. 260.

[2] A. G. van Hamel, "Gods, Skalds, and Magic," art. in *Saga Book of the Viking Club*, 1935, pp. 129-53.

[3] Grettir's Saga, c. 78-9.

and waken trolls"[1]—dangerous ogres, which were perhaps emana-
tions of the troubled earth. Certain place-names suggest this. Trölla-
dyngiar (Ogres' Bowers) is the name of some clinker caves in the
lava field near Ølfusa, formed in 1000 while a critical meeting of the
Althing was adopting Christianity, and neighbouring lava cones are
called Tröllabörn (Giants' Children).[2] These natural dug-outs are
now used for sheepfolds and storm shelters. The eccentric Bishop
Gudmund owed his early popularity to his incantations, which were
held to keep trolls out of mischief and undo the work of sorcery.

Nevertheless, in spite of the practical influence of bishops and
clergy and the injunctions of Canon Law, sorcery was too deep-seated
in Icelandic nature to be cured outright. Priests and pastors were to
be found among the sorcerers. Professor van Hamel records how Sira
Snorri of Húsavik took zealous steps to keep his parishioners from
ghostly commerce, with the result that they sent him a staff covered
with verses. He looked at the writing and went blind; but with
presence of mind at once he composed a counteracting verse and
recovered his sight.[3]

Little harm was done to social life until foreign influence dominated
legal administration, for in earlier days a personal settlement concluded the business. Latterly Church or State had to intervene.
Gudmund, prestur of Arnabæli, lampooned his servant for losing his
ponies. The boy subsequently fell and fractured his legs, and in
consequence the minister was removed from office and ended his
days as a labourer.

The most interesting and scholarly of these traffickers with the
powers of darkness was Jón Gudmundsson (1574-1658), a poor per-
secuted farmer, friend and biographer of the elves, author of magic
poetry, against whom his rural dean wrote a diatribe. This layer of
ghosts, with his pastor son, was outlawed at the instigation of the
governor in 1635, and would have been in hapless plight had he not
been befriended by the magnanimous Bishop Brynjolf.[4]

The witchcraft which darkens the pages of Icelandic annals in the
seventeenth century was not so much a cloud of magic suddenly
appearing as an epidemic of sadism in dealing with a chronic Icelandic proclivity. For Iceland is a tolerant country; the harshness of
nature appears to mitigate human feelings, so that little or no official

[1] E. J. Oswald, *By Fell and Fjörd*, pp. 230-2.
[2] E. H., pp. 270-1.
[3] A. G. van Hamel, "Gods, Skalds, and Magic," art. in *Saga Book of the
Viking Club*, 1935, pp. 129-53.
[4] *Islandica* XV reprints his *Natural History* with Introd.

vindictiveness pursued such offences as might be included under witchcraft, or even breaches of faith and morals. But owing to foreign influence this period was marred by a visitation of capital punishment almost absent in the preceding century. "At every session of the Althing people flocked to witness the hangings, burnings, decapitations, drownings, the floggings, brandings of offenders under the harsh (Danish) laws."[1] This must have left a deep and damaging mark on the social, intellectual, and moral life of the whole people. Severe punishment against murder, adultery, and incest was normal, but that age added superstitious vengeance against supposed witchcraft.

From 1625 to 1690 about a score of people were burned at the stake for witchcraft. In this persecution pastors, some of them eminent and otherwise scholarly, co-operated with officials. A provost appeared as leading instigator, Páll Björnsson, a learned arch-deacon, who fancied himself attacked by this or that private enemy, and in nearly all his writings dealt with the baleful influence of witchcraft.[2] The only redeeming feature on this dark page is the fact that the victims in Iceland, unlike those in the rest of Europe, included only one woman witch.[3]

Iceland cherishes a similar but more picturesque inheritance in its ghosts. Of the sagas it has been said: "Few literatures possess more impressive ghost stories."[4] Later and more prehistoric records amply show people's preoccupation with buried men and women who "walked afterwards." We read of a midnight Mass of the departed (kirkjugardrinn risi) on All Souls' Eve celebrated by a ghost priest and attended by all those buried in the churchyard.[5] Individual ghosts were more provocative, and bodies had to be dug up and reburied, often after being cut up, to prevent their walking after.

Eminent priests are to be found amongst ghost-layers, notably Halfdan Narfason of Skagafjörd in the sixteenth century and Eirik Magnusson of Vogssos in the seventeenth. Miss Oswald recalls a tale she heard of a girl called Solveig of Miklibaer, whose love was

[1] Gj., pp. 316-7.
[2] Magnus Stephensen, *Island in det 18de aarhundrede*, pp. 165 *sq.*; J. H., II, pp. 179-81.
[3] In England witchcraft persecution was at its height during the Commonwealth, and ended in 1712. Even the learned doctor Sir Thomas Browne condemned a woman witch.
[4] W. A. Craigie, *Icelandic Sagas*, p. 34. See Laxdale S. 76; Njál's S. 77; Egil's S. 58; Eyrbyggja S. 33-4; Hardar S.; and especially the vivid tale of Glám in Grettir's S.
[5] E. J. Oswald, *By Fell and Fjörd*, pp. 230-2.

spurned by the prestur Odd Gislason in 1781, so that she died by her own hand, making a last request to be spared a suicide's burial (Dysjadur). But the bishop insisted, so she walked afterwards, and Sira Odd never again dared ride alone after dark. However, one night he left his escort near home, and soon the roof rattled and he was never seen again. He has left his own memorial in an altarpiece still in use at Miklibaer Church.

But latter-day ghosts more often prove harmless. As Henry More the Platonist wrote of Iceland (*Pre-existency of the Soul*, 1647):

> Here wandring ghosts themselves have often shown
>   As if it were the region of the dead,
> And men departed met with whom they've known
>   In seemly sort shake hands, and ancient friendship own.[1]

(*c*) We pray for all sorts and conditions of men that they may be relieved of their afflictions of mind, body, or estate. Pirates attacked the Icelander's estate, witchcraft delusions his mind, while many a body was ravaged by leprosy, which took the form of elephantiasis. The scourge is supposed to have been introduced into Europe by the Romans and to have been reintroduced by Crusaders, who brought it back from the East. Seamen carried it to Norway and to the southern and western coasts of Iceland, where it has remained much longer than elsewhere in Europe. At the Reformation the monastic revenues of Selja Island in Norway were devoted to founding a leper hospital at the neighbouring town of Bergen. In the seventeenth century in Iceland the malady, like tuberculosis and other diseases, found a congenial breeding ground in the poverty and ill-nourishment of the people, and above all in the fetid and filthy conditions of the dank, dark, half-buried cabins in which they lived.

Andrew Boorde, an English writer, described in 1542 how Icelanders of his day have "no corn, and little bread or none . . . they be beastly creatures, unmannered and untaught. They have no houses, but yet do lie in caves altogether like swine."[2]

Sir Thomas Browne gave professional help to some lepers from Iceland, which led to correspondence in Latin about the conditions of the country with the pastor of Hitardal, whose letters have survived and show the characteristic curiosity of an Icelander about English personal traits and customs.[3]

---

[1] *Ap.* Seaton, *Literary Relations*, pp. 17, 367.
[2] Cp. Seaton, *Literary Relations*, p. 13.
[3] Edmund Gosse, *Sir Thomas Browne*, p. 146, who compiled for the Royal Society in 1663 an "Account of Island alias Iceland."

Four small hospitals, one in each Quarter, were established in 1652, and granted the endowments of four Crown farms, confiscated a century earlier from monasteries. In addition they received certain fines and an interesting fish-tax—half the catch of six-oared boats on the first fishing day after Easter.[1]

At the beginning of the nineteenth century each of these hospitals under the direction of the governor and the bishop contained not more than eight inmates, though in 1770 there were twenty lepers living in one small district alone, the peninsula of Seljarnarnes near Reykjavik, and the southern diocese had ninety-nine.[2] Most lepers, therefore, had to carry on their normal mode of life. Poignancy is added to the writings of the most arresting and helpful of Icelandic poets, the prestur Hallgrim Pétursson, by the fact that he was a leper.

It is satisfactory to record that about thirty years ago all lepers were segregated into one hospital where the disease could be properly tackled. No fresh cases have occurred, so that after the death of the dozen present patients the scourge should be merely an unhappy memory.[3]

(ii) ANTIQUARIES

In front of the altar at Hólar Church may be seen the tombstone of Bishop Gudbrand, "Jesu Christi peccator," supported on the sanctuary walls by two portraits of that evangelical master-printer, one worked in wool by his illegitimate daughter.

(a) This doyen of Icelandic bishops was succeeded by his grandson, Thorlak Skúlason (1628-56), the picture of whose florid countenance also hangs at Hólar, together with those of his three wives. Thorlak continued the biblical work of his predecessor, producing in 1644 a new edition of Gudbrand's Bible, the first to have the text divided into verses. He received royal support on condition that he adapted the Icelandic version to that of Denmark—i.e., probably the Christian IV Bible, published in Copenhagen in 1633.[4] Thus Thorlak's edition became the authorised version of Iceland, and was reprinted in 1747 under the supervision of Bishop Harboe, and again in 1813, at the expense of the British and Foreign Bible Society. Unfortunately, in 1826 this pure and dignified version underwent the

[1] F. J. III, pp. 460-1. All hospitals had lapsed before 1809.
[2] Stephensen, l.c., p. 342.
[3] The names of Dr Saemundur Bjarnhjedinsson (1883-1936) and his wife Kristophine Jörgensen should be held in remembrance as chief workers in this self-sacrificing achievement, as well as much Danish interest and generosity.
[4] E. H., p. 485; ct. F. J. III, p. 729. Rvk Museum has a copy.

questionable process of a revision on up-to-date lines, and a fresh translation from original texts was made for the Bible Society in 1912.[1] An ordinal was published at Hólar in 1635 to conform to King Christian's edict of 1607.

. Bishop Thorlak continued also the antiquarian side of Icelandic post-Reformation scholarship, initiated under the leadership of Odd Einarsson, whose long tenure of the see of Skálholt overlapped his own. Odd's junior collaborators, Jón Gizurarson and Jón Egilsson, who specialised in Annals and Lives of Bishops, were encouraged in their historical researches by Bishop Thorlak. His most important personal achievement was the saving from decay of the Sturlunga Saga and the older bishops' sagas, biographies of the first bishops, neglected and forgotten, like the rest of the country's literature, since the numbing ecclesiastical aggressions of the fifteenth century. His work helped the men of his generation to envisage, if not to recapture, the robust and radiant spirit of early Icelandic churchmanship.

Many personal documents demonstrate the lively interchange of information existing after the Reformation between students, in particular ecclesiastics, in Iceland and scholars in England and other parts of Europe. Shakespeare reflects his country's interest in the "prick-ear'd cur of Iceland"—a popular sixteenth-century pet. Henry More, the Cambridge Platonist, portrays Icelandic ghosts. Bishop Gudbrand, the Bible-maker, found time to send a descriptive letter to the Rev. F. Branham, of Harwich, which Hakluyt translated (IV, 196). Gisli Magnússon, chemist, of Hlidarendi, corresponded with the learned Ole Worm, and visited England.[2] From its inception in 1662 the Royal Society showed much interest in Iceland, sending many questionnaires as to conditions in the country. These perhaps stimulated the surveys made by Sira Arngrim Jónsson and a succession of lesser antiquaries over two centuries.[3]

Much attention was paid during this period to the pedestrian work of copying old manuscripts, with the result that, in addition to Pálssaga being thus preserved, the priceless account of the Settlers called *Landnámabók* and the story of the coming of Christianity— *Islendingabók*—would have been lost to posterity had they not been carefully copied by Jón Erlendsson in 1651. Jón Halldórsson (1665-1736) and Ketill Jorundsson (1638-70), prestur of Hvamm, also prominently assisted in this saving work.

Denmark secured the originals of these and most other ancient

---

[1] Gj., p. 421.   [2] His son died in Oxford on June 12, 1642, from the heat.
[3] Seaton, *Literary Relations*, pp. 33, 180-8.

records collected and copied by Icelandic ecclesiastics of the day. Many of the manuscripts perished in the great fire in Copenhagen in 1728.[1]

The Hólar printing press was claimed by Bishop Thorlak's son Thordur, Bishop of Skálholt (1674-97), who devoted it, except for one Harmony of the Gospels (Skálholte, 1687) to the valuable work of reprinting Icelandic classics such as *Landnámabók*, Kristnisaga, Olaf's Saga Tryggvason, and the Skedi (*Islendingabók*) of Ari the Learned.[2] Thordur also published a treatise on Iceland to counteract exaggerations of foreigners. Every generation seems to need some such antidote.

In spite of the rights of inheritance, it is satisfactory to record that the press was bought by Björn, Bishop of Hólar, in 1704 and restored to its original seat, at which one more edition of the Bible was printed in 1728 and some other books down to 1799, when it was removed with the see itself to the south.[3]

In its long and chequered history by its means great and imperishable good has been effected.

(*b*) The outstanding collector and antiquary of the seventeenth century was Brynjolf Sveinsson, Bishop of Skálholt 1639-74, whose life reflects much of the light and shade of Icelandic churchmanship.[4] A biography of him was written by his nephew Torfi Jónsson and is included in the second series of *Biskupa Sögur*. Owing to his scholarship, bearing, and force of character, he was regarded, like the old chieftain-bishops, as a king in Iceland.

Descended on his mother's side from Jón Arason, the Catholic stalwart in the Reformation struggle, he had much of that fiery prelate's energy and incisiveness—at least in speech; and owing, perhaps, to this consanguinity his Lutheran churchmanship showed few signs of negative protestantism. "The mediæval church," he used to say, "had indeed a scabbed head, but Luther took a curry-comb to it, and scraped off hair and scalp and all." Bishop Brynjolf used to pray with his eyes on a crucifix, and, like his contemporary Archbishop Laud, he faithfully observed ecclesiastical rules and feasts and fasts, refusing even to start on a journey on the eve of Sunday. But in morals he was puritanically strict. Torfi records that in Brynjolf's coffin were placed a Greek New Testament and four gospels translated by Bishop Jón Arason. But as an in-

---

[1] Vigfusson, *Sturlunga S.*, Prolegomena, pp. cxli *sq.*
[2] E. H., pp. 110, 488-9.   [3] E. H., pp. 486-7.
[4] F. J., pp. 602 *sq.*; Vigfusson, *Sturlunga S.*, Prolegomena, pp. xxii *sq.*

ventory of Hólar after Bishop Jon's death mentions only a breviary,[1]
Torfi probably meant this, which would suit Brynjolf's Catholic
proclivities.

In appearance the bishop was a big, stern, proud-looking man with
a mop of red hair and a forked red beard. He made a great impression
on the youth of his day, some of whom he adopted in the ancient
Icelandic manner with a view to undertaking their education.
When they wrote to him from Copenhagen in Icelandic he would
remind them forcibly that he had sent them abroad to practise their
Latin, not the vulgar tongue he heard round him all day. Scholars
must use with one another a befitting scholarly language. To this
day, as Henderson and Lord Dufferin testify, and one at least of the
British Army chaplains can confirm, some presturs and farmers will
help out the average Englishman's linguistic incapacity by conversing
in Latin. Brynjolf was a great linguist and carried on extensive
learned correspondence with scholars on the Continent, such as the
famous Ole Worm, one of the earliest Danish archæologists, and
Thomas Bartolin the historian, which helped to put Iceland once
more on the map of Europe.[2]

The bishop marked his books with one capital L superimposed on
a second L (Ꮮ) to indicate Lupus loricatus (brynjadur ulfur), mailclad
wolf. He signed himself Brynjolfus R. as if it indicated Rex; but it
probably signified Rufus. Vigfusson suggests that it stood for
"Ragnheid's son," as the bishop had a great affection for his mother
Ragnheid, great-granddaughter of Jón Arason.

However that may be, it brings us to the tragedy in this fine old
scholar's life. He had a well-loved son and daughter, on whom he
set his hopes. His son Halldor (* Dec. 8, 1642) became a merchant
seaman, and after some years in Norfolk, where he became friendly
with Sir Thomas Browne's household, died at Yarmouth on December 28, 1666. His father sent a Latin epitaph for his monument,
erected in 1723.[3] His only daughter Ragnheid (* Sept. 8, 1641),
remarkable for unusual beauty and intellectual powers, received
tributes from many scholars associated with her father, notably a
holograph of Hallgrim Pétursson's Passion Poems, dedicated to her
with ominous congruity "as a token of dear friendship in the love of
Christ" (as we may still read). Ragnheid was regarded by her

---

[1] H. Hermansson, *Gudspjallabók*, Introd.
[2] Christian (son of Ole) Worm edited Ari's *Islendingabók*, published at
Oxford 1696-1716. Brynjolf was the second M.A. in Iceland.
[3] Seaton, *Literary Relations*, pp. 180-1.

father as the apple of his eye (Finnur Jónsson's phrase is "instar ocelli"), and yet, with the unwisdom of the learned, he appointed as her tutor his foster-son Dadi, an attractive scoundrel who seduced her. The bishop found himself unable to regard this outrage as a lover's uncontrolled passion, for he learnt that Dadi had violated his maidservant about the same time. The father was beside himself with horror and rage. He could not forgive Dadi, but he would not deprive him of Orders, though he refused to let Ragnheid see him or her baby again. He petitioned the Crown for letters of rehabilitation for his daughter; and, no doubt to expedite the matter, he sent almost all his valuable and treasured manuscripts, to the Royal Library. But Ragnheid, who was twenty-two years old, died a few months later from shame and terror at her father's bitter grief, and the deprivation of her child.[1]

(c) Brynjolf's expiatory sacrifice of his library inaugurated the transfer of the historic Icelandic vellums to Denmark. Arni Magnusson (1663-1730) was the last of this notable line of antiquaries, the chief reaper of the harvest of manuscripts sedulously accumulated for more than a century under the leadership of Bishop Odd, Prestur Arngrim Jónsson, and the learned Bishop Brynjolf.

Arni was a son of the parsonage, and after studying at Copenhagen became secretary to the historian Thomas Bartolin, at whose suggestion he devoted forty years of his life to collecting old Icelandic manuscripts, which he carried off to Denmark. Their disappearance from the country of their origin is regrettable, especially after the patriotic labour devoted to their collection; but had they been left in Iceland they would probably have perished altogether, for in their latter days Arngrim and Brynjolf lost heart, and after them little antiquarian interest was shown. The people went through a period of calamities. Many lives were lost and much depression caused by volcanic outbursts in the seventeenth century, and, as we shall see, in the following century national life was almost brought to an end. So the manuscripts, mostly neglected in damp and scattered farms, were saved from perishing and destruction.

The fire at Copenhagen destroyed many Icelandic vellums, but the Arna-Magnean Collection in the University Library there now houses 2,000 Icelandic manuscripts and 6,000 Icelandic documents.[2] Thus was the work of Icelandic pioneer collectors completed; for the

---

[1] F. J. III, pp. 643-4; G. Kampan, *Jómfrú Ragnheidur*, Cpn, 1930; trans. Evelyn Ramsden, *The Virgin of Skálholt*, London, 1936.
[2] Gj., p. 315.

real credit for initiating and establishing this serviceable undertaking is due to native antiquaries.

The generalisation has been made that "the Church in Iceland by
becoming Lutheran slipped into a backwater of culture." This
notion does not appear to be supported by the evidence. In the years
which preceded the Reformation all interest in the national literature
had been stifled. The Roman protagonist, Bishop Jón Arason,
boasted in a poem that he knew no Latin, and even though this may
have been one of his jokes it shows no pride in scholarship. But
when positive principles prevailed the love of learning and literature
inherent in Icelanders once more blossomed into the flowers and
fruit of poetry and history.[1] "In no land was the number of talented
and well-educated leaders relatively so large."[2] The clergy had
become the most influential class and nobly played the part of Help
in the slough of despond into which the nation had fallen. Leading
ecclesiastics recovered the buried treasures of their country's
incomparable ancient sagas, revived their people's pride in their
national records, and by their industry and assiduous propaganda
induced other nations to take an interest in the chronicles of their
country, which has continued to this day. Interest in the history and
literature of Iceland rightly precedes latter-day curiosity in the
country's unusual natural phenomena. For the achievements of the
people are of more real concern and importance than the wonders of
the land.

(iii) A Mystical Poet and a Preacher: Hallgrim Pétursson and
Jón Vidalin

Bishop Brynjolf's influence, in accordance with the genius of the
Icelander, was personal rather than pastoral. He worked through
individuals more than in national or social spheres. The most
interesting and famous of the young men he discovered and trained
was Hallgrim Pétursson (1614-74), whose compositions Vigfusson
hails as "the flower of Icelandic poetry old and modern."

Hallgrim's father held the honourable but ill-paid job of bell-
ringer at Hólar Cathedral in the memorable days during which his
cousin Bishop Gudbrand compiled the first Icelandic Bible. The lad
gave up his schooling to go to sea with some German merchants and
finally became a blacksmith's apprentice in Copenhagen, where he

---

[1] This sentence has caught the alliterative taint without which no poem or
saga is considered passable in Iceland.
[2] Gj., p. 313.

was (as men say) accidentally discovered by Bishop Brynjolf. The bishop was always on the lookout for promising young men. One of the leading priests of the day, Provost Jón Halldórsson, compiler of ecclesiastical biographies, recalls what a lasting impression it made on him when the great bishop, coming out of a meeting of the Althing, went up to a group of boys, and, putting his hand on the head of Jón, then nine years old, said in the cryptic, pithy Icelandic manner: "Age is upon me, but youth is upon thee." Jón Halldórsson (1665-1736), father of the historian Finnur Jónsson, grew up to become a valuable prestur, "imposing in presence, a fine preacher, and an unusually learned man."[1]

In connection with the young blacksmith the story is told that the bishop passed his shop and heard him swearing with a surprising mastery of language. Recognising misdirected talent in this eloquence, the bishop entered the shop and, finding Hallgrim and he were distantly related by marriage, offered to adopt the youth. The bishop sent Hallgrim, now eighteen years old, to the cathedral school in Copenhagen, where he did well and passed out in 1635 as student. In that year the miserable group of Icelandic captives were ransomed from Algiers and returned home. It was found that after seven years of exile they had almost entirely forgotten their Christian religion, so Bishop Brynjolf appointed Hallgrim to teach them. The youth fell in love with one of the captives, Gudrid Simonsdóttir, who was nearly old enough to be his mother. She was married, though she had not heard of her husband since they were parted by the slave-traders after her capture. Nevertheless, Hallgrim took her to live with him, and they had a son. After the husband's death they married, but had much obloquy to meet. For some years they lived on next to nothing at Hvalsnes in the south-west, and in 1644, on the next vacancy in the poor parish there, Bishop Brynjolf ordained Hallgrim to take charge. In 1651 he moved to Saubaer on the lovely shores of Hvalfjord, where he rebuilt the dilapidated ecclesiastical buildings and did other practical and personal Church work. Occasionally travellers would look in. One mother in Israel later recorded how inspired she was when, as she passed that way as a young girl in a subordinate capacity, Hallgrim, whom she did not recognise as the poet, bade her be of good cheer, as great work lay before her.

His Passion Hymns, the great achievement of his life, were beaten

[1] J. H. II, p. 242, ut sup., p. 172. He wrote Biskupa-aefi (Lives of [later] Bishops).

out on the anvil of his many-sided personal experience. Sorrow and suffering made Hallgrim a poet. He was deeply moved by the loss of his daughter Steinunn, who was four years old when she died. After that he began to pour out his soul in his Passion Hymns, a "crucifix of song," which he dedicated in 1661 to Ragnheid, Bishop Brynjolf's daughter. Hallgrim's last years are hidden in the mists of his retreat. Poverty weighed him down and his health began to fail. Even at the beginning of the nineteenth century the income of Saubaer benefice was not more than £6 a year, with "a small farm capable only of affording pasture to a few sheep and cattle."[1]

In Hallgrim's last ten years leprosy attacked him, and increased with such malignity that in 1667 he had to give up work and appoint an assistant (adstodarprest), *rara avis* in Iceland. Then he went to live with his son at an adjacent farm, where he died on October 27, 1674, as his grave at Saubaer shows.[2]

Hallgrim's reaction to death is shown in his most famous poem, "Allt eins og blómstrid eina," which has stood the test of nearly 300 years' use at funerals in Iceland:

> All life is like the flower
> That grows upon the plain,
> And meets the morning hour
> In grace without a stain;
> But in a moment flying
> Time cuts its beauty down,
> And leaves and colours dying,
> Like human life, are flown.
>
> No rank or shining raiment
> I find beneath the heav'n:
> The Soul as loan, not payment,
> Is to the body giv'n.
> From God came the concession;
> He claims my latest breath;
> And so, my Lord's possession
> I yield his herald, Death.[3]

The afflicted poet wrote out three original copies of his *Passiusál-mar*, one of which is treasured at the National Library in Reykjavik.

---

[1] E. H., p. 394 (who does not mention Hallgrim).
[2] His wife outlived him by eight years and died (and was buried) at Saubaer in 1682, aged eighty-four. See Halfdan Einarsson, *H.P. Salmar og Kveldi*.
[3] Trans. Watson Kirkconnell, *Icelandic Verse*, pp. 109-11.

The book was first printed at the Hólar press in 1666 and soon made its way throughout the country. These Passion Hymns met a heart-felt need of the people for comfort and inspiration in days of famine, isolation, and penury. Hallgrim was a man of like passions with themselves who had suffered in body and mind, and had experienced the bitterness of deprivation and death, which had driven him to taste the pungent medicine of repentance. Bringing all his "sorrow, sin, and care," he had followed his Saviour through Gethsemane on to Golgotha, and laying his burden at the foot of the Cross had there won assurance of pardon and the spirit of heroic fortitude.

His poems lack the robust simplicity of Luther's noble hymns and reflect the resignation of the pietists.   Like Johann Rist's Lutheran hymns, they were "pressed out of him by the Cross," but they stop short at the Cross and fail to bring the Christian to meet his conquering Lord in the garden, at work on the shore, or on the road of life.

Nevertheless, they satisfied the then Icelandic mood. The distressful people felt they were not alone as they stumbled along their Via Dolorosa. A poignant example of the value of Hallgrim's work is provided by the use made by Ragnheid of his Passion hymns, which became the sole consolation of her death-bed. She kept the slim volume under her pillow and turned often to the poet's own favourite lines:

> A stronghold ever I shall find
> Beneath His mantle purple-lined,
> There I my guilt will cover.

Hallgrim's funeral hymn was first sung at Ragnheid's burial. It fitted her sweet, short, tragic life.[1]

At the poet's tercentenary, Professor Haraldur Nielsson said: "Generation after generation [Hallgrim's Passiusálmar] have been sung winter after winter in every home in the land, and this is still being done. Generation after generation many have committed them to memory, and for 250 years nearly every person has learned some of them. During these years scarcely an Icelander has been buried either at home or abroad unless some stanzas of the hymn "Allt eins og blómstrid eina" have been sung at his bier. Since Hallgrim's time the teachings of Christ have been instilled into the souls of the children through his hymns. The first prayers which our mothers and sisters taught us they had learned from the lips of Hallgrim Pétursson."[2]

---

[1] Kampan, *op. cit.*   [2] Gj., pp. 311-2.

A verse from Hallgrim's poem on the superscription over the Cross
indicates his method and general aim:

> Grant, Lord, that this my mother tongue,
> dear Jesu, I beseech thee,
> cleansed from all wickedness and wrong,
> as crucified may preach thee
> through this dear land at thy command,
> that so, thy name confessing,
> thy folk who dwell by Iceland fell
> may know thy gracious blessing.[1]

Hallgrim wrote another book of religious poems, Gospel verses for
Sundays and holy days, anticipating John Keble's *Christian Year*.
Though every Icelander loves a book, he responds more readily to
poetry than he does to prose. This accounts for the fact that after
the Reformation not only the Psalms, but many of the historical
portions of the Bible were paraphrased in verse, notably by poets
such as the pastors Jón Thorsteinsson, slain by pirates in 1627,
and Sigurdur Jónsson (†1661), composer of hymns still sung, and
author of a notable poem on the Seven Last Words. Hallgrim's
paraphrases of Scripture in his *Christian Year* reach a high level
and have been unfairly neglected. They widen the scope and outlook of his achievement and illustrate the fertility of his mystical
thought. Some of them are in the vein of his contemporary George
Herbert (1593-1633). Thus:

Trinity III (St Luke xv)

> Son, silver, sheep when they
> all lost and wandering were,
> father, wife, herd straightway
> to seek and find did fare.
>
> In mercy so God's Son
> bears rich and ready aid;
> by each repentant one
> God's angels glad are made.
>
> A son, a silver coin
> of price, a sheep of thine
> make me, my Lord divine.[2]

---

[1] Trans. Bp E. V. Pilcher, *Icelandic Meditations on the Passion.*
[2] W. C. Green, Trans. from the Icelandic.

B. Jón Vidalin, Bishop of Skálholt 1698-1720, also endowed Icelandic literature with a religious classic, *Húspostilla* (Family Sermons), "the most notable theological book Iceland has ever produced."[1] He was, furthermore, an outstanding bishop, worthy to be rated alongside Gudbrand and Brynjolf for a solid and lasting contribution to his Church and nation. He inherited his surname from his learned ancestor Arngrim Jónsson, and (as the homely old sagas would have put it) a lot more besides that.

All his life Jón Vidalin had difficult problems to face. He lost his father when he was eleven years old, and to support himself worked as a fisherman and afterwards served in the Danish Marines. Knowing what poverty meant, in later life he never turned the needy from his door unhelped.

Vidalin was trained for the ministry in Denmark, and nobly upheld the Icelander's devotion to learning and languages and readiness to impart his knowledge freely to others. It is clear from his writings that his scholarship was both profound and wide. At this time Danish theologians enjoyed contacts with England, and Vidalin shows acquaintanceship with English Church history, and clearly derived inspiration and edification from the *Whole Duty of Man* (published in 1657-8), which he translated into Icelandic. His sermons contain many quotations from Greek philosophy and reflect credit on the writer and their innumerable readers. As one of his contemporaries has recorded: "He knew many languages and was deeply versed in history, philosophy, and the Holy Scriptures."

Vidalin devoted much time and trouble to helping young people and training young pastors. In his comprehensive and well-docu-mented account of this noble-hearted bishop, Dr Möller recalls the story of a young pastor of Skálholt who took his sermons to the bishop every Saturday for two years to receive his criticism and advice.[2]

When Vidalin became bishop the chief topic of conversation, especially at the Althing, was the grievous distress in the country, chiefly due to harsh conditions of trade and enforced labour imposed by Denmark. Successive deputies proved cruel and grasping ad-ministrators, against whose tyrannies bishops and clergy waged unequal war. In 1707, as the result of years of lowering conditions, a plague of smallpox carried off 18,000 people—almost one-third of the population. In Skálholt diocese twenty-six pastors and almost all

---

[1] F. York Powell in *Enc. Brit.*, *s.v.* Icelandic Literature.
[2] Arne Möller, *Jón Vidalin*, pp. 58, 304.

the theological students died. The bishop took drastic measures to meet this emergency, by grouping parishes, ordaining adolescents, augmenting stipends, and establishing a pension fund for pastors' widows. To deal with his people's plight he called a synod which drew up a gravamen for the State official to lay before the king.

But Vidalin was a preacher and writer rather than an economist. Gudbrand and Brynjolf had dealt chiefly with individuals, students and scholars. Jón Vidalin catered also for the masses cowering in their wretched homes. He saw that, however sorely their bodies wanted food, their tragic need was sustenance for their despairing spirits. Hungry and thirsty, their souls fainted in them. Both Hallgrim in his poems and Vidalin by his sermons recalled the people to religion: one rather as a balm, the other as a goad. The Passion Hymns led those who were losing heart to find consolation and endurance (to use his phrase) in "the Sacred Heart of Jesus."[1] The cottage sermons stirred them to a change of mind, leading to a new life according to the will of God. Both books were individualist and reflective, eminently suitable for an independent and thoughtful people.

For "cottage sermons" Vidalin's discourses are remarkably scholarly. It speaks well for the learning of Icelanders that even in the calamitous days that followed they found in "Master Jón's" enobling utterance an appeal to their heads as well as to their hearts.

Vidalin used the evangelical instrument of preaching as it had never been used before in his country. The other great media of Bible-reading and hymn-singing had been successfully adopted. "Vidalin was an orthodox Lutheran of the great reformer's own type. Adhering to the written Bible word with a sincerity which left no room for peradventure or hesitation, he combined with the intellectualism of orthodoxy an ardent faith and an impassioned eloquence which gave him great power over his hearers. He sought to stir the conscience of his people by preaching repentance and conversion rather than the gospel message of salvation through Christ. Raising his mighty voice like one crying in the wilderness, he summoned his people to repent, lighting up their secret sins with the burning torch of the Word of God."[2]

As his life drew near its close in 1718, he had his sermons printed in black letter, and, like Hallgrim's Psalms, they went into almost every house in the land. Their popularity continued for a

---

[1] Passion Hymns 48, ver. 14, "Gegnum Jesu helgast hjarta."
[2] Gj., pp. 312-3.

century and a half, so that twelve editions have been required. They brought into homely use the words of the Bible as given to the Icelandic Church after the Reformation by Odd and Gudbrand, so that its clear, direct phraseology has passed into the current talk of every day.

For devotional purposes also Vidalin's Family Sermons have proved their value. Should age or illness, driving rain or snow, hurricane or long hours of darkness keep a household from making a long and hazardous journey to their parish church, they would assemble in the living-room, and, beginning with a hymn, or in Lent with one of Hallgrim's Passion Psalms, offer prayer, and then, getting out a much-fingered volume, familiarly called "Jón's Book," they would read one of Vidalin's sermons, concluding with another hymn and a kiss of peace.[1]

The words on the memorial to Sir Robert Shirley (1599-1656) in the church which he founded at Staunton Harold (the only church built in England in the stormy days of Cromwell) may be applied to Hallgrim and Vidalin: "whose singular praise it was to have done the best things in the worst times, and hoped them in the most calamitous."

---

[1] E. H., p. 306; Baring-Gould, *Iceland*, p. 151. The official title of Vidalin's sermons was Hwss (or Hús) Postilla. Postilla was first used of Corvinus' work (*supr* p. 145), and then of Gudbrand's translations (p. 163). The word came from the beginning of a priest's sermon: Post illa (verba)—after those words—*i.e.*, the text.

CHAPTER XI

STORM AND STRESS (1720-1820)

THE eighteenth century—the most sombre in the history of Iceland—was a time of almost unrelieved material disaster with a melancholy outcome from which the nation has only just begun to recover. Storm and stress serves as a description of the whole period in three spheres: (i) elemental, (ii) political, (iii) bodily and mental.

(i) THE ELEMENTS AGAIN

(*a*) The population at the beginning of the century was 50,444. In 1800 it was 47,086. The increase in the nineteenth century, in spite of the loss of about 20,000 by emigration to Canada and U.S.A., amounted to 31,400, so that it may be said the diminution of population between 1700 and 1800 in effect meant there were 35,000 fewer people in the country in 1800 than there would have been in tolerable conditions—a loss of about 40 per cent.

It is a remarkable fact that the first census in Europe was taken in Iceland in 1700—a hundred years before such a step was contemplated in Great Britain, when the House of Lords rejected the proposal chiefly on the biblical ground that it was "tempting Providence" to bring on some national calamity. Such objectors might well have pointed to the experience of Iceland's population, the sequence, though not the result, of their census enterprise. The census was made from the full and accurate parish registers kept by pastors as the outcome of their regular visitations. Whatever charge can be made against Icelandic bishops and pastors, their systematic visitation of their people is exemplary. Such contacts did much to sustain the people in this century of plague, pestilence, and famine, from which we pray in the Litany to be delivered, with no thought of what such calamities demand in strength of character and depth of religion. In Iceland this century saw a concentrated outbreak of storms and volcanic eruptions, followed by earthquakes, devastating large tracts of the few habitable green valleys on the island. Except for the bishops and the holders of the half-dozen Crown benefices,[1] the clergy shared the life and the poverty of their people, following their precarious occupation of farming, and occupying

---

[1] In 1736 there were four "good livings"—*i.e.*, over £20 a year—in Skálholt diocese: Breidabólstad, Oddi, Stadarstad, Hitardal; and fifteen "mediocre." For Hólar we may add Grenjadarstad, £30 (F. J. III, p. 502).

parsonage houses no different from the labourers' cabins scattered
along sparse river valleys and an ungracious seaside.

(b) In this century many pastors had to endure the loss of church,
home, and family while exhorting their people to stoical endurance
and Christian resignation, if not hope. This is apparent in the vivid
account of the poignant experiences of his parish in the eruption of
1727 by Jón Thorlaksson, prestur of Sandfell in South-East Iceland:

"In the year 1727, on the 7th of August, which was the tenth
Sunday after Trinity, after the commencement of divine service in
the church of Sandfell, as I stood before the altar, I was sensible of a
gentle concussion under my feet, which I did not mind at first; but,
during the delivery of the sermon, the rocking continued to increase
so as to alarm the whole congregation; yet they remarked that the
like had often happened before. One of them, a very aged man,
repaired to a spring, a little below the house, where he prostrated
himself on the ground, and was laughed at by the rest for his pains;
but, on his return, I asked him what it was he wished to ascertain ?
to which he replied, 'Be on your guard, Sir; the earth is on fire !'
Turning, at the same moment, towards the church-door, it appeared
to me, and all who were present, as if the house contracted and drew
itself together. I now left the church, necessarily ruminating on what
the old man had said; and as I came opposite to Mount Flaga, and
looked up towards its summit, it appeared alternately to expand and
be heaved up, and fall again to its former state. Nor was I mistaken
in this, as the event shewed; for on the morning of the 8th, we not
only felt frequent and violent earthquakes, but also heard dreadful
reports, in no respect inferior to thunder. Everything that was
standing in the house was thrown down by these shocks; and there
was every reason to apprehend that mountains as well as houses
would be overturned in the catastrophe. What most augmented the
terror of the people was, that nobody could divine in what place the
disaster would originate, or where it would end.

"After nine o'clock three particularly loud reports were heard,
which were almost instantaneously followed by several eruptions of
water that gushed out, the last of which was the greatest, and completely carried away the horses and other animals that it overtook in
its course. When these exundations were over, the ice-mountain
itself ran down into the plain, just like melted metal poured out of a
crucible; and, on settling, filled it to such a height, that I could not
discover more of the well-known mountain Lomagnupr, than about
the size of a bird. The water now rushed down the east side without

intermission, and totally destroyed what little of the pasture-grounds remained. It was a most pitiable sight to behold the females crying, and my neighbours destitute both of counsel and courage; however, as I observed that the current directed its course towards my house, I removed my family up to the top of a high rock, on the side of the mountain, called Dalskardstorfa, where I caused a tent to be pitched, and all the church utensils, together with our food, clothes and other things that were most necessary, to be conveyed thither; drawing the conclusion that should the eruption break forth at some other place, this height would escape the longest, if it were the will of God, to whom we committed ourselves, and remained there.

"Things now assumed quite a different appearance. The Yökul [glacier] itself exploded, and precipitated masses of ice, many of which were hurled out to sea; but the thickest remained on the plain, at a short distance from the foot of the mountain. The noise and reports continuing, the atmosphere was so completely filled with fire and ashes, that day could scarcely be distinguished from night, by reason of the darkness which followed, and which was barely rendered visible by the light of the fire that had broken through five or six cracks in the mountain. In this manner the parish of Øroefa was tormented for three days together; yet it is not easy to describe the disaster as it was in reality; for the surface of the ground was entirely covered with pumice-sand, and it was impossible to go out in the open air with safety, on account of the red-hot stones that fell from the atmosphere. Any who did venture out had to cover their heads with buckets and such other wooden utensils as could afford them such protection.

" On the 11th it cleared up a little in the neighbourhood; but the ice-mountain still continued to send forth smoke and flames. The same day I rode, in company with three others, to see how matters stood with the parsonage, as it was most exposed; but we could only proceed with the utmost danger, as there was no other way except between the ice-mountain and the Yökul, which had been precipitated into the plain, where the water was so hot that the horses almost got unmanageable; and, just as we entertained the hope of getting through by this passage, I happened to look behind me, when I descried a fresh deluge of hot water directly above me, which, had it reached us, must inevitably have swept us before it. Contriving, of a sudden, to get on the ice, I called to my companions to make the utmost expedition in following me; and, by this means, we reached Sandfell in safety. The whole of the farm, together with the cottages of two tenants, had been destroyed; only the dwelling-houses remained, and a few spots of the túns. The people stood crying in the church. The cows, which, contrary to all expectation, both here and elsewhere, had escaped the disaster, were lowing beside a few hay-stacks that had been damaged during the eruption. At the time the exundation of the Yökul broke forth, the half of the people, belonging to the parsonage, were in four newly constructed sheepcotes, where two women and a boy took refuge on the roof of the highest; but they had hardly reached it when, being unable to resist the force of the thick mud that was borne against it, it was carried away by the deluge of hot water, and, as far as the eye could reach, the three unfortunate persons were seen clinging to the roof. One of the women was afterwards found among the substances that had proceeded from the Yökul, but burnt, and, as it were, parboiled; her body was so soft that it could scarcely be touched. Everything was in the most deplorable condition. The sheep were lost; some of which were washed up dead from the sea, in the third parish from the Ørœfa. The hay that was saved was found insufficient for the cows, so that a fifth part of them had to be killed; and most of the horses, which had not been swept into the ocean, were afterwards found completely mangled. The eastern part of the parish of Sida was also destroyed by the pumice and sand; and the inhabitants were, on that account, obliged to kill many of their cattle.

"The mountain continued to burn night and day, from the 8th of August, as already mentioned, till the beginning of summer, in the month of April the following year, at which time the stones were still so hot, that they could not be touched; and it did not cease to emit smoke till near the end of summer. Some of them had been completely calcined; some were black and full of holes; and others were so loose in their contexture that one could blow through them. On the first day of summer, 1728, I went in company with a person of quality to examine the cracks in the mountain, the most of which were so large that we could creep into them. I found here a quantity of saltpetre, and could have collected it, but did not choose to stay long in the excessive heat. At one place, a heavy calcined stone lay across the aperture; and as it rested on a small basis, we easily dislodged it into the chasm, but could not observe the least sign of it having reached the bottom.

"These are the most remarkable particulars that have occurred to me with respect to this mountain; thus God hath led me through fire and water, and brought me, through much trouble and adversity, to my eightieth year. To Him be the honour, the praise, and the glory for ever."[1]

(c) The disasters of the eighteenth century were unique in the history of the country, not by their occurrence, but on account of their concentrated intensity. Annals down the ages record volcanic eruptions followed by floods and earthquakes, losses of farms and cattle. Floods changing the courses of rivers occur owing to the intense heat of the eruption melting a glacier or mountain ice-cap and precipitating it into the plain. The fourteenth and seventeenth centuries with recorded dates of ten or a dozen local disasters are typical of almost any century, indicating the constant warfare these few and scattered people have had to wage against the elements.

In 1693 Hekla's seventeenth recorded eruption occurred, spreading ashes all over the island and casting dust 1,000 miles east and south over the seas to Norway and Scotland. The Icelanders' small meadows or túns and scantier cultivated patches became unproductive, and, as the Danish trade monopoly impeded food imports, wide-spread famine developed, intensified by excessively severe winters, so that the country lived up to its name and became ice-bound.[2] Many died in 1702, including 120 in the district of Thingvellir alone. In 1706 violent earthquakes in the region of Ølfüs destroyed 24 farms with many cattle. In 1707 an epidemic of small-pox carried off 18,000 of the underfed peasants, nearly one-third of the population.[3] At this period the suffering people were saved from despair by the bracing sermons of Bishop Jón Vidalin, who had lost many of his clergy. His theme was based on Dr Johnson's epigram, "it matters not how a man dies, but how he lives." Any natural feelings his hearers may have cherished that they were helpless in face of visita-tions of an angry Creator were transformed into stoical fortitude based on Christian repentance.

It was easy to see that a strong statesman-bishop of the ancient chieftain type would have withstood the despotic State officials and corrupt monopolists. Individual tyrants may be faced and slain, but bureaucratic vested interests are hydra-headed monsters too much for a modern St George on his own. Bishop Vidalin used with effect the method at his disposal and sublimated his people's suffer-ings; so that

"still even here content can spread a charm,
redress the clime and all its rage disarm."

[1] E. H., pp. 208-12.   [2] Espolin viii, 26.   [3] Gj., pp. 320-2.

In the years 1724-30 the north-east part of the island was inundated by a lava-flood after eruptions from Krabla, so that the district has hardened into a state resembling the arid mountains of the moon or the neighbourhood of the Dead Sea, the "seat of desolation," with boiling fetid mud pools locally regarded as lakes of hell.

Local farms were destroyed and their lands rendered unworkable. The church at Reykjahlid remained intact with the church farm on a mound, an oasis in the lava desert. When making my way in 1941 over this wilderness to visit the troops in the east, I broke the long, tiring journey at this little farm. I was given coffee and pancakes, for which no payment would be accepted. This should be stated, as some summer tourists have given a different impression of Icelanders. Nevertheless, in this region the inhospitable countryside has not produced an inhospitable people.

Krabla had no sooner subsided than the historic tracts of the south-east seaboard were devastated in 1727-8 by an eruption of Øraefa-jökull, Iceland's highest mountain (7,420 feet), whose glaciers dip down into the sea. The local results have been tellingly described by the octagenarian pastor of Sandfell, whose calm courage and leadership speak well for the country churchmanship of Iceland in this testing epoch.

Four years later the outbreaks moved westwards, and Rangarvellir —the fields by the Crooked River, often changing its course—had a dozen farmsteads destroyed and forty damaged.

In 1755 the eruption of Katla, another fissure in the great southern volcanic massif, immediately destroyed thirteen farms and spread lava and ashes so thickly over the district that fifty other farms had to be abandoned. Severe winters followed (as often), leading once more to famine, of which 2,500 persons died in the diocese of Skálholt in 1757. Sheep disease broke out in 1761, reducing the flocks in two years from 491,934 to 112,054. Sheep and cattle were provided by the landlord and replaced if they died of old age; but many landlords, including the Bishop of Skálholt's steward, held that disease was the fault of the tenant and demanded payment from the helpless crofter.[1]

(d) The climax of this century of calamities was the eruption of Laki in Skaptajökull in 1783, followed by a widespread earthquake and severe frosts. The Rev. Ebenezer Henderson, visiting the district less than a generation afterwards, describes this national disaster in his Journal in a way which catches the spirit of that day:

"The eruption of 1783 not only appears to have been more

[1] Gj., p. 325.

tremendous in its phenomena than any recorded in the modern annals of Iceland, but it was followed by a train of consequences the most direful and melancholy, some of which continue to be felt to this day. Immense floods of red-hot lava were poured down from the hills with amazing velocity, and, spreading over the low-country, burnt up men, cattle, churches, houses, and everything they attacked in their progress. Not only was all vegetation, in the immediate neighbourhood of the volcano, destroyed by the ashes, brimstone, and pumice, which it emitted; but, being borne up to an inconceivable height in the atmosphere, they were scattered over the whole island, impregnating the air with noxious vapours, intercepting the genial rays of the sun, and empoisoning whatever could satisfy the hunger or quench the thirst of man and beast. Even in some of the more distant districts, the quantity of ashes that fell was so great, that they were gathered up by handfuls. Upwards of four hundred people were instantly deprived of a home; the fish were driven from the coasts, and the elements seemed to vie with each other which should commit the greatest depredations; famine and pestilence stalked abroad, and cut down their victims with ruthless cruelty; while death himself was glutted with the prey. In some houses there was scarcely a sound individual left to tend the afflicted, or any who possessed ·sufficient strength to inter the dead. The most miserably emaciated tottering skeletons were seen in every quarter. When the animals that died of hunger and disease were consumed, the wretched creatures had nothing to eat but raw hides, and old pieces of leather and ropes, which they boiled and devoured with avidity. The horses ate the flesh off one another, and for want of other sustenance had recourse to turf, wood, and even excrementitious substances; while the sheep devoured each other's wool. In a word, the accumulation of miseries, originating in the volcanic eruption, was so dreadful, that, in the short space of two years, not fewer than 9,336 human beings, 28,000 horses, 11,461 head of cattle, and 190,488 sheep perished on the island."[1]

Seventy-eight farms were obliterated, 94 ruined, and 372 badly damaged. Over 500 houses were wrecked and 1,459 completely destroyed. Little was left of the historic cathedral and episcopal school at Skálholt.

The worst feature of this national disaster was the loss of a fifth of the population, with possible reactions on the minds and spirits of those who remained.

[1] E. H., pp. 220-1 (? some exaggeration in the figures).

Sudden and unexpected catastrophes may unnerve a whole nation and lead, as in the Far East, to an epidemic of bodily disease. The high mortality in Iceland during this period was due not to mental agony, but to the physical concomitants of tremendous volcanic eruptions. In many parts of the island people lived literally on the edge of a volcano, and they were braced to endurance by constant experience of hardships, close contact with the soil, and their moral equipment. The terrible volcano of Laki bears in its name a resemblance to Loki, the Scandinavian spirit of evil "in the earth beneath." But the people did not collapse in fear of an unknown fate overhanging them. Their intolerable burden came, not from within themselves (the source of most burdens), nor from the inscrutable forces of Nature, but from the grinding tyrannies of the State. In spite of their inexplicable visitations they might have cried with David, "I am in a great strait: let me fall now into the hand of the Lord; for very great are his mercies: but let me not fall into the hands of man."[1]

(ii) Church and State

After the devastating eruption and earthquake of 1783-4, the miserable population, reduced to 40,000, was faced with extinction. The country had suffered from prolonged ravages from the forces of Nature, and even more from the inefficiency, greed, and callousness of the Danish administration, a corrupt trade monopoly, and rack-rent and villeinage in the system of land tenure.

The immediate economic result of the disaster of 1783-4 was the abolition of the trade monopoly and the centralising of ecclesiastical and educational administration in Reykjavik.

(a) The tyranny of State officialdom and the harsh working of the trade monopoly may be illustrated by two instances out of a series of black records given in Stephensen's account of the eighteenth century in Iceland. In 1699 a poor peasant convicted of offering a few fish for sale outside his district was flogged in the presence of the amtmadr, or local governor, Christian Müller. The following year three men were sentenced to imprisonment with the confiscation of their household goods because they had bought two ells of kersey from an English fisherman.[2]

Increasingly high fees were paid for the trade monopoly by Danish merchants, who added these State charges to their prices; and as Icelanders had little money, the merchants sold inferior goods and

---

[1] 1 Chron. xxi, 13.　　　　[2] *Lovsamling for Island* I, pp. 406, 481.

falsified weights and measures.[1] The introduction of absolute rule
in 1661 led in Iceland to the dominance of a corrupt and lawless
bureaucracy, in which bishops and clergy, now appointed and paid
directly by the State, took their place as State officials, and, whether
they liked it or not, became involved in the grinding system of
exploiting the people.

In the earlier part of the century, as in 1699, protests initiated by
the bishops were sent to the king, but, though commissions were
appointed, usually the only result was an increase in the number of
officials. Nevertheless, the Government showed growing disquietude
about the affairs of a land that had become their dependency, to the
extent of instituting a series of enquiries, followed by reports on the
state of the country.

In 1741 Ludvig Harboe, the learned and influential Bishop of
Seeland, was appointed Visitor-General to investigate the state of
religion and education.[2] Undaunted by disasters, he remained four
years in the country, and by his presence and counsel instilled much-
needed staying power. It may be suggested that in our day a similar
though unofficial visit from a learned and sympathetic bishop of a
sister Church would do much to help the Church in Iceland to tackle
unusual modern problems due to a strange concomitance of un-
paralleled commercial world contacts and internal isolation. A noble
tribute was paid to Harboe's achievement by Finnur Jónsson,
Bishop of Skálholt 1754-85, in dedicating to him the fourth volume
of his monumental *Historia Ecclesiastica Islandiae*, completed up to
the year before Harboe came to the country. Bishop Harboe made a
report on the conditions of Iceland, paying special regard to education,
and in the spacious manner of the time not neglecting natural
history;[3] but the only immediate practical outcome of his visit seems
to have been the issue of a new edition of the Bible in 1747, reprinted
from the admirable text of 1644, for which a tax of 1 riks-dollar
(=4s.) was levied on every parish. A thousand copies were printed
and sold at 2½ dollars each. As this price was more than most people
could afford, in 1750 a New Testament was published to sell at
3 marks a copy (=2s.).[4]

In 1772 the Icelanders Eggert Olafsson and Bjarni Pálsson,
commissioned in 1751 by a well-disposed king to report on the
country, made such a comprehensive survey of its economic conditions and natural features that it evoked widespread interest in

---

[1] Gj., pp. 335-9.
[2] J. H. II, pp. 251-65.
[3] Trans. into English, published 1758.
[4] E. H., pp. 489-91.

Northern Europe and led to a series of visits from influential foreigners.[1] The earliest and most distinguished of these, Dr (afterwards Abp) Uno von Troil, chaplain to the King of Sweden, and Sir Joseph Banks, later President of the Royal Society, took steps to make known their conclusions and the desperate plight of the people owing to the callous administration of the Danish Government.[2] Sir Joseph Banks (privately) reported that the bishops and the two State officials were the only men of authority in the country, and the settlement of the bishop and his retainers at Skálholt was the only attempt at a town.[3]

(b) The voice of protest that the Church should have raised was weakened by the implication of bishops and the richer clergy in the State system of land tenure. According to the *Liber Villarum* of 1695, the Bishop of Skálholt owned 304 farms; the Bishop of Hólar 345; 640 were allotted to parochial glebes, 45 to pensioned pastors, 16 to the poor, and 4 to leper hospitals. The Crown held 718 farms confiscated from the monasteries; so that there were only 1,847 free farms in the country, while the Crown and Church held 2,112.

A farm was generally leased at one-twentieth of its taxable value. The rent was not lowered in spite of deterioration owing to natural causes, and if the land was so damaged that the rent could not be paid a levy was made on the tenant's household goods. Subletting was extensively practised. Some pastors followed the demoralising example of officials and sublet the farms they leased to tenants who could barely make a pittance from their husbandry, and were required to render a service as well as rent. The severity of these exactions is amply illustrated in the accounts of Iceland in the eighteenth century. A farmer ordered to row a deputy across a fjörd refused to do it for nothing, and was brought before the Lawman, now not much more than a tool in the hands of the State, who sentenced him to be flogged twice. Individual bishops and pastors denounced the travesty of government exemplified by this kind of tyranny, and bitter struggles between clergy and officials were frequent; but the Church produced no outstanding champion of the people, so that indignation took the form of personal and local

[1] Reise igiennem Island, Soroe 1772; epitome, London, 1805. Eggert (* 1726, † 1768—drowned) was also a patriotic and religious poet and reformer (*Islandica* XVI).

[2] Von Troil, *Letters on I.*, trans. London, 1780.

[3] *Islandica* XVIII, pp. 26, 29; cp. *inf.*, p. 201. Scandinavia only recently has taken to towns. In Iceland tún implies a farmstead. Reykjavik, the capital, was no more than that until 1752 (*Dic. C.V.*). Cp. p. 37.

quarrels, in which any protest that reached Denmark was discounted by the fact that the State itself and even the Church were involved in the corrupt administration.

(c) The first step in practical opposition to the tyranny of officials and merchants and in restoring independence and self-reliance to the depressed Icelanders was taken in 1784 by the appointment of a native administrator, Skúli Magnússon (1711-94), to succeed the notorious Christians Müller and Dresse. He was a man of vision and action. With the co-operation of King Frederick V in 1752 he built mills at a hamlet on the south shores of Faxafjörd called Reykjavik, and bought an open sea fishing fleet. He imported foreigners to teach weaving and farming.[1] The monopolists' reaction was speedy and forceful. The merchants, seeing their profits in danger, refused to handle the goods; whereupon Magnússon sued them for past corruption, and the company was dissolved. But its successor deemed that it had bought its "goodwill," and attempted the same exploitation with some success, until they brought to dump on Iceland flour condemned in Copenhagen, so full of worms and mildew that not even the omnivorous cattle would touch it. Magnússon encouraged the people to throw it into the sea, and had the company heavily fined.[2]

This vigorous resuscitation of the old Icelandic spirit, together with the national disasters of 1783-4, led to the abolition of the trade monopoly in 1787.[3]

After Skálholt was destroyed it was natural to establish in Reykjavik the new cathedral and school, for it was rapidly becoming the commercial and fishing centre of the country. But it became evident that there was more in the transference than convenience when the ancient ecclesiastical and educational centre at Hólar in the north was also suppressed and its cathedral and school merged in the new Reykjavik establishments.

The leader in this centralising movement was the ambitious and versatile Magnus Stephensen (1762-1833), whose affinities are significantly advertised in the Danish way in which he spelt his name. He led the people, battered by a century of physical calamities, to look to continental culture rather than to national resources for the country's salvation. He maintained that pride in Icelandic literature and ideals was no more than futile nostalgia, so that men for

[1] *Lovsamling for Island* I, pp. 107 *sq.*
[2] Gj., pp. 340-2.
[3] This measure freed trade only for all Danish citizens, and Icelanders were too poor for many years to take advantage of it. Free trade for all nations was not granted until 1854.

a time ceased to find inspiration in the ancient historic centres of national life.

The destruction of Skálholt provided a reasonable excuse for abandonment of its time-honoured institutions; but even so, Skálholt school with forty students had as many as the congested establishment at Bessastadir ever contained.[1] And the suppression of Hólar with its thirty-four scholars did an injustice to the families in the north and east of the island, which Sir Richard Burton found in 1872 to be still a "prime grievance."[2]

This centralisation brought about also the lapse of the two episcopal theological colleges, so that training of candidates for the ministry was seriously handicapped until the University of Reykjavik was founded in 1911.

Impartial judgment on the merging of the two cathedrals is difficult for a student who has traced the moving story of their vicissitudes for 700 years. It is easy to see the expediency of the move, but for the people, for whom the past means much, it must have been a grave loss to abandon the local and historical associations of St Jón of Hólar and St Thorlak of Skálholt. Moreover, there is more than sentiment in the pronouncement of Isleif, the first bishop and founder of the mother-church of the country at Skálholt: "There shall always be a bishop's chair there, while Iceland is inhabited and Christianity endures." It is significant that Christianity was at its lowest ebb in Iceland when the bishop's chair was moved.

Centralisation generally raises more problems than it solves and tends to destroy the only spirit that can grapple with them.

(iii) Poverty, Apathy, and Rationalism

The centralising movement which was the outcome of the disasters culminating in 1783-4 took some time to alleviate the burden of poverty accumulated in that sombre period, and aggravated rather than lessened the growing deadness of spirit accompanied by a loss of faith sometimes dignified by the term "rationalism."

(a) For the relief of the sufferers of the earthquake Denmark collected about £8,000, but only about a quarter of it reached the

---

[1] P. P., pp. 365 sq. The "Latin," i.e. Grammar, school, set up in Rvk 1801-5 was moved to Bessastadir 1805-46, after which it returned to the capital. For bad conditions, see E. H., p. 287.

[2] Ultima Thule I, p. 155; II. pp. 44-6. So in 1814 E. H., p. 110; Hooker (1811) I, p. 352.

unfortunate victims. The rest went on expenses of a survey and on general administration.[1] The removal of the trade monopoly only freed commerce for all citizens of Iceland-Denmark, and, as Icelanders were too poor to trade, Danish merchants, as before, charged what they liked. A plan was actually considered for removing the whole population of Iceland as a colony to the plains of Jutland; but at this time the north was comparatively immune from disaster, and Icelanders would rather starve in their own homeland than grow fat elsewhere. As Seneca says, "Nemo patriam amat quia magna, sed quia sua."

However, a generation later the whole country was in danger of starvation. For in the Napoleonic wars England stood at bay against the conqueror of the European continent, and, unable as ever to brook an enemy on her flank, she destroyed the Danish fleet at the Battle of Copenhagen, 1801,[2] and afterwards blockaded the ports of Denmark, which would have cut off most of the food supply of Iceland. But Sir Joseph Banks, the Privy Councillor who visited Iceland in 1772, prevailed on the British Government to allow trade via Leith, and so matters were eased. This friendly gesture is set out in an Order in Council dated February 7, 1810, which declares that "His Majesty being moved by compassion for the sufferings of these defenceless people . . . orders that they be exempted from attack . . . and be regarded as Stranger Friends under the safeguard of His Majesty's royal Peace, and in no case to be treated as alien enemies."[3]

The treaty of peace in 1814, though it ceded Norway to Sweden, left Iceland tied to Denmark, with which it had no original historic connection (as it had with Norway, especially since 1262). Nevertheless, conditions slowly improved and the population increased, so that in 1823 it again numbered 50,000—the figure of 1703, though that was no larger than the total in the eleventh century, when Bishop Gizur had a tithe census made.

The poverty of the clergy and the squalor in which they lived is emphasised in the accounts, both classics in their way, written by visitors of different temperaments and avocations, Sir W. J. Hooker (1809) and the Rev. Ebenezer Henderson (1814-5). Stipends appear miserably small, the richest income being about 200 riks-dollars

---

[1] Gj., pp. 343-4.

[2] This victory was chiefly due to Nelson, second-in-command, who (according to Southey) turned his blind eye to the Commander's signal to break off action in view of losses. He showed then his instinct for vigorously engaging the enemy at his weakest point (the "Nelson touch").

[3] E. H., pp. 402-4.

(£40). Most pastors received about 35 riks-dollars and the poorest of them about 5. This income came from the State, being a partial reimbursement of the money which the Crown retained from confiscated Churchlands, for only in that sense can Icelandic clergy be said to be State-paid. In addition, pastors had a glebe-house and farm rent-free with some fees, so that in this respect they were better off than their country parishioners. The prestur of Thingvellir in 1809 received £5 a year with glebe sufficient to pasture 5 cows and 28 sheep. His parsonage, like most country homes of the period, was a mere cabin, dark, damp, and squalid, with a small window of membrane of a sheep's womb or stomach, and a roof of turves laid on driftwood or on ribs of a whale. The food would consist of dried fish or, once or twice in winter, of mutton, occasional sour ryebread or imported biscuits, bread made from lichen or wild oats, with rancid butter. This acidulous diet on occasions would be helped down with a delicious dessert of skyr or curds mixed with crowberries, the only native fruit.[1] At Middalur the prestur received £4 and worked as a blacksmith.[2] It is not surprising that to support their families clergy laboured as farmers or fishermen, as carpenters or blacksmiths, though there is nothing unapostolic in this.

It must have been helpful to their own lives and to those of their people that pastors shared in the incessant and precarious toil of wresting a subsistence from their ungracious and aggressive countryside or on their grim grey seas.

The clergy had two or three professional means of uplift not readily open to the laity, which served to keep them human in an existence lived too close to the soil—pastoral visitation, teaching, and study. Study, though more advanced in clerics, has been the laudable practice of all Icelanders. Pastoral visitation was thorough and systematic. Mention has been made of the fact that the earliest census in Europe was made possible by the accuracy of details entered in the parish registers. Not only were "characters" recorded as in a school report, but also religious and educational progress. Parents acted as teachers and clergy as catechists, so that, despite stress of poverty, traditional Icelandic scholarship was not dis-

---

[1] Von Troil, *Letters on Iceland*, pp. 99-112. Earlier observers note the liking for eating "candles" (*i.e.*, whale-oil, a help against extreme cold); cp. Andrew Boorde, 1542: "When I eat candle ends I am at a feast. Talow and raw stockfish I do love to ete." For hovels see Mackenzie, *Travels*, p. 115.

[2] Hooker, *Journal* I, pp. 96, 129-30; E. H., p. 33; Burton, *Ultima Thule* I, p. 164. Average clerical incomes in England, eighteenth century, £30-60 (O. M. Trevelyan, *Blenheim*, pp. 46-7).

EXTRACT FROM GLÆSIBÆJAR PARISH REGISTER, 1785

Farm.	Name.	Occupation.	Age.	Confirmed.	Able to read.	Conduct.	General Abilities.
Hladir in Thelamörk.	Markús Markússon	Householder	63	Yes	Able to read	Trustworthy Pious	Ready to render service. Clean.
	Bergthóra Arnadóttir	His wife	64	Yes	Able to read	Pious Peaceable	Ready to render service and industrious.
	Arni Markússon	Their son	23	Yes	Able to read	Well-behaved	Good general knowledge. Intelligent.
	Thorgerdur Markúsdóttir	Their daughter	27	Yes	Able to read	Mediocre	Slow to understand.
	Thorbjörg Benediktsdóttir	Fosterchild	13	No	Able to read	Well-behaved	Can read prayers.
	Helga Olafsdóttir	A pauper	30	Yes	Able to read	Peaceable	Dull and ignorant.

Books in the house: Vidalin's Sermons, Choral Book, 2 books by Jon Arndts, Sermons by Gerhardi, 2 vols. Hallgrim's Passion Hymns, Fons Vitæ 1598 (in Icelandic translation), Hymn-Book, the New Testament, and several other books.

continued.[1] Icelandic parish clergy may have neglected their priesthood and become too wayworn or callous to be arresting prophets,
but they faithfully exercised their ministry as sedulous pastors. The
Church, though poor in itself, did not neglect the evangelical duty
of almsgiving. In pre-Reformation days paupers used to be supported by a fourth part of the tithe and on Church estates, the founders
of which often stipulated that a poor relation should be a first charge
on the endowment. Afterwards a nidursetningur ("one who is
down") was kept by inhabitants of his native parish in turns.[2]
Retired pastors and widows were supported by those who had the
richer benefices and by a portion of the State reimbursements.[3]

Personal sublimation of poverty is finely illustrated in two sketches
of pastors given by Dr Henderson in 1814. Sira Jón Jónsson, prestur
of Audabrekka, he writes, is the doctor, counsellor, and leader of his
people. "His house is literally a Bethesda," his parlour does duty as
library and apothecary's shop. He zealously instructs his flock,
especially the rising generation, whom he regards as the most
important part of his ministerial charge. In his parish register he
enters regularly the character and circumstances of his parishioners,
who number 400. Crime, especially drunkenness, has decreased
owing to the high price of spirituous liquors. "Our poverty," the
prestur avers, "is the bulwark of our happiness."

A neighbouring pastor, Jón Thorlaksson, over seventy years of age,
was found in August, like most of his brethren, helping in the hay-
field. He lived in one tiny room, 8 feet by 6 feet, with a door 4 feet
high and a window 2 feet square. His endowment amounted to about
£6 a year. His bookshelves contained English, French, and German
works, and he had acquired merit by making an Icelandic version of
Milton's *Paradise Lost*.[4] He embodied in a verse his reflections on
his state:

> "Pale poverty hath dogged my steps
>   Since in this world my life did start;
> For threescore years and ten our ways
>   Have seldom wandered far apart.
> Whether in heaven I'll shake her clear
> He only knows who joined us here."[5]

---

[1] E. H., p. 285; see reproduction on opposite page.

[2] E. H., pp. 122-3. Arngrim Jónsson states that inveterate beggars were
castrated (*Isl. Tractatus*, p. 437). Vagabond in Icelandic =hlaupingi; ? hence
land-loper, later land-lubber, often a sailor.

[3] A widow enjoyed for a year of grace the benefice income (F. J. III, p. 337).

[4] E. H., pp. 98-102.   [5] Trans. Watson Kirkconnell, *Icelandic Verse*.

(*b*) Such men of God were exceptional in their resignation. Isolation and hard conditions drove many people to apathy. Those who depended for their living on the sale of cod, whale oil, or their home-spun wadmal, found for more than a century that they had to barter their hard-won goods for a trifle. Injustice and oppression hardened their outlook on life and made them less eager to face their native difficulties and disasters. The iron entered into their souls. As Milton reminds us, "Our torments may also in length of time become our elements " (*P.L.* 274).

In 1772 von Troil described the Icelanders he saw as "of a good honest disposition, but so serious and sullen that I hardly remember to have seen any one of them laugh."[1] A generation later the traveller Hooker considered that their amusements were "not of a kind to dispel the gloomy habit which continually hangs about them." He reports their amusements to be an occasional game of cards and the recounting of their past history.[2] But what actually was depressing in those days was not that, like Englishmen, they took their pleasures sadly, but that they found no joy in their work. When the worker is deprived of the fruits of his labours, even so skilful and hazardous a pursuit as fishing, or one so exhilarating as haymaking, becomes drudgery, and the human spirit is abased.[3]

Thus unjust trade conditions reinforced the depression induced by calamities and isolation; but although individual pastors showed a sense of duty and devotion, the chief clergy evinced no real leadership. The general tendency of religion in the country at this time was quietist and fatalistic—passive resignation to the divine and human powers harshly regulating Icelandic affairs. The "higher" clergy escaped from an unfeeling and materialistic economy and the devastating forces of the universe into a world of literary study, patient sermonising, and personal benevolence. A typical example of their apathy is illustrated in Finnur Jónsson's tombstone-like eulogy of Stein Jónsson, Bishop of Hólar 1711-39, at a time when a large part of his diocese had been ruined by six years of volcanic eruptions, and thousands had died of hunger:

"Tall, bearded, strong, he was placid, affable, easygoing, humane,

---

[1] *Letters on Iceland*, p. 27; similarly Sir Joseph Banks, *Islandica* XVIII, pp. 28, 37.

[2] *Journal* I, p. lxxxix. He notes the decline of glima (wrestling), pony-racing, and chess. An old law forbids gambling.

[3] Today when the country is being over-commercialised the slave-driver is industrialism.

. . . popular, . . . never angry, scarcely ever moved, kindly to the wretched and needy. . . . With State officials he maintained good relations, for he never hurt or worried anyone, and overlooked the delinquencies of others. He was a competent student, and his writings breathe a spirit of singular piety and patience."[1] In his episcopate of twenty-eight years he ordained sixty-eight priests.

Subsequent bishops and richer clergy show a similar complacency, but, with the exception of the historian Finnur Jónsson, Bishop of Skálholt 1754-85, less literary powers. Their hands were tied by their monetary dependence upon the Crown.

After his popular visit in 1772, Sir Joseph Banks considered that the prevailing apathy was due not only to the succession of disasters, but to the prolonged trade oppression and State profiteering; and on that account advocated the taking over by England of the administration of Iceland either by purchase or annexation. He thought that, if force were needed, 500 soldiers would be sufficient for the capture of the two bishops and the two State officials, the only men of any standing in the island; he had reason to know that the unhappy people would welcome such a step.[2]

In the dark days at the end of the century, the only leader to strike a helpful note was Bishop Hannes Finnsson, son of the historian. In the earthquake of 1783 he was ill in bed at Skálholt, when the buildings collapsed over him; nevertheless, he lived to succeed his father as bishop (1785-96), and in 1796 published a notable treatise "On the decrease of population in Iceland," with the double motive of rousing Danish or other governments to action and, by depicting the heroic endurance of his countrymen through difficult centuries, to kindle new hope in the hearts of his people.[3]

(c) Through contact with Europe brought about by centralisation the apathy of many hardened into rationalism. Stolid Icelanders had survived a century of physical disaster, but the economic earthquake which followed almost made havoc of their faith. In his estimate of the country in 1809 Hooker makes a naive comment: "Many works on divinity have appeared since the Reformation, but happily for Iceland metaphysics do not appear to have occupied the attention of Icelanders to a great degree."[4] Deprived thus of philosophy and with

---

[1] F. J., pp. 749-50. His publications through his press included three editions of Vidalin's Sermons, a Triumphal Psalter and Hymn Book, and an anthology of Lassenius, Tarrapress, and Rachlow.
[2] *Islandica* XVIII, pp. 28 *sq.*, 83-5.
[3] J. H., *H. F. Biskup i Skálholti*, Rvk, 1936.
[4] W. J. Hooker, *Journal* I, p. lxxxi.

their religion at a low ebb, it is not surprising that intercourse with the complexities of commercialism drove them to freethinking and secularism.

In spite of its independent spirit, Iceland is a law-abiding country, and has always been free from open heresy and schism. In the first half of the eighteenth century Bishop Finnur Jónsson records only two cases of marked Socinianism, a Unitarian tendency latent in Icelandic Lutheranism. But Icelanders are tolerant and Lutheranism is a liberal creed. Much Unitarianism existed unchecked, especially when bishops were infected. At the end of the century, when intercourse with the larger world increased, a wave of "enlightenment" broke on the hard grey shores of Icelandic realism. On the crest of this movement rode the versatile continentalised leader Magnus Stephensen.[1] His abolition of the historic bishoprics, hard fact as it was, proved to be symbolic of his desire to remove or at least "improve" the Faith for which they had stood for 800 years. Arising out of a State order issued in 1784, he produced with the help of a future bishop a revised hymn-book, as the old psalter called Grallarinn was considered "mystical" and therefore "out of date." His new book, published in 1801, had the appeal of sentimental rhymes and ideas. The old hymns were purged not only from obsolete and difficult words, but also from what were considered difficult doctrines, such as the Divinity of Christ and the Atonement, and the Person and Work of the Holy Spirit; so that the result was a Socinian hymn-book.[2]

The work met with strong opposition. Many country parishes refused to introduce it. Nevertheless, clergy and people and the bishop (for by this time Iceland had only one) were influenced by this new theology. Many young men sent to the capital to school came back indifferent or sceptical. In those days began the tendency, still much in evidence, of emphasising the practical rather than the devotional side of Christianity. Hooker's report of the introduction of Pope's Universal Prayer into church worship can only refer to an isolated instance,[3] but the theme of a sermon preached at Holmar on August 28, 1814, "Christ's life on earth, a life of benevolence and usefulness," is typical of Icelandic sermons from that day to this.

The wave of Stephensen's influence soon spent itself. For the strength of the Church lies, not in such opportunist devices as his hymn-book, but in the steady witness of the homes and lives of its

---

[1] Gj., pp. 348-9.   [2] E. H., pp. 169-70.
[3] Journal I, p. 279; E. H., p. 171.

adherents. That the negative force of the time-spirit failed to quench this witness is shown by examples noted by many visitors. Some churches may have been neglected and used as storehouses, and services intermitted through lack of faith or congregations; but in 1814-5 Henderson found "the exercise of family worship attended to in almost every family from Michaelmas to Easter." Distances are so great in Iceland that two or three families, isolated in the desert, would meet at a house of prayer (bœnahús) twice a year for Communion, and services or family prayers were held in cottage parlours.[1] Personal piety was marked. On setting out for a journey it was customary for men to remove their hats and ask for God's protection; and similarly when they set their ponies to ford a river. Fishermen putting out to sea would likewise pray for a blessing and guidance.[2] This custom still continues. Icelandic hymn-books provide a prayer for sailors to use called "sjóferdasálm," and one for other travellers called "ferdabaen." Moreover, when it was realised that religion embraces the whole of life, grace before meals became natural, according to the injunction of the Shorter Catechism. "It is" (Henderson records) "universally the custom in Icelandic families to give thanks to God with clasped hands before and after meals." When the opening grace is finished guests "turn to the master of the house (the mistress never sits at table, being engaged in serving) and says: 'Gif mér mat med Guds fridr'" (Let me now partake in the peace of God).[3]

There may be poverty there, but not apathy or lack of faith.

---

[1] E. H., pp. 95, 163, 285, 306, 375.
[2] E. H., p. 123; von Ţroil, *Letters*, p. 89.   [3] E. H., p. 100.

CHAPTER XII

REORGANISATION (NINETEENTH CENTURY)

(i) NATIONAL REBIRTH

THE *Aufklarung* movement of Magnus Stephensen faded when Iceland lost contact with Denmark and the Continent from 1800 to 1814, during the European war. The downfall of Napoleon led to a revival of ideals of independence, not least in the northern countries; and the grant of a constitution to Norway (to which Iceland was attached by origin and traditions rather than to Denmark) provided a spur to Iceland's aspirations to autonomy.[1]

The realistic impulse spent itself in a pessimism which it found and increased in the national temperament, though it found there also its solvent in the people's romantic admiration of the past and its heroic achievements. At the approach of Iceland's Millennium in 1874 it led to a threat of wholesale emigration, staved off by one of the church leaders.[2] But although it had little political influence, it was responsible for the country's modern novels, bringing home to the people the complexity of the industrial world and the fact that they should not drift on listlessly dreaming in a saga mentality.

(*a*) If a date is to be given for the rebirth of national idealism, it may be found in the Revolution in France in July, 1830. Just before that the Icelanders had been roused from apathy by Baldvin Einarsson, 1801-33, a student in Copenhagen who founded a patriotic magazine in which he demanded the restoration of the Althing. He died young, but the torch of his enthusiasm was taken up by a young prestur, Tómas Saemundsson, who with able supporters established a periodical, *Fjölnir*,[3] the second of such rallying tracts for the times. After seven years of leadership his inspiring personality also burnt itself out († 1841). But he handed on the fiery cross of freedom to a successor, destined to lead the country along the thorny path of political agitation to the dizzy height of self-government. This was Jón Sigurdsson, an outstanding scholar and statesman, built on the lines of the great Snorri Sturluson. Jón Sigurdsson (1811-79) was the founder of modern Iceland.[4] Step by step he won for his people almost all their ancient rights, teaching them for over thirty years

---

[1] Gj., pp. 370 *sq*. Gj. is exceptionally full on this period.
[2] Gj., p. 409; "Nordenfari" for Aug. 23, 1872.
[3] Fjölnir = wise, attribute of Odin.
[4] Gj., pp. 375 *sq*.

by his periodical *Ny Félagsrit*, in which he discussed problems of government, education, trade, and finance. He harnessed the romantic idealism of the Tómas Saemundsson group to constructive politics and national responsibility. Tradition by itself may evaporate in romanticism; freedom without a background tends to be individualistic and irresponsible. It was the merit of the patriot Jón Sigurdsson to claim his country's liberty on the basis of historic tradition.

The chief problems concerning Iceland forced on the consideration of Denmark by the persistence of Jón Sigurdsson were constitutional and financial. Icelanders held the firm conviction that the only connection between their country and Denmark was the personal link of the Crown. They maintained that the Act of Union with Norway in 1262—the Gamli sáttmáli, establishing the Jónsbók as the Code of Law for Iceland, though modified in respect to the Crown by the Kalmar Union of 1397—was still in force, as the king had renounced the absolute monarchy claimed in 1662.[1]

Under pressure of events and the influence of Sira Tómas' movement, the Althing, abolished in 1800, was re-established on March 8, 1843, and met at Reykjavik in 1845. With few representatives and fewer powers, it was a mere shadow of its traditional self. This was a victory for the national idealists, but so unsubstantial that it was from the start regarded as a fulcrum.

The next stage in the struggle—to make the Althing properly representative and consultative—owed much to the work of patriotic pastors. For a century or more bishops had taken little part in championing the real grievances of their people against Danish aggression, as their economic dependence on the State made them, however unwillingly, State officials. In an equalitarian society such as Iceland the clergy always had considerable influence, and effected much, though Bishop Finnur Jónsson sectionalises his great history, produced under royal patronage, chiefly under the headings of kings and bishops, and Bishop Jón Helgason's account unduly emphasises episcopal achievements. But in the struggle for autonomy in the nineteenth century it is evident that pastors played a leading part.

In 1848 a liberal nationalist newspaper (*Thjodólfr*) was founded by Sira Sveinbjörn Hallgrimsson, demanding a constitution for Iceland. This led to an informal meeting presided over by Pétur Pétursson, afterwards Bishop of Iceland (1866-89). In 1853 a similar meeting

---

[1] Burton, *Ultima Thule* I, p. 104.

was called on the historic site of Thingvellir by Sira Hannes Stephensen. Probably it was due to this stirring of public opinion that the
next year saw the end of a long-standing grievance—the Danish
trade monopoly. Crown agents were abolished and trade was made
free to all. (April 15, 1854.)

(b) The restoration of the Althing and the establishment of Free
Trade were indeed marked advances in the direction of autonomy,
but most Icelanders regarded them as mere stages on the road to
freedom, as neither the constitutional problem nor the financial
grievance had been settled.

Somewhat rashly, the Danish Government raised the question of
finance on the doubtful ground that Iceland contributed nothing to
its own support, but rather made a perpetual drain on Danish
resources. The Icelanders admitted that the cost of administering
the scanty medical and educational services and payment of the
bishop and officials, costing about 60,000 dollars a year, came from
the Danish treasury, but pointed out that the Icelandic estates which
had supported the bishops and schools were sold in 1785 by the
Crown on condition that the treasury met these charges.[1] Furthermore, the moneys from sales of Church estates had all been claimed
by Denmark, in addition to fees for the trade monopoly, so that a
substantial balance was actually due to Iceland.[2]

The bishop in 1809, as part return for the sale of the episcopal
estates, received 1,248 riks-dollars, with an augmentation of 600
dollars, making 1,848 dollars a year. The Reykjavik prestur received
22. As a comparison it may be stated that the Lecturer in Theology
was paid 600 dollars.[3] Holders of Crown benefices and some other
clergy were granted some reimbursement for parish glebes confiscated at the Reformation; but in all cases Icelandic ecclesiastical
estates put into the treasury more than was returned. Only in that
sense was the Church State-supported.

The Danish Government realised the strength of Icelandic claims,
and subsequently went far to meet them. But after comparatively
generous financial offers by Denmark in 1867-71 it became clear that
the economic question would not be settled until Iceland was given
a real decision in her own affairs.

(c) The attitude of the country on the constitutional question was

[1] Most monastic estates were sold in 1674 for 24,162 riks-dollars, and the
Crown claimed the proceeds. In 1809 Iceland had only six doctors.

[2] P. P., pp. 149-54; Hooker, *Journal*, 1809, p. xxxi; Burton, *Ultima Thule*
I, p. 164 (1875). In 1875 Bp=3416r.d., but money had halved in value.

[3] In 1809 1 doll.=6 mks=about 4s., so the Bishop received £369.

idealistic, going far back into the history and traditions of the nation.
Thus the appointment of officials, judges, and laws by an external
power was regarded as a breach of time-honoured privilege. And
though Danish efficient bureaucracy and the growing commercial
prosperity of Reykjavik tempted some to compromise, idealistic poets
eloquently supported their country's campaign by raising their voices
against the nation selling its soul for a mess of pottage.

A leading schoolmaster, Steingrim Thorsteinsson (1831-1913),
thus epitomises the rival appeals:

> The lion often hungers, and yet
> Though the swine be well fed and all that,
>   Higher the desert is set
> Than the sty where the others grow fat.[1]

Bjarni Thorarensen (1786-1841) and Jónas Hallgrimsson (1807-
45), poets of loftier genius, had already appealed to the national
tradition and character and to the glories of the history and nature
of their country. Jónas, son of a parsonage, was a co-founder of
Fjölnir. He died young, an exile lonely and destitute, but his lyric
poems mark him out as a pioneer of modern Icelandic literature.
Thorarensen, magistrate and amtman, a devout Christian with an
intense love of the traditions and beauty of his native land, had been
chiefly responsible for the fall of the Stephensen continentalising
movement. He conjures up the heroes of the past and bids people
imitate the fortitude and heroism of their forefathers. He shows how
the rugged grandeur of the country is to be preferred to the flat fields
of Denmark. "Why should not Icelanders take heart ? Let them fight
again, as of old against fire and frost, against enervating foreign
influence. Better die with honour than live in shame."[2]

One of the favourite heroic epithets in the sagas is "skörungr,"
which contains in it the element of scaur, an isolated rock in the sea,
a beacon of unyielding strength.[3] This national attribute is finely
expressed by Thorarensen in the following poem:

> The skerry away in the fjörd
>   So deep in the sea's unrest
> In silence endures for ever
>   The foam that beats on its breast.

---

[1] Trans. Vilhjálmur Stefánsson in *Icelandic Lyrics*.
[2] Gj., pp. 368-9.   [3] Applied in Hv. to Bps Magnus, Klaeng, etc.

Mean is the man who is weaker
Than senseless rock in the strife,
And yields to the clash of the billows,
The countering currents of life.[1]

These pioneers of the nineteenth-century idealistic school were
followed by a succession of able pastor-poets, of whom the most
notable were Valdimar Briem, whose literary energies, after the
achievement of independence, were devoted to composing the most
inspiring of modern Icelandic hymns; and Sira Matthias Jochumsson,
perhaps the greatest national poet of the century, famous for his
Millennial National Anthem.

(d) The granting of a constitution to Iceland, the outcome of a
prolonged though not bitter struggle, aptly coincided with the
advent of the country's millennium in 1874—Iceland's thousand
years. For some time before this the national prospects appeared so
hopeless that thousands proposed to follow the hundreds who through
poverty had begun to seek a home across the Atlantic, but this counsel
of despair was overruled (see page 222).

In June, 1873, a public meeting about the constitutional question
was held, significantly at Thingvellir and not in Reykjavik. From
this self-appointed but representative assembly a petition was sent
to the king asking for a constitution giving the Althing legislative
power and control of the country's finance. This move was successful.
On June 5, 1874, Iceland was granted self-government. Icelanders
were guaranteed freedom from forced labour (the bane of the
previous century), freedom of the press (poets had been imprisoned),
security of private property, and sanctity of the home. The Lutheran
Church was recognised as the State Church, though liberty of
conscience was granted to all. There were some privileges withheld
which the country regarded as necessary for its complete independence, but it was recognised that time was on its side and all would
eventually be won.[2]

It was not, however, contemplated that final freedom would come
when most of the continent of Europe was enslaved. Full independence was granted on December 1, 1918, the only union between
Iceland and Denmark being at last recognised as the king. "Dane-

---

[1] Trans. Miss E. J. Oswald. The poem echoes the counsel of Marcus
Aurelius quoted at the beginning of Stefán Stefánsson's valuable *Handbook
for Tourists*: "Stand firm like a rock, which stands unmoved though the
waves batter against it, and they fall at last." (For word see *Dic. C.V.*)

[2] Gj., pp. 410-1; Bayard Taylor, *Egypt and Iceland*, pp. 269 *sq.*

brog" was struck, and the hardly-won Icelandic national flag—a red cross on a blue ground—was hoisted, the symbol of a sovereign state. "We pray God," said the minister, "to help us to carry our flag to honour. . . . So let us hoist the flag!"[1] A treaty was signed, open to revision by either side after twenty-five years. But the occupation of Denmark by Germany in 1940 made communication impossible, and in 1941, on June 17, Jón Sigurdsson's birthday, the Althing, having decided not to renew the treaty, elected a regent and became a republic. Icelandic flags were flying from every building; arctic terns darted over the sea and lake in the clear air, and the sun went not down that night. Three years later the Republic was proclaimed and Sveinn Björnsson was appointed its first President.

Such acquisition of freedom should be a good omen for the countries groaning under an oppressor, for, as Montesquieu reminds us, "Scandinavian liberty is the mother of the liberties of Europe." However, it must not be forgotten that, although Denmark's political and economic hold on Iceland has been crippling, the strong cultural and spiritual ties between the countries will remain.[2]

The Millennium (874-1874) so aptly epitomises Iceland's dogged and persistent struggles for freedom and heralds its new birth that it may well conclude this section.

The occasion was celebrated as a great national and religious festival. To present the country with its new constitution, King Christian IX came over from Denmark himself—the first crowned monarch ever to land in the country.[3] Delegates from many foreign countries brought greetings which were read at a public festival at Thingvellir. A commemorative service was held in the national cathedral, at which Bishop Pétur Pétursson preached; but the climax of the service was a Psalm of Praise, specially written by Sira Matthias Jochumsson and since regarded as the National Anthem of Iceland. Its tune is solemn rather than festal or grandiose, almost a dirge, as befits the words and the country:

> God of our land, our country's God,
> We praise Thy hallowed, hallowed name.
> The heavens have woven the sun and stars
> To make Thee a crown of flame.

---

[1] Gj., pp. 439-45, 446-8.
[2] Cp. pp. 160-1, 166-7, 171, 175, 177, 181, 192.
[3] Except King Rörek, banished by King Olaf Haraldsson, who died in N. Iceland 1020 (*Heimskringla* VI, 86).

A day before Thee is a thousand years,
    And a thousand years as a brief day lies,
A flower of the infinite, touched with tears,
    That worships its God and dies.

Iceland's thousand years—
A flower of the infinite, touched with tears,
That worships its God and dies.[1]

(ii) CHURCH BUILDINGS

Early Icelandic churches normally formed part of the farmstead constructed by chieftains or franklins, enclosed by a stone-and-turf wall with their houses and outbuildings together with the meadow or tún, which, as the most valuable part of the farm, gave its name to the touns and towns of Britain.

(a) The first churches were built of timber, most of it brought from Norway, since trees in the country, though more abundant than in later centuries, did not produce sufficient wood for large buildings.[2] The Laxdale Saga recalls the importance of timber for a church planned by Thorkell, Gudrun's fourth husband († 1026), and the disaster that befell it owing to stormy seas. *Hungrvaka* records St Olaf's gift of timber for the first church at Thingvellir. Repairs to churches were often made with driftwood, a veritable godsend to the coasts of Iceland, and part of the endowment of some benefices, such as Hólar. A sermon preserved in the mediæval Book of Homilies brings out the symbolism of a wooden church resembling the Norwegian stave-kirk, so Icelanders must have been familiar with buildings of that style.[3]

The use of stone was unusual, as the basalt found all over Iceland is porous. It is noted as remarkable that Bishop Audun of Hólar in the fourteenth century equipped his cathedral with stone pillars and a stone altar. Most church roofs until recently were made of turf —*i.e.*, sods—which became useful, well-drained grass plots, duly mown or, if accessible, grazed. The wooden church at As, repaired with a "thack" or turf, lasted from 984 until 1250. A distinction of the large and solid cathedral church at Hólar was its lead roof.[4]

---

[1] Trans. Watson Kirkconnell in *The North American Book of Icelandic Verse*, pp. 151-2 (N.Y. and Montreal, 1930).
[2] *Lndbk* I, 1, 14; 2, 2, 21, etc.; Eyrbyggja S. 26, 33, 35; Njál's S. 32; Laxdale S. 74-6.
[3] *Homiliu-bók*, pp. 16-7.   [4] Jónssaga 9, 1.

Steeples in the wind-swept land were few. Skálholt Cathedral
was given a tower in the thirteenth century by the munificence of
Bishop Pál, to form a memorial to its patron saint Thorlak rather
than to house its bells, and to be used as a chapel where Pál kept his
coffin in the usual Icelandic fashion. Hólar steeple fell down at
Christmas, 1392, in one of the storms that so frequently assail the
much-vexed country.

Bells, though usually small, have always been popular. St Olaf's
foundation gift to Thingvellir included a bell. The bells of Hólar,
the best in Iceland, were rung when Laurence's election to the
episcopate was proclaimed in 1324, and when he rebuilt Mödruvellir
monastic church he presented "apostle bells and singing maids."[1]
Of all the monasteries, Videy was richest in bells, which must have
been inspiring as they rang out from the island over the waters of
Faxafjörd.[2] The bells of Thingeyrar Abbey, according to the Annals
(s.a. 1299), tolled of themselves at the passing of the saintly abbot
Björn. And folk like to think the same about the great funeral bell
of Hólar, Likaböng, which made the valleys ring again as the body of
its fighting bishop Jón Arason was borne to its last resting-place.
Likaböng was broken in two in 1624 when a hurricane destroyed the
cathedral, but happily was recast 250 years later.[3] King Christian IV
in 1638 ordered parish church bells to be restored; so that in spite of
the poverty of the country in post-Reformation days, even turf-
built churches were given bells, which were usually hung in a rack
over the door. The pair at Vidimyri are dated 1630, those at
Grenjadarstadir 1663 and 1740.

Well-built timber churches may last for centuries, as is shown by
the remarkable stave-kirks of Norway, which the earliest Icelandic
churches would have resembled. But they are specially liable to
catch fire, and in Iceland are also exposed to hurricanes and floods of
molten lava, which is perhaps the chief reason why Icelandic churches
are built as a rule on rising ground.

(b) A résumé of the history of Skálholt Cathedral illustrates the
vicissitudes to which most buildings have been subject down the
ages. Soon after 1000, when the country adopted Christianity, a
church was built by the chieftain, Gizur the White, at his homestead,
and rebuilt by his son Bishop Isleif. Twice enlarged by his successors,

[1] Lárentius S. 52-61; ut sup., p. 123.
[2] F. J. I, p. 174, IV, p. 93.
[3] Sigfus Blöndal, *Islandske Kultur-billeder*, p. 47; Hans Reynolds,
Island, pp. 63-5. In Iceland during earthquakes church bells often ring of
themselves (as, *e.g.*, in 1896).

the reconstructed church was burnt down in the winter of 1309 (according to the Annals) "as swiftly as men eat and drink at a meal." The new building was given a steeple a hundred years later by Bishop Wilkin, but was destroyed by fire a few years before the Reformation. It was nobly renewed by Bishop Øgmund, whose cruciform cathedral, known as Kross-kirkja, survived until the middle of the eighteenth century, when it was replaced by a large wooden building which was overthrown by the earthquake of 1784.[1] After that the see was moved to Reykjavik and a small and insignificant shanty, used but occasionally, took the place of the spacious cathedral which had been the mother-church of Iceland and the daily focus of its life. Few memorials of Skálholt's storied past remain, as much perished in the earthquake. The mediæval altar-stone, of white marble blackened by use, together with a mediæval chalice and a silver wafer-box, are preserved in the National Museum. Many generations of worshippers used to point with reverence to the coffin-shrine of their own St Thorlak, and with even greater pride to the altar frontlet, which was decorated by silver plates from the girdle of Thorgunna, the heroine of Eyrbyggja Saga. Sir Joseph Banks in 1770 was shown also Sharphedon's halberd, which is praised in Njál's Saga. Such seeming incongruity is an indication of the Icelandic integration of life.

Hólar Cathedral also had its great days and great men, some of them literally church-builders, such as Jón the Saint and Audun the Red. On October 2, 1801, it was decreed that the see of Hólar should share the fate of Skálholt,[2] but its eighteenth-century church remains. Though it illustrates the poverty of post-Reformation architecture, it shows enterprise in the use of local stone. Its memorials of the past are unusually numerous and interesting for Iceland, where so much has been destroyed or carried out of the country. The tomb of the Bible-maker Bishop Gudbrand may be seen beneath the floor. Reference has been made to the mediæval crucifixes, stone altar and pre-Reformation altar-cloth, and quaint sixteenth-century portraits. The gold chalice, said to have been given by the Pope to the first bishop, was carried off to Copenhagen in the sixteenth-century spoliation and replaced by one of silver-gilt. Hólar has a branched candlestick dated 1679 and a stone font dated 1674.[3]

---

[1] For drawings of Skálholt church, town, and bishopstead (made 1772), see *Islandica* XVIII, Plates 7 and 8.
[2] P. P., p. 205. The buildings now form an agricultural college.
[3] Baring-Gould, *Iceland*, pp. 236-7.

The ancient parishes of Breidabolstad and Kirkjubaer own mediæval chalices, of such unusually fine workmanship that they were thought to have been wrought by elves.[1] The stone church at Bessastadir, which appears to float on the sea on its wind-swept peninsula near Reykjavik, preserves a battered effigy of the crusader type, which one could wish might represent the great historian-statesman Snorri Sturluson, owner of that estate in the thirteenth century. Some alabaster reredoses preserved in museums show signs of English workmanship.[2] A few runic sepul-chral inscriptions, roughly incised on basaltic pillars, survive at Borg, Kirkjubaer, Grenjadarstadir, and (in particular) at Hallbjarnareyri, near Helgafell.[3] Iceland's memorials are not written on stones, but on vellum and parchment, setting forth in undying sagas the heroism of her ancient people.

(c) Reykjavik, which succeeded to the honours but hardly to the glory of the dispossessed historic sees, was not much more than a village up to the beginning of the present century; so that the national cathedral of Iceland (Dómkirkjan) is a small stone building, whose only pretension to ecclesiastical dignity is its simple solidity. In front of the altar stands a finely carved white marble font of Italian design, the work and gift of the eminent sculptor Thorvaldsen, whose father was an Icelander († 1844).[4] The Lutheran Free Church is a well-built, well-fitted corrugated-iron building with a slender spire, happily placed by the lakeside. The small Roman Catholic cathedral in Reykjavik, constructed of grey reinforced concrete in Early English style, complete with tower and deep-toned bells, is the most striking place of worship in the country. The building is narrow, giving the interior a sense of height, and stands out well on its hilltop site. This effective use of modern material should be considered for church building in England after the war, particularly in new housing districts. A fine concrete church on more ordinary lines was com-pleted in 1941 at Akureyri, the northern capital, where one of the consecrating bishops is in charge. It has twin spires and is well placed on a height over the beautiful Eyjarfjörd. Reykjavik has only

---

[1] W. G. Collingwood and J. Stefánsson, *Pilgrimage to Sagasteads*, pp. 26-7; E. J. Oswald, *By Fell and Fjörd*, p. 153.

[2] *Archæological Journal*, lxxvii, 1920, pp. 192-7.

[3] E. H., p. 328, who reproduces the last inscription.

[4] Born Cpn Nov. 19, 1770, son of a carver of ships' figureheads and a Jutland peasant woman, grandson of Thorvald Gottskalksson, pastor of Miklibaer (see Eugene Plon, *Thorvaldsen, Life and Works*, trans. Mrs. Cashel Hoey, London, 1874.

two Lutheran places of worship for 40,000 people, of whom 98 per cent. are Lutheran. It is proposed after the war to build two large new churches, defraying the cost by a State grant and lottery subscriptions, by which expedient the cost of the impressive university building was met.

The oldest church in Iceland goes back to the first half of the seventeenth century, a small wood-and-turf structure at Vidimyri on the wild mountain road from Blöndúos to Akureyri.[1] Its sides are so banked with grass sods that sheep and even ponies can walk up and graze on its roof. The west front is made of deal planks painted white, with a pent-house over the door holding the two old bells already mentioned. The gable apex is fashioned into horns like the helmet of a viking. The interior walls and rafters are as rough as the outside suggests, but its sequestered situation has preserved a finely-made double screen and a worn mediæval pulpit. The crude picture over the altar illustrates its inscription: "Quotiescunque commedistis . . . ii Cor. xi." Its date (1616) shows that post-Reformation Icelandic churchmanship had no fear or ignorance of Latin.

These turf-and-timber churches that replaced the mediæval wooden buildings of Iceland's more spacious days were very small. Mossfell Church measured only 13 feet by 9, standing up on its rocky mound over the valley like Noah's Ark.[2] Its successor, perched high on the mountain-side with its red roof, white walls, and neat bell-cote, resembles at a distance a child's toy in a miniature Swiss landscape.

Most modern country churches are similar small homely erections of corrugated iron or concrete. The fact that they are painted white inside shows up the woodwork to the best advantage, and gives good effect to the brass candelabrum which is often their most prominent feature. Personality counts for much in Icelandic Christianity, and it is a custom to have portraits of notable pastors on the chancel walls. Altars retain their accustomed position and fittings, with one or more candlesticks and generally a cross. The pulpit is not allowed to obscure the altar, and any obstructive tendency of the organ is avoided by its being placed on a gallery at the back of the nave. The font stands by the altar—a shallow basin on a wooden pedestal. It is rarely used, for almost all baptisms are taken in houses. Interesting souvenirs of seventeenth-century practice remain in engraved brass baptismal bowls, which hang by chains on some chancel walls. Perhaps the best specimen of these is a bowl at Munkathvera (once

---

[1] See sketch, p. iv.   [2] E. H., p. 54; Baring-Gould, *Iceland*, p. 46.

monastic) Church, having a hart finely carved in high relief on a background of oak-leaves, illustrating Ps. xlii, 1.[1]

Earthquakes, hurricanes, fire, and floods have left little remains of ancient churches and their furniture, so that only seven old stone structures still exist and a few time-worn memorials and fittings. The strength and glory of Icelandic churchmanship lie not in its buildings and appurtenances but in the stalwart character of the people. After a hasty view during a month's summer holiday, visitors have expressed disappointment at the poor ecclesiastical show the country can produce. But those of us who endured long, hard, dark winter months in Iceland and have enjoyed the use of its places of worship constantly marvelled that any traces of churches and churchmanship have survived at all.

(iii) Church Order, Organisation, and Worship

(a) The Reformation in Iceland made a break in what ecclesiastically has become known as Apostolic Succession. Priests ordained under the Roman obedience and converted to Lutheranism were originally commissioned as superintendents by the learned Dr Palladius, appointed by Luther's coadjutor Bugenhagen, Primate of Denmark. But neither the title nor the office of superintendent found favour in Iceland, and subsequently such men were consecrated as bishops. The matter was regularised; and only on the theory that the Church depends on the bishop rather than the bishop on the Church can it be considered questionable.[2]

Following old tradition in the first phase of the Reformation, Gissur Einarsson was elected by the Althing in 1539 to succeed Øgmund Pálsson as Bishop of Skálholt; and in 1540 he received the royal sanction, being consecrated two years later by Palladius in accordance with the new order. Similarly, Olaf Hjaltason duly succeeded at Hólar in 1551 after the doubtful execution of his predecessor. Thus the old office and title of bishop never fell into abeyance in Iceland, and have won the recognition and respect of all knowledgeable men to this day. The title of priest (prestur) has also been retained.[3]

In grappling with the moral, economic, and physical difficulties and dangers which followed the Reformation in rapid succession

---

[1] Baring-Gould, *op. cit.*, p. 132.   [2] Cp. *sup.*, p. 159 and ref. in note 2.
[3] *Presta-tal* (Lists of priests in each parish from earliest years), Svein Nielsson, Cpn, 1869.

down to the middle of the nineteenth century, bishops in Iceland had
no inclination or occasion to question their status in the Church
Universal, especially as their position was paralleled in the sister
Churches of Norway and Denmark. Only in Sweden was outward
ecclesiastical continuity unbroken. But in the years 1865-7 some
English clergymen raised the question, and the historian Pétur
Pétursson, the bishop-elect, expressed his willingness to have an
English bishop assisting at his consecration. This met with the
approval of King Christian IX, but the Primate, Dr Martensen,
strongly objected, so that the matter dropped.[1]

In order to satisfy the scruples of the doubtful, it would be a help
in the promotion of reunion if Apostolic Succession could be technically restored to the Church in Iceland by the concurrence of a
Swedish or English bishop in the next consecration. But if this is
done it should be made plain to those who follow Luther and St
Augustine in this matter that such a theory is of practical more than
doctrinal value, being of the *bene esse* rather than the *esse* of the
Church, and that such a step would cast no slur on the ministry of
post-Reformation Icelandic bishops and pastors who have been
"ordained in accordance with the Apostolic rule, with prayer and
laying on of hands, and who have celebrated the sacraments according
to the command of our Lord."[2]

Like its sister Church of Sweden, Iceland after the Reformation
found little and finally no use for the order of deacon. Parishes had
scanty populations and very small endowments, and at times of
famine and disaster could hardly fill the ranks of the ministry, so that
it became the custom to ordain men direct to a parochial charge
without even a *per saltum* diaconate. After the Reformation pastors
of five of the largest parishes had unordained assistants styled
deacons, who helped with preaching and confirmation classes. This
system has now lapsed. The last deacon of that type was Provost
Svein Nielsson, who assisted at Grenjadarstadir 1827-35.[3] The
lapsing of the order of deacon and of its post-Reformation substitute
is unfortunate. Icelandic pastors suffer from the isolation and loneliness of their life, which makes heavy demands on their spiritual and
intellectual background. Some of the consequent secularity and

[1] See *Church Chronicle*, Aug. 1, 1866; *Scotsman*, June 12, 1867. Helga
Thordarson, Bp of Iceland 1846-66, favoured it.
[2] Cp. A. C. Headlam, *Doctrine of the Church and Christian Reunion*,
pp. 261-9, 293-4.
[3] Grandfather of the present Dómprofastur, Fridrik Hallgrimsson, to
whom I am indebted for brotherly encouragement and information.

abandonment of orders would be prevented by a revival of the diaconate.

Confirmation in Iceland is administered, as in the Eastern Orthodox Church, by prayer and laying on of hands, not of the bishop, but of the presbyter.[1] It is perhaps significant that the prestur begins the service in his vestments, but removes them for the laying on of hands. Almost everyone in Iceland is confirmed as a matter of course as a completion of baptism after unusually careful preparation; nevertheless, many rarely receive the sacrament of Holy Communion afterwards, appearing to treat Confirmation as a ticket of exemption from Church worship until they reach middle age.

(b) The bishop is elected (according to the law of June 27, 1921) by the clergy and theological professors from three candidates they nominate.[2] Any candidate receiving three-fifths of the votes is elected; otherwise the Government appoints one of the candidates. Up to 1909 the bishop-elect was consecrated in Denmark. Since then two consecrating bishops (vigslubiskupar) have been retained in Iceland for that purpose. These bishops have no other episcopal rights or powers, serving generally as cathedral or rural provosts, one in the south and the other in the north.

Pastors are elected by secret ballot by all parishioners of full age, and then appointed by the Government. If half of those entitled to vote do so, the applicant who obtains a majority of votes is elected. Failing this, the Government appoints one of the applicants on the bishop's recommendation. Since June 17, 1941, Denmark has had nothing to do with the government of the country, which is vested in the historic Althing under a President. The Church had ably helped the long and worthy struggle for independence and deserved to be among the first institutions to share its benefits.

There are twenty-one provsties or deaneries. The provost is elected by the clergy of the deanery and receives an honorarium of about £12—two principles in advance of the present English system. In accordance with the traditional historic custom, deaneries form a very real part of the Icelandic Church organisation, and thus the parishes are given a proper interest in central ecclesiastical matters and the evils of bureaucracy are obviated.

There were in 1939, 276 parishes in Iceland, but as two or three

[1] But cp. Headlam, op. cit., 295-6. In the Church of the East the "matter" of the rite is the chrism (always blessed by the bishop). Canon Law allows a priest to confirm on occasions.
[2] Jón Helgason, Bp 1917-38 († 1942); Sigurgeir Sigurdsson, Bp 1938-.

are usually served by one pastor the number of resultant parishes is 111 and the total of clergy 109. Their annual stipend ranges from 2,500 to 3,000 kronur (*i.e.*, about £92-112), together with marriage and funeral fees and a small house and glebe, the farming of which occupies most of their time.

A general parochial meeting is held once a year, which elects a council of from three to five members every six years, serving to help their pastor to maintain order, morality, and seemly worship. It superintends also the religious instruction of the young, which finds no place in the otherwise admirable State schools. As is well known, Icelanders, like other Scandinavians, are distinguished for their devotion to learning, for high intelligence and width of scholarship.[1] Down to the middle of the nineteenth century this achievement was largely due to the Church, for all instruction used to be given by parents and pastors in the homes and in the cathedral schools. It has been noted that the parish registers kept by the clergy as a result of their visitations form a remarkable feature of Icelandic Church life and are so full and thorough that they are used for all civil and official purposes.[2] It would not be hard to prove that the fact that 98 per cent. of the population remain members of the National Church is largely due to the tradition of pastoral visitation of their vast and scattered parishes, carried on by the bishops and clergy of Iceland.

There are two methods of church maintenance: (1) State-owned churches which have recently come under congregational management through a committee appointed to collect the customary dues; (2) farmer-owned churches, for which the owner is responsible and is empowered to collect 1·50 kronur (about 1s. 2d.) annually from parishioners.

The population of Iceland is 125,915, of whom more than 98 per cent. are Lutheran. According to the census of 1930 there were 782 "secularists," who contract out of paying Church rates by paying a tax for the university. Roman Catholics number about 300, served by a bishop, 4 (Dutch) priests, and 38 sisters. Almost all of that persuasion in Iceland are foreigners. Their mission began in 1859, but freedom of worship was not granted until 1874, and the work only began vigorously in 1895. In addition to their striking concrete

---

[1] So much so that mistakes in history and ancient literature in the script of the *Midnight Sun* (a paper I edited for the Forces in 1940-1) would be corrected by any of the compositors.

[2] Gregersen, *L'Islande—Son Statut* . . ., pp. 416-20.

cathedral, the community own two small churches, two schools, a convent (Carmelite), and three efficient hospitals.[1]

Some 9,500 Lutherans belong to the Free Church (Frikirkjan), who own and entirely support two places of worship, and so are relieved from subscribing to the State Church. These two congregations have self-government and choose their own ministers, though they are ordained by the bishop, and are subject to his jurisdiction, being members of the synod. The Free Church has the same ritual and ceremonial as the National Church, and except for the matter of congregational autonomy remains part of it, as do the Salvation Army, the "Liberal" Congregation, Christian Scientists, and other small communities who sometimes worship separately.[2] Thus in a measure the problem of unity without uniformity is solved.

A college for ordinands was established at Reykjavik in 1847, which was merged in the University of Iceland at its foundation in 1911. The theological faculty at the university, which has a beautiful chapel, is comparatively large and influential. Out of its 200 students recently, 20 were studying theology. Not all of them proceed to ordination, but any who obtain the degree or diploma may act as lay readers and preach in church at the request of a prestur. They are entitled to attend the synod, and to add "Cand. Theol." before or after their names.[3]

(c) The ancient custom is maintained (as it is in the East) of beginning the day at 6 o'clock on what we should call the previous evening. Thus Christmas and Easter commemorations begin on the eves of the festivals, for which there is much to be said. Shops are shut at 4 o'clock, and town churches are crowded for services at 5 and 6 o'clock. On Sundays, in town, services are held in the afternoon and entertainments at night, which is perhaps the reason why many English visitors feel that there is no atmosphere of Sunday in Iceland, though some of them help to contribute to that feeling.[4] A more serious reason is the fewness of services in country churches,

[1] Bp M. Meulenberg (1929-41), succeeded by Bp Johannes Gunnarsson in 1943. Sisters=33 of St Joseph's Order, 5 Franciscans, 3 nuns.

[2] *E.g.*, Theosophists (who have a temple) and Adventists. There are some Fundamentalists, few but vociferous. The number of adherents of all of these half-religions is diminishing. A Society of Psychical Research was founded in 1905.

[3] *E.g.*, in the telephone directory (where entries are made under Christian and not surnames) and on tombstones, as: "Jón Jónsson, Cand. Theol., Bankafehirdir" (cashier).

[4] Hooker, *Tour* (1811) II, p. 326, and many since.

due to grouping of parishes and consequent non-residence of pastors, with difficulties of distance increased by adverse weather conditions.

The principal Sunday service retains its pre-Reformation name of Hámessa, though it usually breaks off in the middle in the manner of Table Prayers or Ante-Communion. The Nicene Creed is never used, and the Apostles' Creed used only at Baptism and Confirmation. Otherwise the service follows the ancient liturgy—psalm, kyries, gloria and responses leading up to the sermon, the climax of a Lutheran service.[1] This service is completed with the reception of the sacrament only occasionally, though much is made of Easter Communion, with services leading up to it on Palm Sunday and Holy Friday.[2]

The Iceland Psalm- or Hymn-Book was revised in 1871 and a new book issued in 1886. The collection now contains 870 hymns, though the grand, solemn hymns of Luther maintain their popularity. The Free Church has added a modern supplement and the Ministry of Church Affairs has just completed a further revision.

Though fonts are given a prominent place in churches, baptism, contrary to post-Reformation injunctions,[3] is administered almost invariably in the homes of the parents. Marriage services are held in the pastor's house, generally in his study, where a table is furnished for the occasion with lighted candles and perhaps a cross. None but witnesses can be present. Strangely enough, in at least one parsonage a separate room, as in Norway, has been provided and equipped as a chapel for such purposes. These domestic services probably owe their origin less to Low Church predilections than to the low temperature of the churches during most of the year. For shades of churchmanship are largely conditioned by climate and environment.

A great feature is made of funerals, which are apparently the best attended of all services. Part of Hallgrim Pétursson's famous funeral hymn is sung, a special sermon is preached and often broadcast from the local radio station. Icelanders have been taught to regard death

---

[1] For description of services see Hooker, *Tour* (1811) I, pp. 173-8; E. H., pp. 50-1, 119, 342; Baring-Gould, *op. cit.*, pp. 291-5.

[2] Garstang in N. Lancs twenty years ago had some old parishioners who liked to make their communions "three times a year" on Palm Sunday, Good Friday, and Easter Day, as was their custom there in the eighteenth century (cp. *Diary of Thos. Parkinson*, curate 1700-29).

[3] *E.g.*, of Bp Odd Einarsson at the Synod of Thingvellir in 1590. (F. J. III, p. 336.)

as the "herald of the Lord," and those who answer his summons are given a great send-off.

The British Forces who occupied Iceland in the World War owe a debt of gratitude to the bishop and clergy of that country, who from the start, in face of misunderstanding, put their places of worship at our disposal. We were strangers and they took us in. The opportunity granted us was deeply appreciated. This brotherly hospitality enabled us to realise some of the difficulties of organisation and worship in a country whose circumstances are unusually forbidding. We realised how the people's faith and worship could not escape being coloured outwardly by their environment. But though in expression we differed in emphasis, we recognised that in fundamentals we were closely akin. We found parish churches which in their form and arrangements greatly resembled our own, and in the faith and worship they represented proved able to help men of varying shades of belief and devotion. Normally we worshipped separately; but some Icelanders came to our services, and some of us went to theirs.[1] And occasionally we held a united service, as when one Christmas morning the Dean (Dómprofastur) preached to a great congregation of troops and nurses of the United Nations. One picture remains that recalls the "first fine, careless rapture" of early Christian worship. At a small town on the western coast (where a great whale had just been cast up) a troops' Confirmation had been arranged in the parish church, which the pastor and some of his people wished to attend. Scots bishop, Icelandic prestur, and English chaplain stood in the chancel; and when a hymn was announced from the Army Prayer Book, the prestur announced a similar hymn from his psalm-book. Sometimes Icelanders sang a translation of the English words, but sometimes they sang a different hymn, which fitted the tune we were using. Thus in spirit the curse of Babel was annulled. "Solvitur orando."

The Icelandic Church down the ages has fought a good fight against grim, adverse forces within and without its borders. Today it has emerged secure in itself after centuries of struggle against an aggressive environment and against acquisitive civil and ecclesiastical external powers. But at the moment this small Christian community stands almost alone and not without scars of conflict. Its present enemies are isolation and secularity. The times are full of anxiety; but a Church which has shown so great a power of survival through

[1] Si fueris Romæ, Romano vivito more; si fueris alibi, vivito sicut ibi (St Ambrose).

such appalling vicissitudes cannot ultimately fall out of what its noble bishop Gizur Isleifsson called "God's battle."

So may Iceland cease to be last among lands.[1]

NOTE ON ICELANDIC COLONIES IN AMERICA

(See Gj., pp. 458-71)

Pastors have played a leading part in the large and flourishing colonies of Icelanders which have established themselves in U.S.A. and Canada.

The movement began in 1872, when freedom, for which the country had striven so long, seemed unattainable at home. Three hundred left Iceland for North Dakota, where the settlement was organised by Sira Páll Thorlaksson († 1880). In 1873 150 went to Canada, making a home, not without difficulty, along the shores of Lake Winnipeg, where the virile colony now numbers about 7,000.

Many individual Icelanders have attained high positions in the service of their adopted countries, but the settlements as a whole have shown their motherland's love of independence, maintaining separate newspapers, schools, and Lutheran synods. In 1905 an Icelandic synod was founded at Winnipeg, with 37 congregations, which had increased to 58 by 1919.

To help higher education the learned and able pastor Jón Bjarnason inaugurated at Winnipeg a scheme for an Icelandic college, which was founded in his memory in 1914, the year in which he died, though recently it has been incorporated in the university.

The doggedness of character which has distinguished Icelanders down the ages, together with their traditional love of learning and native integrity, have made good in the new world overseas, and should make men eager to look unto the rock from which they were hewn.

[1] Nec sit terris ultima Thule (Seneca, *Medea* II, 371).

CHRONOLOGY

870.	First settlers find traces of Columban Christianity.
870-930.	Period of Settlement (Landnámstid).
930.	Commonwealth of Iceland inaugurated. Althing established at Thingvellir.
930-1030.	Saga age (Söguöld).
981-5.	Missionary visit of Thorvald Kodransson and Bp Fridrek.
996-9.	Olaf Tryggvason, King of Norway, sends Stefnir Thorgilsson and then Thangbrand as missionaries.
1000 (June 24).	Christianity officially adopted.
1016.	King Olaf "the Stout" (afterwards St Olaf) gets remaining heathen customs abolished.
1024.	King Olaf attempts to annex Iceland.
1030-1118.	Peace period (Fridaröld).
1056 (May 26, Whit-Sunday).	Isleif, son of Gizur the White, consecrated first bp (†1080).
1082-1118.	Gizur, son of Isleif, Bp of Skálholt.
1096.	Tithe system introduced.
1100.	Bp Gizur's census: 4,500 landowners = c. 50,000.
1102.	Northern bishopric of Hólar founded.
1102-1121.	Jón Ogmundson its first bp. afterwards Saint.
1122-1133.	Code of Church Law compiled by Bps Ketill and Thorlak.
1133.	Monastery founded at Thingeyrar (Benedictine). First nunnery, Kirkjubaer, 1186.
1133.	Death of Priest Saemund the Wise, founder of the school at Oddi.
1148 (Nov. 9).	Death of Priest Ari the Wise, father of Icelandic history.
1152.	Bishops in Iceland put under new archdiocese of Nidaros in Norway. Abp Eystein Erlendsson (1157-88).
1198.	Bp Thorlak Thorhallsson and (1200) Bp Jón Ogmundson canonised by the Althing.
1200-1264.	Civil war of Sturlunga clans.
1202-1237.	Bp Gudmund Arason's buccaneering campaign.
1238.	Two Norwegians appointed bishops in Iceland.
1241 (Sept. 14).	Snorri Sturluson, historian, assassinated.
1262-4.	End of the Commonwealth. Norwegian rule accepted.
1267-1313.	Jörund Thorsteinsson, Bp of Hólar for 46 years.
1269-98.	Arni Thorlaksson, Bp of Skálholt, vigorous administrator, compiled second code of Church Law, passed by Althing 1275.
1271-3, 1281.	Codes of Law—Jarnsida and Jónsbok—promulgated.
1295.	Norway and Iceland join the Scottish-French alliance.
1300, -8, -11, -13, -39, -70, -90, -91.	Devastating earthquakes.

1323-30.	Lárentius Kalfsson, Bp of Hólar, saintly teacher.
1380.	Iceland with Norway passes under Danish rule.
1397.	The Kalmar Union with Sweden.
1392-1430.	"New" Annals, last contemporary accounts till *c*. 1600.
1394-1405.	Wilkin Hinriksson (Danish), Bp of Hólar, benefactor.
1402-4.	Great Plague (and 1494).
1491-1518.	Stefán Jónsson, Bp of Skálholt, able administrator.
1521-41.	Ogmund Pálsson, Bp of Skálholt.
1524-50.	Jón Arason, Bp of Hólar.
1539.	Sack of monastery on Videy.
1540.	N.T. published in Icelandic by Odd Gottskalksson (1515-56).
1539.	Gissur Einarsson appointed Superintendent, in 1542 Bishop, of Skálholt; †1548.
1541.	New Church ordinance adopted for Skálholt Diocese; Hólar 1551.
1550 (Nov. 7).	Bp Jón Arason and his two sons beheaded.
1567-1648.	Arngrim Jónsson revives interest in old Icelandic history.
1584.	First Bible in Icelandic published by Bp Gudbrand Thorlaksson, Bp of Hólar for 56 years (1571-1627).
1618-19, 1625, -36, -60.	Volcanic eruptions cause great destruction and loss of life. Earthquakes: 1614, -33, -57, -61.
1607.	New Church code imposed by King Christian IV.
1614-27.	Raids of Spanish, English, and Algerian pirates.
1625-90.	Witchcraft burnings.
1639-75.	Brynjolf Sveinsson, Bp of Skálholt, antiquary (*1605).
1662.	King of Denmark proclaimed absolute monarch.
1674.	Death of Hallgrim Pétursson, author of "Passion Hymns" (*1614).
1698-1720.	Jón Vidalin, Bp of Skálholt, author of family sermons.
1703.	Population = 50,444.
1707.	18,000 die of smallpox, following earthquakes in 1706.
1726-57.	Great eruptions and earthquakes destroy many farms and cattle. Thousands die of hunger.
1754-85.	Finnur Jónsson, Bp of Skálholt, historian of the Icelandic Church (*1704).
1783.	Devastating eruption of Laki. Earthquake destroys Skálholt Church and ruins 38 farms.
1784.	Earthquake in south wrecks 133 farms and ruins 1,700 houses. Over 9,000 people die and much cattle.
1785-1801.	Bishoprics of Skálholt and Hólar (and their schools) abolished and merged in one bishopric of Iceland with cathedral at Reykjavik Oct. 2, 1801.
1798.	Althing meets for last time at Thingvellir.
1800.	Population = 47,086.
1811 (June 17).	Birth of Jón Sigurdsson, patriot (†1879).

1843.	Althing re-established, meets at Reykjavik.
1847.	Theological college established at Rvk.
1854 (Apr. 15).	Danish trade monopoly abolished.
1874.	Religious and civic celebration of Millennium.
1874 (Aug. 1).	King Christian IX grants constitution to Iceland.
1890.	Population 70,927.
1901.	Population 78,489.
1911 (June 17).	University of Reykjavik founded.
1918 (Dec. 1).	Home rule of Iceland under King of Denmark acknowledged.
1920.	Population=94,696; 1937=118,000 (Rvk=17,976).
1940.	Population=120,264 (Rvk=40,000); 1943 = 125,915.
1941	Independence of Iceland proclaimed and Regent elected.
1944 (June 17).	Republic proclaimed. Sveinn Björnsson appointed President.

REFERENCES

CHAPTER I

(i) *Islendingabók*—a short history of the years 870-1120 by Ari Thorgilsson, *c*. 1134, in Origines Islandicae (Oxf. 1905). Introd. and trans. by Halldor Hermannsson in Islandica, Vol. XX. (N.Y. 1930; Cpn 1930).
Ditto. Finnur Jónsson: Island fra Sagatid til Nutid. Cpn 1930.
Landnámabók by Sturla Thordarson (*c*. 1150), Book of the Settlement (874-930). Trans. T. Ellwood, Kendal 1898. Also in O.I. (Also Cpn 1925).
Alexander Bugge: Vesterlandenes Inflydelse, paa Norboernes—esp. chap. IX, "Norse Colonies in Relation to Celtic Culture" (Christiania 1905).
Jón Helgason: Kristnisaga Islands, Vol. I, pp. 3-6 (Rvk 1925).
W. A. Craigie: Proc. Soc. Ant., S. XXXI, 1897, pp. 247 *sq.*

(ii) *Laxdale Saga*—Romantic account of years 892-1206, trans. by Muriel Press, Temple Classics (Lon. 1899).
Ditto, with Introd., maps and tables, illd. ed. E. O. Sveinsson (Rvk 1933).
Njál's Saga, Introd. and trans. by Sir G. W. Dasent. 2 vols. (Lon. 1861). Trans. only in Everyman's Library (Lon. 1912). Notable introduction.
K. Gjerset: History of Iceland, pp. 12-29 (N.Y. 1924).
For pre-Christian Religions see Eyrbyggja S. in Saga Lib. 1892. Viga-Glum's S., trans. F. Head, 1866; ed. G. Turville-Petre (Oxf. 1940).

(iii) *Thorvald's Saga vidförla*, from the Latin of Gunnlaug (†1218). (Trans. O.I.) (B.S. I, pp. 33-50)—largely legendary.
Vatnsdale Saga, antiquarian acct. of Thorvald's converts.
Kristni Saga—summary of Church history 981-1118, expanded from Ari († 1148) (in O.I.) (B.S. I, pp. 1-32).

CHAPTER II

(i) *Kristni Saga* 6-9.
Olaf's S. Tryggvason 73, 84, 188, 216. Trans. J. Sephton, in Northern Library, Vol. I (Lon. 1895). Ed. F. Jónsson, 32, 76, 80, 91, 103.
Laxdale S. xli, etc. For Thorgils see the romantic Floamanna Saga.
(ii) Also Islendingabók 7, and Njál's Saga 75, 135.
Eirikur Magnússon, art. in Saga Bk of the Viking Club II, 1901, pp. 348-76.
(iii) *Heimskringla*: Saga of Olaf the Saint. Trans. in Everyman's Library. Ditto. Ed. and trans. E. Monsen (Camb. 1932). Ed. F. Jónsson (Cpn 1900).
Eyrbyggjasaga 41, 51, 53 (an account of the years 884-1031, written *c*. 1200; trans. Saga Lib. II.).
Hungrvaka 1-11 in B.S. I, 57-86, in O.I. (sub-contemporary story of the first five bps of Skálholt (1056-76). Ed. with Latin trans. and notes; Cpn 1778.
Hid Islenzka Fornritafélag, Vol. IV (Rvk 1933-5).
Bogi Th. Melsted: Islendinga Saga (an accurate and thorough account to 1200). 3 vols. (Cpn 1916-30).

CHAPTER III

(i) and (ii) *Hungrvaka*. See sub II (iii).
Flatey Book ii, pp. 140-2 (O.I.), gives the story of Isleif's courtship; also in B.S. I, pp. 51-6.

Islendingabók has a summary of Lives of Isleif and Gizur.

Adam (Canon) of Bremen (1072-5) wrote a History of Christian Missions in the North (788-1072), at the suggestion of Abp Adalbert. Mon. Germ. Hist., 2nd ed. G. Waitz (Hanover 1876).

Saxo Grammaticus: Gesta Danorum, ed. J. Olrick and H. Raeder; Cpn 1931.

G. Storm: Studies on the Vinland Voyages (Cpn 1889).

G. H. Gathorne Hardy: Norse Discoverers of America (Lon. 1922).

For Greenland, see Islendingabók 17, and Saga of Eirik the Red, trans. Rev. J. Sephton (Liverpool 1880).

Vilhjálmer Stefánsson: Greenland (Lon. 1943).

(iii) Gizur's Genealogy is given in Kristni S.; that of Ari the Wise in Lndbk ii.

For Feuds see Sturlunga S. i, 5-25; Grettir's Saga, trans. G. Hight; and the Story of Burnt Njál, trans. G. W. Dasent, both in Everyman's Library.

Saemund and his successors: see art. by Halldor Hermannsson in Islandica, Vol. XXII (Ithaca 1932).

Church Law—Kristin Rettr: see Islandica IV, pp. 12-15. A sumptuous edition of the Codex Regius of Grágás with Eng. Introd. by Páll Eggert Olason was pubd at Cpn 1932.

Literary Development : see Bertha S. Phillpotts: Edda and Saga, pp. 215 *sq.* (Lon. 1931).

CHAPTER IV

(i) (*a*) and (*b*) *Hungrvaka*, and see sub II (iii).

Mrs Disney Leith, *Stories of the Bishops of Iceland*, a summary of *Hungrvaka* (Lon. 1895).

Gj., pp. 158-60, deals with Abp Eystein's reforms, giving the letter he wrote to the Iceland bishops from F. J. I, 237 *sq.*

Diplomatarium Islandicum, Vol. I, ed. Jón Sigurdsson (Cpn 1857-76).

(ii) (*a*) *St Jón of Hólar* is given three Lives in B.S. I., pp. 149-260:

1. Saga in Latin written *c.* 1220 by Gunnlaug the Monk at the request of Bp Gudmund.

2. Two translations into Icelandic, thirteenth century.

3. Later unhistorical compilation *c.* 1310.

For Saemund's alleged black magic see art. by Helen T. McM. Buckhurst in Viking Soc. Saga Bk, 1934, and especially Islandica, Vol. XXII.

(iii) (*b*) *St Thorlak:* B.S. I, pp. 261-404, including a service for St Thorlak's Day from Brev. Nidrosiense.

Two versions of a Life by a contemporary, *c.* 1206. The first, or "Elder," saga resembles *Hv.*, and O.I. considers them the work of the same author. The "Younger" S. completes Thorlak's career by the addition of incidents of his campaign to obtain Church property (cp. Oddaverja S. and Sturlunga S.). A fourteenth-century expansion adds miracles.

The MS exists of the eulogy read by Bp Pál to the Althing in 1199, and a contemporary MS (AM 645) of the first Thorlak Saga.

CHAPTER V

(i) Finnur Jónsson: Hist. Eccl. Isl., Vol. III, pp. 96-7, IV, 1-124.

Jón Helgason: Kristnisaga Isl. I, pp. 101-3.

K. Gjerset: Hist. of I., pp. 136-7, 212, 302.

H. Hermannsson: Icelandic MSS in Islandica, Vol. XIX.

(ii) Gudmund Vigfusson: Prolegomena to Sturlunga S. (O.U.P. 1878).
W. P. Ker: Collected Essays, Vol. II, Nos. 27-30 (Lon. 1920).
W. S. Craigie: The Icelandic Sagas (Camb. 1913). Useful handbook.
Bertha S. Phillpotts: Edda and Saga (Lon. 1931).
Biskupa Sögur. 2 vols. (Cpn 1858-78). Invaluable.
(iii) 1. Dipl. Isl. esp. Vol. II, ed. Jón Thorkelsson (Cpn 1893).
2. Aage Gregersen: L'Islande—Son Statut à travers les Ages (Paris 1937).
3. Einar Arnórsson and Jón Thorkelsson: Islenzkur Kirkjurettr. Rvk 1912.
4. Finnur Jónsson, *op. cit.*; Church Law I, pp. 455 *sq.*, 551 *sq.*
5. Ancient Laws of Norway and Iceland—Bibliography by Hermannsson in Islandica IV.
6. Origines Islandicae has sections on Ecclesiastical Law and Church Charters, from which our translations are mostly taken.

CHAPTER VI

Pétur Pétursson, Commentatio de jure ecclesiarum in Islandia (Cpn 1844).
(i) *Pál's Saga*, by the author of Hungrvaka, a contemporary of the bishop. B.S. I., pp. 125-48; trans. O.I.
(ii) 1. *S. of Gudmund the priest* (1161-1202); by Hrafn, in Sturlunga S. ? abridged from B.S. I, pp. 639-76.
2. *Aronssaga Hjörleifssonar*, written 1200-55; part about Gudmund (B.S. I, pp. 619-39).
3. *S. of Gudmund the bp* (1202-37), composed in the latter part of thirteenth century by different author from 2 (B.S. I, pp. 405-558).
4. Ditto by Arngrim, Abbot of Thingeyrar (†1361), probably original in Latin; a variant of 1 and 2 with miracles added (B.S. II, pp. 1-220).
G. Turville-Petre and E. S. Olszewska; Life of Gudmund the Good, Bp of Hólar. Introd. and trans., Viking Society 1943.
(iii) *Sturlunga S.* (a history of Iceland 1100-1263). Ed. with valuable Prolegomena by G. Vigfusson. 2 vols (Oxf. 1878). Official documents and letters in Dipl. Isl., Vol. I.

CHAPTER VII

(i) *Arni Biskupasaga*, by a contemporary (not trans.) (B.S. I, pp. 677-786).
For lay ownership of churches see Stutz in Encl. der Rechtswissenschaft V, pp. 301 *sq.*; Pollock and Maitland, Hist. of Eng. Law, 1898, I, p. 497; Addy, Church and Manor, 1913; Thomas, Le Droit de propriété des Laïques . . . et le patronage laïque . . . (Paris 1906).
(ii) *Lárentius S.* by Einar Haflidason, written *c.* 1350, with Annals and appendix (B.S. I, pp. 787-914).
Trans. The Life of Laurence, Bp of Hólar, by O. Elton (Lon. 1890).
Law : Jón's Bók, 1578. Facsimile and Introd. by O. Larusson (Cpn 1934).
Grágás. Ditto (Cpn 1932) (see III (iii))—sumptuous volumes.
(iii) *Saints* : Postola Sögur; Heilagra Manna S. (2 vols); and Mariu S., ed. Prof. C. R. Unger (Christiania 1874-7).
Lilja : In Icelandic with Latin trans. (F. J. II, 398 *sq.*).
Ed. and trans. by Eirikur Magnusson (Lon. 1870).
Le Chante du Lilja . . . P. de Rivière (Rome 1883).
Lilja, ed. in German (Freiburg 1884).
Lilja, ed. Gudbrandur Jónsson (Rvk 1935).

GENERAL.
Annals : 1263-1392 by Einar Haflidason *ut sup.* VII (ii).
Gustav Storm: Islandske Annaler to 1578 (Chr. 1858).
Islenzkir Annálar (803-1430) with Latin trans. (Cpn 1847 and Rvk 1922).
Dipl. Isl., Vol. II, 1269-1415, ed. Jón Thorkelsson (Cpn 1893).
Jón Espolin: Arbaekur Islands in Sögu-formi, 1262-1832. 12 vols. (Cpn 1821-55).

CHAPTER VIII

For physical features of Iceland.
Bp. Gisli Jónsson: MSS on Nat. Hist. 1558-87.
Arngrim Jónsson: Brev. Comm. de Isl. (Cpn 1593). Introd. and trans. by Hakluyt, IV, 1-88. Crymogœa 1609-30; Specimen 1643. Jón Gudmundsson († 1658): Nat. Hist. with Introd. Islandica, Vol. XV.
La Peyrère: Relation de l'Islande, 1644.
For later notices see ref. in Travellers' Accounts, Ch. XI.

Historical (fifteenth century).
    1. Dipl. Isl., Vol. IV, 1265-1449; V, 1330-1476, also VIII-IX. Annals as sub Ch. VII.
        New Annals 1392-1430.
            Jón Egilsson (*c.* 1625), Biskúpa Annálar (Cpn 1856).
            Björn á Skardsá († 1635). Ditto.
            Gustav Storm: Islandske Annaler (Chr. 1858). Part trans. in Rolls Series in 88, 4.
    2. Finnur Jónsson; Hist. Eccl. Isl., Vol. II, pp. 225-50, 353-89, 465-521.
        Jón Helgason: Kristnisaga Isl. I, pp. 220-65.

Literary.
Icelandic Poetry of fifteenth and sixteenth centuries: a treatise in Danish by Jón Thorkelsson (* 1822).

CHAPTER IX

REFORMATION.
Diplomatarium Islandicum, esp. Vols. IX-XIII (Rvk 1913).
Jón Egilsson: Biskúpa Annaler (Cpn 1856).
Ditto, ed. Jón Sigurdsson in Safn til Sögu Isl.
Björn of Skardsá: Annaler; cp. Rolls Series 88, 4.
Gustav Storm: Islandske Annaler (-1578) (Chr. 1858).
Biskupa Sögur, Series II, Skálholt, Rvk 1907, Hólar, Rvk 1914.
Finnur Jónsson: Hist. Eccl. Isl., Vol. III, pp. 1-449, giving original documents.
Thorkell Bjarnason: Hist. of Refn in I. (in Icelandic) (Rvk 1878).
For Bp Øgmund, B.S., II, pp. 265-314. F. J. II, pp. 521-71.
For Bp Jon Arason, B.S., II, pp. 316-507. F. J. II, pp. 644-754.
    W. P. Ker; art. repr. fr. Saga Bk of Viking Society, 23 pp. (Lon. 1914).
For Bp Gissur, B.S. II, pp. 249-51; F. J. II, pp. 540 *sq.*, III, 299-80.
For Bp Gudbrand, B.S., II, pp. 685-709. F. J. III, pp. 368-443.

LITERATURE.
N.T. of Odd Gottskalksson, reprint with Introd. by Sigurdur Nordal (Cpn 1933).
Gudspjallabók, ditto. Halldor Hermannsson (Cpn 1933).

Halldor Hermannsson: Icelandic Bks of sixteenth century, art. in Islandica IX (N.Y. 1916): XXIX (1942).

E. Henderson: Journal, App. I, Icelandic Scriptures, pp. 468-82 (Edinb. 1819).

For Lutheran Catechism, Confession, etc., see Documents of the Chr. Church, . . . H. Bettenson (Oxf. 1943).

CHAPTER X

(i) Björn of Skardsá, Account of Algerian Pirates called Tyrkjaránssaga. Jón Espolin, Arbaekur—Pirates IV, pp. 398 *sq.*; Witchcraft V, pp. 29 *sq.* H. Haengsson and H. Hrólfsson; Litil Saga um herlaup Tyrkjans a Islandi, arid 1627 (Rvk 1852). (Including Olaf Egilsson: Travels; and Klaus Eyjulfsson, Annals.)

N. Annandale: The Faroes and Iceland, pp. 69-92 (Oxf. 1905).

(ii) *For Bp Thorlak Skulason*, F. J. III, pp. 715-25.

For Bp Brynjolf Sveinsson, ditto, pp. 602-64. Life by Torfi Jónsson in B.S., Series II.

(iii) *For Hallgrim Pétursson.* Arne Möller, H.P. 212 pp. (Cpn 1922).

Aevi Hallgrims Peturssonar og Saubaer, ed. V. Gudmundsson. 68 pp. (Rvk 1934).

C. V. Pilcher: Passion Hymns of Iceland (Lon. 1913).

Ditto. Icelandic Meditations (Lon. 1923).

For Bp Jón Vidalin. Arne Möller. J. V. og hans Postil (Odense 1929).

F. J. III, pp. 682-95.

Literary.

Halldor Hermannsson: Icelandic Bks of the seventeenth century, Icelandica XIV (N.Y. 1922): XXIX (1942).

Ethel Seaton: Lit. Relations of Eng. and Scandinavia in seventeenth century (Oxf. 1935).

Brit. Mus. Catalogues: Bks printed in I. 1578-1844.

Conditions of the People.

Jón Espolin: Arbaekur VIII, 42.

P. E. Olason and Th. Jóhannesson: Saga Islendinga, Vols. IV, V. (1600-1770) (Rvk 1942-3).

CHAPTER XI

Magnus Stephensen: Island in det 18de aarhundrede (Cpn 1808).

Jón Espolin: Arbaekur V-X. (Cpn 1821-55).

Th. Thorodssen: Observations on Eruptions and Earthquakes in Iceland. Trans. by G. H. Boehmer (Cpn 1897).

Jón Jónsson: Skuli Magnusson, landfogeti (Rvk 1911).

Finnur Jónsson: Hist. Eccl. Isl. to 1740; continued by Bp Pétur Pétursson to end of 1840 (Latin) (Cpn 1841).

Reports and Travels.

Bp Ludvig Harboe: Nat. Hist. of I. Report of 1741-5; Eng. trans. 1758. Eggert Olafsson and Bjarni Pálsson: Reise igiennem Island . . . Soroe 1772. Uno von Troil: Letters on Iceland 1772; Eng. trans., Lon. 1780. Sir G. S. Mackenzie: Travels (esp. scientific) (Edin. 1810). Sir W. J. Hooker: Journal (1809) of a Tour in I. 2 vols. (Lon. 1811). Ebenezer Henderson: Iceland—Journal 1814-5 (Edin. 1818). Hermannsson: Sir Jos. Banks and Iceland, Islandica XVIII (N.Y. 1926).

CHAPTER XII

(i) Sigfus Blöndal: Isl. Kulturbilleder (Appendix on Jón Sigurdsson) (Cpn 1924).

K. Gjerset's History of I. is very full on nineteenth century and on Icelandic Colonies in America.

Poetry.

Watson Kirkconnell: N. Amer. Book of Icelandic Verse (N.Y. and Mont. 1930).

Icelandic Lyrics (Rvk 1930).

(ii) *Travellers' Accounts.*

R. F. Burton: Ultima Thule. 2 vols. (Lon. 1875).

S. Baring-Gould: Iceland, its Scenes and Sagas (Lon. 1863).

E. J. Oswald: By Fell and Fjörd (Edin. and Lon. 1882).

W. G. Collingwood and J. Stefánsson: A Pilgrimage to the Sagasteads of I. Illd. (Ulverston 1889).

(iii) Aage Gregersen: L'Islande—Son Statut à travers les Ages (Paris 1937).

Handbook—Iceland 1936, pubd by Nat. Bank of I. (Rvk 1936).

INDEX

abb.=abbot, abbess; *bp*=bishop; *ch.*=church; (*H.*)=Hólar; *kg*=king;
pr.=priest; *qu.*=quoted; (*S.*)=Skálholt.

Printed in Great Britain by
Billing and Sons Ltd., Guildford and Esher
F2349